AF778034

The Handbook for Divorce Valuations

The Handbook for Divorce Valuations

Robert E. Kleeman, Jr.
R. James Alerding
Benjamin D. Miller

JOHN WILEY & SONS, INC.
New York • Chichester • Weinheim • Brisbane • Singapore • Toronto

This book is printed on acid-free paper. ♾

Copyright © 1999 by John Wiley & Sons, Inc. All rights reserved.

Published simultaneously in Canada.

No part of this publication may be reproduced, stored in a retrieval system or transmitted in any form or by any means, electronic, mechanical, photocopying, recording, scanning or otherwise, except as permitted under Sections 107 or 108 of the 1976 United States Copyright Act, without either the prior written permission of the Publisher, or authorization through payment of the appropriate per-copy fee to the Copyright Clearance Center, 222 Rosewood Drive, Danvers, MA 01923, (978) 750-8400, fax (978) 750-4744. Requests to the Publisher for permission should be addressed to the Permissions Department, John Wiley & Sons, Inc., 605 Third Avenue, New York, NY 10158-0012, (212) 850-6011, fax (212) 850-6008, E-Mail: PERMREQ @ WILEY.COM.

This publication is designed to provide accurate and authoritative information in regard to the subject matter covered. It is sold with the understanding that the publisher is not engaged in rendering professional services. If professional advice or other expert assistance is required, the services of a competent professional person should be sought.

Library of Congress Cataloging-in-Publication Data:

Kleeman, Robert E.
The handbook for divorce valuations / Robert E. Kleeman, Jr., R. James Alerding, Benjamin D. Miller.
p. cm.
Includes index.
ISBN 0-471-29966-9 (cloth : alk. paper)
1. Equitable distribution of marital property—United States.
2. Divorce settlements—United States. 3. Business enterprises-
I. Alerding, R. James. II. Miller, Benjamin D. III. Title.
KF532.7.K58 1999
346.7301′66-dc21 99-17588

Printed in the United States of America.

10 9 8 7 6 5 4 3 2 1

As the principle authors, my co-authors indulged my desire to dedicate this volume.

To my wife, Judy, and the rest of my family, who hassled me, cajoled me, put up with papers spread all over the house, forgave me for my inattention to them while working on this project, and, more importantly, provided moral support and encouragement throughout this project.

To the many members of my firm who supported my efforts over the project term and kept encouraging me to stay the course.

—Bob Kleeman

About the Authors

ROBERT E. KLEEMAN, JR., is a member and the Director of Litigation and Valuation Services for Clifton Gunderson L.L.C., a large regional public accounting firm. Mr. Kleeman has been providing valuation services since 1975, and has limited his practice to litigation support and business valuation since 1982. Mr. Kleeman is a certified public accountant licensed to practice in Colorado, Illinois, and Texas. In addition, Mr. Kleeman holds the Accredited in Business Valuation (ABV) credential from the American Institute of Certified Public Accountants, the Accredited Senior Appraiser (ASA) credential from the American Society of Appraisers, and the Certified Valuation Analyst (CVA) credential from the National Association of Certified Valuation Analysts.

Mr. Kleeman has served a three-year term on the AICPA Business Valuation and Appraisals Subcommittee, and currently is a member of the AICPA ABV Credentials Committee. He has served on the AICPA's Steering Committee for both the National Conference on Divorce, as well as the National Business Valuation Conference (including chair of the 97 conference). He is also completing his third year on NACVA's Education Board, having been the Chairman during 1996 and 1997.

Mr. Kleeman is a frequent author and lecturer for the AICPA, American Bar Association, state CPA societies, state bar associations and other professional organizations. He is also the author of the AICPA CPE Course "The CPA—Valuator, Expert Witness."

R. JAMES ALERDING, JR. is a member and regional coordinator of Litigation & Valuation Services for Clifton Gunderson L.L.C., Certified Public Accountants and Consultants. Previously, he was director of taxation and director of valuation and litigation support services for Blue & Co., L.L.C. Mr. Alerding is a certified public accountant licensed to practice in Maryland and Indiana. He holds the Accredited in Business Valuation (ABV), Accredited Senior Appraiser (ASA), Business Valuation, and Certified Valuation Analyst (CVA) certifications. Mr. Alerding currently services on the Business Valuation & Appraisal Subcommittee for the AICPA. He is a member of the Maryland Institute of CPAs, the Indiana CPA Society, the National Association of Certified Valuation Analysts, and the American College of Forensic Examiners Advisory Board. He is a frequent lecturer and has authored numerous articles and publications. He is an instructor and author for the AICPA Accredited in Business Valuation Exam Review Program and an instructor for the State CPA societies in Illinois, Indiana, Michigan, New York, North Carolina, South Carolina, Texas, California, Washington, and Virginia.

About the Authors

BENJAMIN D. MILLER is a manager and regional coordinator in the Litigation and Valuation Services Group for Clifton Gunderson L.L.C. Mr. Miller has been providing business valuation services since 1985. He holds the Accredited Senior Appraiser (ASA) credential from the American Society of Appraisers.

Mr. Miller has written articles on business valuation and, as a previous employee of John Wiley & Sons, Inc., was a primary designer of several business valuation software programs, including *ValuSource Pro, Value Express 5.0, Midmarket Comps,* and the MGMA/Wiley *Physicians' Compensation and Production Survey.*

Contents

Foreword

This book is clearly oriented to litigation over the value of a business or professional practice in a marital estate. It takes the reader all the way through the process from accepting the engagement through surviving cross examination, and then adds a chapter on marketing divorce practice. Although there are other useful books dealing with valuations for divorce, there is not another "A to Z" primer such as this.

The authors' experience and insight in the litigation arena particularly show through in one of their comments about the engagement process: "The case you initially accept is rarely the same case you take to trial." They explain how the dynamics of litigation may require multiple engagement letters or amendments, and why each change should be committed to writing.

This book focuses more than any other on the divorce valuation cases encountered most frequently: disputes over the value of small businesses and professional practices. In fact, the chapter on goodwill (often the most controversial issue) has considerable focus on the sole proprietorship and the sole professional practitioner. It addresses differences among states in treating personal versus entity goodwill, and offers extensive lists of factors that may be considered in quantifying the value of goodwill.

I could not agree more with the authors' admonitions that the appraiser needs to get a grasp on the standard of value accepted in the relevant jurisdiction. This varies greatly from one jurisdiction to another, and can only be understood by a study of the precedential case law. Furthermore, even the precedential case law is subject to frequent change, and sometimes appears to be contradictory on an issue within a single jurisdiction.

Equitable distribution is generally interpreted to give courts wide discretion, and only a minority of states adhere strictly to the standard of fair market value. It is helpful that the authors make extensive reference to the interpretation of fair market value by the Internal Revenue Service and the U.S. Tax Court, and such interpretations often are taken into consideration in family law courts. The important caveat, however, is that the appraiser should not assume that all (or even most) family law courts will accept all the tenets of the standard of fair market value, and the appraiser faces the challenge of interpreting from precedential cases in the relevant jurisdiction where departures from a strict fair market value standard may be appropriate or necessary.

I was surprised to learn from the Preface that most CPAs that perform business valuations spend less than 15 percent of their charge hours in that area. The chapter on depositions and the three chapters on court trials will be extremely useful to those with limited court experience. Every marital dissolution valuation engagement should be approached assuming a likelihood that it will go to court.

I also congratulate the authors on their handy and useful appendixes. There is a fairly lengthy list of references. Several sets of professional standards and Revenue Rulings are reprinted in full. In particular, the set of forms provides a valuable tool for the practitioner with limited experience.

Most business appraisers experience their first court appearance in conjunction with a marital dissolution valuation engagement. Some go so far as to build a practice where they spend 100 percent of their time on business and practice valuations for marital dissolutions. It is a fertile field of practice, and growing.

Unfortunately, the quality of business valuation practice in family law courts often has been sadly lacking. This has resulted in poorly served clients, unnecessarily costly appeals and remands, and some unfortunate precedential case law. The sophistication of business appraisers in family law situations has been gradually increasing. The reader of this book should help contribute to the trend toward improved practice.

Shannon P. Pratt, CFA, FASA, CBA
Willamette Management Associates
Portland, Oregon
April 9, 1999

Preface

Based on the demographics of the attendees of the American Institute of Certified Public Accountants (AICPA) National Business Valuation Conference, most CPAs who perform business valuation (BV) services spend less than 15 percent of their total charge hours in that area. It is probably fair to say that most BV engagements performed by CPAs are performed in the divorce or marital litigation arena. This area is also where most CPAs find themselves as expert witnesses. Neither BV skills nor expert witness skills were part of the curriculum that led to our undergraduate degrees. With those two premises as the seed, this book began germinating.

When I was first approached about creating this book, I asked why the profession needed another BV book. What would make this book special and different from what was currently out there? Thinking about where most CPAs perform these services, I settled on the concept of a practical how-to book on providing BV services in the marital litigation area. But I decided not to stop at the issuance of the BV report, but rather to take the reader through the rest of the engagement, which includes depositions and direct examination and cross examination.

Early in this process, I enlisted the assistance of R. James Alerding, another member of Clifton Gunderson LLC, and Benjamin D. Miller, a manager with the firm. As the process went forward, Jim and Ben went from a resource to coauthors. A good part of these materials are their direct efforts. The project became a joint project that added value to the final product.

We have made some basic assumptions in putting this manuscript together:

- We have assumed that the reader of this book already has a basic understanding of BV procedures. We are not trying to be an introductory or basic reference text to all of the BV principles and methodologies. Many volumes are available to provide that information.
- We focused on divorce valuations only. Information regarding valuations for other purposes is not included in this book. Keep that in mind as you use this text; it is probably not appropriate to refer to the discussions in these materials for nonmarital valuations.
- Because of the wide divergence among various state laws, we did not become state specific on any issue. We assumed that the practitioner would meet with the attorney to determine the specific restrictions that the state places on divorce valuations.

- We assumed that practitioners wanted guidance on how they can better perform an engagement. The CPA is not looking for a "fill in the blanks" approach, but wants reassurance that the steps he or she is taking are in the right direction.
- We assumed that most CPAs have not provided trial testimony and would welcome some ideas to make that process less traumatic and more effective.

We hope that you will find that we succeeded in our goals and that this work will be a useful tool to the practitioner who performs three to six valuations a year, primarily in the marital litigation arena, as well as to the seasoned veteran.

The BV profession is rapidly changing. In the area of marital litigation it changes even faster. State decisions are constantly changing the interpretation and application of BV principles to divorce litigation. Therefore practitioners must stay current with the rules and interpretations of the jurisdiction in which they provide these services.

Robert E. Kleeman, Jr.
CPA/ABV, ASA, CVA

Acknowledgments

Until you have undertaken a project of this magnitude, you never really know how much effort it takes to complete the task. In addition, at the beginning of the project, you underestimate the help that you will need to meet the objective. I have written CPE programs before, but they pale in comparison to having to write a stand-alone text. What I thought would be a simple process turned out to be much more complex that I ever realized. My good friend and fellow member, Jim Alerding encouraged me to take on this project, and as it moved forward, Jim became a coauthor. The same is true of Ben Miller; what started as a promise to help where he could, turned into a significant contribution to this manuscript and coauthorship.

A number of other people were important to the realization of this project. First, we need to thank Randie Dial and Rick Takemoto. Both of these gentlemen are financial analysts with the Litigation and Valuation Services Group of Clifton Gunderson L.L.C. They had to track down volumes of information for our use, research technical information, chase down library materials, and do many other tasks, which they did professionally and with good cheer. We also need to thank Jennifer Lace, our administrative assistant in the Englewood, Colorado, office. Jennifer was chief gopher and chased down permissions and other details that are so important in publishing a work of this type. In addition, she had all of the rotten clerical jobs that we could possibly assign to her.

We also thank the business valuation groups that gave us permission to reproduce their standards and other pertinent information. It is truly exciting to see that all of these groups can come together for the good of the profession. None of these groups hesitated in giving us whatever information we wanted to publish. I have had the opportunity to work with many individuals who are members of all of these groups over the past few years, and was not surprised by the cooperation. Quite to the contrary, there was never a roadblock placed in my way by any of these groups.

Last, I think we all owe thanks to the business valuation giants who have been active in the development of this profession over the last 20 plus years. I would not even think of trying to name all of them, and I might suggest that it is not necessary to do so. I have been blessed with the privilege to personally know, and count as a friend, many of these individuals, and I am very grateful for that opportunity in my lifetime.

Chapter 1

Introduction

Whether we agree with the concept or not, divorce is a regular happening in the United States. Although there are some very simple divorces, a great many divorce cases today are complex and therefore, require experts. The CPA/accountant is well qualified to take on some of these assignments, and with additional training, may play an even greater role in assisting clients through their divorce. Surveys show that more and more accountants are trying to develop a niche practice, which includes divorce services. The problem is that these services are completely different from traditional services provided by the CPA. These are one-time engagements, they are unpredictable in their timing, and many involve a high level of sophistication. In most cases, we have never met our underlying client, and have no experience with their business. These engagements also tend to require a great deal of senior level involvement. The partner-to-staff ratio on these engagements is quite different from the traditional review or audit engagement. Far too often, we are called in on these engagements in the eleventh hour. Our workproduct is expected on a timely basis, and that time limit may be very short. The good news is that these engagements tend to be professionally challenging, and they can be pleasant to work on.

UNDERSTANDING THE LITIGATION ENVIRONMENT

It is important to understand the environment that you are going to encounter in this practice area. There are myriad rules that govern what you can and cannot do—rules related to whether you are an expert, rules regarding what you need to put in writing, rules related to what you can and cannot testify to. Unfortunately, these rules vary from state to state. The very concept of divorce differs from state to state. You may be practicing in an equitable distribution state, a community property state, or a hybrid state. Each of these concepts may require a different approach in the valuation area as well as other areas. One of your first steps in this new practice area is to find out exactly what the rules are in the jurisdictions that you will practice in. Understand that there are not only state rules, but local courts may also have unique rules. There is no excuse for you not knowing and understanding the rules as they relate to expert witnesses. You find that information by talking to the family law attorneys in your jurisdiction. It is your responsibility to learn the rules that surround your work in a given jurisdiction. You can also obtain information as to the expert rules by reviewing your state's rules of civil practice procedure.

SERVICES TO BE PROVIDED

Setting up the practice requires more than merely saying "I want to do this," and hanging up your shingle. This is not a practice area for the uninitiated and untrained. The practice requires additional skills beyond those learned in undergraduate school. Certainly, parts of the divorce practice utilize your day-to-day accounting and/or tax skills. Reviewing and commenting on tax returns, discussing the tax implications of various potential transactions, preparation of personal balance sheets, perhaps even pro forma income statements, all of these are potentially present in the divorce engagement. However, in preparing business valuation reports, and testifying at trial, new and additional skills are required. In order to qualify to testify at trial you must convince the court that you have specialized skills that have been acquired through experience or training. If you are unable to demonstrate these specialized skills, you may not be allowed to testify as an expert witness. In the last few years, there have been several court cases where the court has not accepted the CPA's valuation testimony, because the CPA could not demonstrate any formal business valuation training.

Valuation Services

Traditionally, marital litigation valuation services fall into three distinct categories. We provide an overview of each so that it is clear what you are and, more importantly, are not providing to your client.

- Valuation Opinion. Valuation opinion is the highest level of valuation service provided. In this service it is your responsibility to provide the client with an unambiguous opinion as to the value of the interest or asset that you are appraising. This means a complete valuation engagement that includes site visits, interviews with key employees, and a review of all of the applicable methodologies. Depending on the jurisdiction in which you are practicing, you may be required to provide a full written report that contains all of your assumptions and conclusions that support your valuation opinion. Your testimony may or may not be limited to the information included in your written report. You need to address this issue with the attorney who has retained you. To the extent that you are limited in your testimony to the information included in your report, you need to be certain that your report is complete as to the work that you have completed, as well as to your ultimate conclusions. (See Chapter 10.)

- Report Review. You may be asked to review and comment on a valuation report prepared by someone else. Your review may be of a report prepared on behalf of your client, or may be the report of the other party's expert. The ultimate use of your review may be a written report by you, and perhaps even testimony as a rebuttal witness. Reviewing a valuation report requires a high degree of valuation expertise and should not be attempted by someone who does not have significant valuation experience. Reviewing a report does not mean substituting your personal judgment for each of the appraiser's assumptions. The first focus of your review is to determine if you can replicate the work of the other appraiser. You need to be able to replicate the work prior to being able to critique the overall workproduct. Obviously, you may also be asked about the methodologies and the assumptions used by the appraiser. You need to let the engaging attorney know when you are questioning assumptions or when you are questioning facts. There is a distinct difference in those two issues. If you are questioning facts, then you need to demonstrate why the facts are not appropriate. Where you are questioning assumptions, you must not only explain why the assumption is questioned, but also why your assumption has more validity in the subject matter. Chapter 19 of Pratt's *Valuing a Business,* third edition (see Appendix A for the appropriate citation) has an excellent checklist that can be used when reviewing a valuation report.
- Estimate or Range of Value. In some instances, you may be requested to provide an estimate or range of value, particularly early in the matter, where the potential of settlement is strong. Estimates of value must be clearly stated as just that, an estimate, which falls far short of a full scope valuation and resulting report. In preparing an estimate of value, it is very important that you explain in your report all of the procedures that you did *not* follow, which could have a significant impact on the ultimate opinion of value. To the extent possible in your local jurisdiction, you should attempt to make any estimate of value not subject to discovery. Again, you need to discuss this issue with the attorney who retained you. It is not unusual for estimates to have as much as a 25 percent to 35 percent margin of error in the amount proffered. Estimates or ranges of value can be very dangerous in litigation matters. Because they are generated before you have all of the information, it is very easy to miss the target by a wide mark. If these estimates of value are obtained by opposing counsel, there may be significant discussions during your cross-examination as to the differences between the initial valuation and the final conclusion that you are testifying to at trial.

Expert Services

You may be asked by your client, or the attorney, to provide expert services in connection with the divorce action. These expert services can take a number of forms, and each has a different responsibility and level of work to be done by you.

- Fact Witness. You may be asked to testify at a deposition or hearing as a fact witness, because you have knowledge of certain information or other facts important to the matter. As a fact witness you are not allowed to provide opinion testimony to the trier of fact. You are only able to testify as to information that you have personal knowledge of. Examples of this testimony may be as to the nature of certain expense items that you deducted in a tax return or the authenticity of certain accounting records that you prepared. If you are the accountant for the entity being valued, you may be called as a fact witness to testify to numerous accounting matters.
- Consultant. Most jurisdictions allow an attorney to hire a consultant, whose identity is not disclosed to the opposing parties. As a consulting expert, your workproduct is generally not discoverable. (Note: Chapter 4 discusses this issue in greater detail.)
- Testifying Expert. This would include both direct and rebuttal testimony. In most jurisdictions, as a testifying expert, all of your workproduct is fully discoverable. In truth, the main difference between a fact witness and the expert witness is that the expert witness has the ability to offer the court an opinion. You need to keep this key distinction in mind at all times. Your expert opinion is being sought not just by your client, but also by the court. In Chapters 13 and 14 there is a lengthy discussion as to how the expert should handle both direct and cross-examination.

ABOUT THIS BOOK

This book focuses on the CPA as both a valuation professional and an expert witness. We do not discuss day-to-day accounting services that you may provide in connection with a divorce, but focus only on the issues discussed previously. Many CPAs provide tax consulting and financial planning to parties in the divorce. Those services are outside the scope of this work. Other books in print cover these services in detail.

As discussed in the Preface, we are assuming that the reader has some basic business valuation skills and is using this book as a tool to refresh prior training and experience. This book is envisioned to be similar to a security blanket, something that you can turn to and see if you are on the right track. Therefore, let us look at what we discuss and how you can best use these materials.

Chapter 2 discusses valuation methodologies and more importantly, the standards of value that may be appropriate in a marital litigation engagement. Understanding the appropriate standard of value is the most basic understanding that the successful business valuation expert must have. Unless you know the standard of value, how do you know what procedures to follow in order to get there? You may think that the appropriate standard of value is always fair market value. Again, this issue is determined by state law, and you need to be certain that you have the appropriate definition. Even when you review state law, you must understand that the standard of value used by a specific jurisdiction may not be the same as the normal definition of that standard. In addition, we briefly review the methodologies that can be used in divorce engagements.

We have also provided a chapter on engagement acceptance and administration. Chapter 3 discusses the nuances of determining whether you should accept the engagement and how you work with an existing client of your firm, as well as other administrative matters. Issues such as engagement letters and conflicts of interest are also included.

Chapters 4 through 6 are devoted to the engagement process, which includes issues such as what your role is in the process and the planning required in an engagement. We discuss the sources of information necessary for you to complete the engagement including information on the subject company. Industry information is discussed to give you an understanding of the sources and makeup of the information. We discuss when certain information is appropriate and when it may not be appropriate. Chapter 7 addresses the issues of comparable companies. Many CPAs just dismiss the guideline company methodology as being unusable for small entities. Although that may be true for the very small entity, the information explosion has made it much more practical to use a guideline methodology on many more closely held business entities.

Chapter 8 addresses the issues of discounts and premiums, keeping in mind that some jurisdictions do not allow the application of discounts for marketability or minority in marital engagements. Chapter 9 discusses the nuances of goodwill in a divorce context. This concept is very fluid and is changing very rapidly. At the same time, the state courts are all over the board on this issue. What may be case law in one jurisdiction may be just the opposite in another. Again, this issue is very critical to address in marital litigation. The expert must not only be aware of what the interpretation of professional goodwill is in a specific jurisdiction, but what the trend and changes are in that jurisdiction. Finally, we discuss the issues of reaching your valuation conclusion and reporting that conclusion.

Chapters 11 through 14 are devoted to issues relating to the CPA as an expert witness. These chapters discuss in detail the deposition process and all of the preparation necessary to provide effective direct examination at trial. We discuss providing the direct examination and how you can more effectively get your points and opinions across to the trier of fact. We finish with a discussion of how to survive cross-examination. Much of this material was taken from the course that Robert E. Kleeman, Jr. wrote several years ago. This course has been part of CPE (continuing professional education) Curriculum (either provided by the Illinois CPA Society or the AICPA) since the early 1980s. Over those years literally hundreds of CPAs have taken the course. Many of you may have taken that course and will recognize the concepts and thoughts. Ninety percent of what is said in these chapters is his personal opinion. These are concepts that he learned and used in his own professional practice over the last 24 years. Others may disagree with some of his personal thoughts, and you need to be aware of that. Short of telling the truth, there are very few hard-and-fast rules as they relate to providing direct and cross-examination. However, the hints and other thoughts contained in these chapters will help you understand the process and allow you to develop your own personal testimonial style.

As a reference source, Chapter 15 provides a discussion of the existing business valuation credentials, as well as the standards for each of the organizations that issues the credentials. Chapter 16 focuses on marketing the divorce practice. Suggested reference materials and selected forms are provided in the appendixes.

We certainly hope that you use these materials on a regular basis to reinforce your thought process when you are working on a marital litigation assignment. We would be very pleased to find out that your copy is dog-eared and well worn. These materials, used in conjunction with the other recognized basic treatises will assist you in a successful marital litigation practice.

Chapter 2

Valuation Approaches and Applicability to Divorce Practice

The topics of this chapter include discussions of the various standards of value used in the appraisal of closely held businesses and an overview on the asset, income, and market approaches to valuation.

STANDARDS OF VALUE

In the valuation of a closely held business, it is imperative for the appraiser to use the appropriate *standard of value* and that all readers of the appraisal report (e.g., business owners, attorneys, judges) are aware of and understand the standard of value used by the appraiser. *Value* is a relative term that, if not explicitly defined, can cause confusion between the writer of the appraisal report and the reader(s) of the report. Most professional business valuation associations require that the appraiser set forth and define the standard of value used in the valuation of a closely held business. For example, in the Business Valuation Standards, as promulgated by the American Society of Appraisers (ASA), the appraiser is required to ". . . identify and define the *standard of value*" (emphasis applied). The Uniform Standards of Professional Appraisal Practice (USPAP) states in Standard Rule 10-2 "Each written business or intangible assets appraisal report must . . . (c) define the value to be estimated."

Two standards of value, fair market value and fair value, are primarily used in the valuation of a closely held business for the purpose of a marital dissolution. Other standards of value that may be used in a divorce proceeding include book value, adjusted book value, going concern value, investment value, and liquidation value. It is incumbent on the expert to be certain that you know the required standard of value for the jurisdiction that you are working in. This standard may vary from jurisdiction to jurisdiction. You also need to be aware of not just the terminology used in the jurisdiction, but how that terminology is actually used. Each of these standards of value is discussed in the following sections.

Fair market value is probably the most widely used standard of value in the appraisal of closely held businesses. Fair market value is defined in the Business Valuation Standards of the American Society of Appraisers as

> The amount at which property would change hands between a willing seller and a willing buyer when neither is under compulsion and when both have reasonable knowledge of the relevant facts.

The Internal Revenue Service, in Revenue Ruling 59-60, defines fair market value in a similar manner as

> The amount at which the property would change hands between a willing buyer and a willing seller when the former is not under a compulsion to buy and the latter is not under any compulsion to sell, both parties having reasonable knowledge of the relevant facts.

Fair market value assumes an arms length transaction between two (or more) parties where each party has *reasonable* knowledge of the facts necessary to make an informed decision to buy or to sell and where neither party is under duress to buy or to sell. In addition, the standard of fair market value assumes a transaction with a hypothetical buyer in the marketplace as opposed to a specific buyer who may pay a different price because of the existence of synergies, cost savings, or other buyer-specific attributes.

Fair value is a statutorily or judicially defined standard of value. Historically, fair value has primarily been used in litigation matters involving a marital dissolution or dissenting minority interest shareholders. When appraising a business using the standard of fair value, the appraiser normally considers all elements of a business's value (such as income or cash flows, risk-adjusted rates of return, or value of assets in place) except for its investment value in the actual marketplace. When using this standard of value, it is critical for the appraiser to be knowledgeable of the applicable state statutes and case law. For example, in certain states, when valuing a closely held business for purposes of a marital dissolution, case law specifically disallows any discounts for lack of control and/or lack of marketability.

Book value is an accounting concept defined by the American Society of Appraisers in the Business Valuation Standards as

> 1. With respect to assets, the capitalized cost of an asset less accumulated depreciation, depletion, or amortization as it appears on the books of account of the enterprise;
> 2. With respect to a business enterprise, the difference between total assets (net of depreciation, depletion, and amortization) and total liabilities of an enterprise as they appear on the balance sheet. It is synonymous with net book value, net worth, and shareholder's equity.

Book value is rarely equal to fair market value. The only exception to that statement is where the assets of the entity are predominantly cash or cash equivalents and the appropriate valuation methodology is an asset-based approach. Book value is an accounting fiction, which only reflects the historic value of the assets as of the date that they were placed on the balance sheet, less a factor for book depreciation, which may have no relationship to actual economic or functional depreciation.

Adjusted book value is identical to book value with the exception that the business's tangible assets and liabilities are adjusted to their estimated fair market values. In some instances, adjusted book value also includes the value of a business's intangible assets (such as patents, trademarks, or goodwill). In many instances, it may be necessary to retain other qualified appraisers (e.g., real estate or machinery and equipment) in order to determine the fair market value of the assets. An expert should not attempt to determine the fair market value of the specific assets unless that expert has the professional qualifications to do so. Remember that your testimony is opinion testimony, but is based on your personal qualifications. Estimating the value of various assets may raise questions about your expertise.

Going concern value is often mentioned in appraisal reports as the "premise of value" used by the appraiser. When the appraiser values a business as a going concern, he is simply assuming that the business will continue to operate in the foreseeable future and not cease operations and liquidate. The ASA defines going concern value in its Business Valuation Standards as

1. The value of an enterprise, or an interest therein, as a going concern (i.e., an operating business enterprise); and
2. Intangible elements of value in a business enterprise resulting from factors such as: having a trained workforce; an operational plant; and the necessary licenses, systems, and procedures in place.

As defined in the foregoing, going concern value is not a standard of value (such as fair market value) but is rather a *premise of value* (i.e., a subset of a standard of value).

Investment value is the value of a business to a *specific* buyer as opposed to a hypothetical buyer as used in the standard of fair market value. When valuing a closely held business using the standard of investment value, the appraiser should consider the specific synergies, cost savings, and other buyer-specific attributes of the target buyer. For example, when using the standard of investment value on an income approach, the appraiser would most likely discount the subject business's projected cash flows at the buyer's cost of capital rather than at a market-based cost of capital. Investment value is rarely used in a marital matter. It is the antithesis of fair market value and only recognizes the value to a specific buyer.

Liquidation value is the value of a business with the assumption that ongoing operations have ceased and that the business's assets will be sold on a piecemeal basis. In general, liquidation value assumes that the business's assets will be sold in an orderly manner in order to obtain the highest possible price. However, *forced* liquidation value assumes that the assets are sold as quickly as possible (such as at auction). A forced liquidation value is almost always lower than the value achieved under an orderly liquidation. Therefore, if liquidation value is used, the appraiser should state whether it is assumed that the assets are sold in an orderly or forced manner.

VALUATION APPROACHES

Conventional appraisal theory provides several approaches for valuing closely held businesses. Although a myriad of valid methodologies exist for appraising businesses, there is general agreement in the appraisal profession that all of the methodologies can be categorized into one of three basic approaches. For a full discussion of the various valuation approaches generally accepted by the appraisal community, we suggest you obtain a copy of Shannon Pratt's *Body of Knowledge.* (See Appendix A for a detailed reference to the work.) The three basic valuation approaches are the income approach, the market approach, and the asset approach.

An *asset approach* values a business's assets and/or equity using one or more methods based directly upon the value of the business's tangible assets less liabilities. This method is analogous to the cost approach in real estate and other appraisal disciplines. An asset approach is primarily used in valuations conducted at the total entity level. It is not normally used to value minority interests because, in theory, minority interest shareholders do not have a direct claim on the business's assets nor do they have the ability to force the liquidation of the assets in order to receive the proceeds from their sale. Generally, the asset approach is not used to value an operating company that is considered a going concern. However, at times, such as when valuing a business with negative or minimal historical and/or projected earnings, an asset approach may give the best indication of value for a control interest.

An *income approach* values a business or equity interest by determining the present value of an expected benefit stream. Depending on the nature of the business, business ownership interest, or security being valued, as well as other factors, expected benefits are usually represented by earnings, cash flows, or dividends. Conversion of those benefits into present value are accomplished by either capitalization or discounting techniques. A capitalized returns method is normally used to value a business when, in the appraiser's opinion, the financial results of a business's current operations are indicative of future operations and annual growth is expected to change at a constant percentage rate. Alternatively, a discounted future returns method is normally used to value a business whose current financial results are not indicative of future operations and/or the expected annual benefit stream is not projected to change at a constant percentage rate. An example where an appraiser would most likely use a discounted future returns method would be in the valuation of a start-up company. Many start-ups incur losses during their initial start-up period before they begin to earn a profit. By using a multiperiod discounted future returns method, as opposed to a single-period capitalization returns method, the appraiser is able to value the business based on the positive earnings expected to be generated after the initial start-up period. The income approach can be used to directly value both control and minority interests. In marital litigation, some jurisdictions do not allow the use of a discounted future earnings methodology due to the fact that the methodology takes into consideration postmarital efforts and investment by the spouse that retains the business. It is the appraiser's responsibility to discuss with the attorney what methodology the jurisdiction allows or does not allow. You can also refer to case law for your state for additional guidance.

A *market approach* values a business or equity interest by using pricing information obtained on "comparable" guideline companies and applying the pricing information to the subject business. This valuation approach has its theoretical basis in the principle of substitution, which states that the value of an asset tends to be determined by the cost of acquiring an equally desirable substitute. Market transactions in businesses, business ownership interests, or securities can provide objective, empirical data for developing value measures to apply in business valuation. Such value measures are frequently derived from guideline companies—companies that provide a reasonable basis for comparison to the relative investment characteristics of the business being valued. Ideal guideline companies usually operate in the same industry as the subject business. However, if there is an insufficient number of guideline companies in the same industry as the subject business, it may be necessary to consider companies who have similar investment characteristics such as markets, growth, cyclical variability, and other salient factors. Depending upon the source of the guideline pricing information, the market approach can be used to directly value either a controlling interest or a minority interest. The guideline company approach is frequently discarded by appraisers in divorce matters because they believe that it is very difficult to find applicable guideline company information. In all but the smallest of valuation, the appraiser should review whether there are indeed guideline companies applicable to the subject company. Some commentators have suggested that the guideline companies can be as much as 50 times larger than the subject company, but the authors are more comfortable with a ceiling of around 25 to 30 times larger. The key consideration is whether the appraiser can locate appropriate information on guideline companies. The availability of data for guideline private company transactions, as well as information regarding the smallest public companies, has dramatically increased in the last couple of years. (See Chapter 7 for a more complete discussion of the source of guideline company data.)

Asset Approach

The asset approach is primarily used to value a controlling interest in a business entity that possesses one or more of the following attributes:

- The business's value is primarily dependent upon its assets as opposed to earnings or cash flows.

- The business is not a going concern entity or there are serious questions about the business's ability to remain as a going concern entity.
- There are little or no earnings or cash flows to capitalize into value.

In business valuation, the net asset value method and the excess earnings method (essentially a combination method that uses both asset and income approaches) are the two most commonly used asset approach methods to value a closely held business.

Net Asset Value Method

The net asset value method develops an indication of value by adjusting a business's component assets and liabilities to their estimated fair market values (or other appropriately disclosed standard of value). Assets are adjusted to either their *value in use* (if the entity is assumed to be a going concern) or to their liquidation value. Assets are adjusted to their liquidation values when, in the appraiser's opinion, the business is worth more dead than alive. When a business's financial statements are prepared on a cash basis, it is sometimes necessary to add certain assets and liabilities that do not appear on a cash basis balance sheet (such as accounts receivable and accounts payable). The most commonly adjusted assets include the following:

- Accounts receivable. This current asset is often overstated on a business's balance sheet and should be adjusted to its net realizable value. In professional practices, accounts receivable often is the practice's largest asset and the appraiser should, therefore, perform a detailed analysis regarding their net realizable value.
- Inventory. In many businesses, inventory is a material asset that may or may not be stated on the balance sheet at fair market value. The appraiser should consider adjusting this asset if inventory is accounted for on a last in, first out (LIFO) basis, is not taken on a regular basis, or large amounts of obsolete items are included on the business's books. The level of analysis detail depends upon the materiality of the asset relative to the business's total value.
- Machinery and equipment. These assets are normally stated on a business's balance sheet at their original cost less accumulated depreciation. Depreciation is often based on tax law as opposed to the assets' true "economic" depreciation. If the value of the machinery and equipment is material to the business entity's overall value, it may be necessary to subcontract an appraiser who specializes in valuing fixed assets.
- Real property. As with machinery and equipment, real property is usually stated on a business's balance sheet at original cost less accumulated depreciation. In many parts of the United States, the value of real property actually appreciates in value and may be materially understated on a business's financial statements. An

appraiser who specializes in real property is often required to be subcontracted in order to adjust the asset to its estimated fair market value.

- Notes receivable. The stated value of a note receivable may not represent its current value. An adjustment to this asset may be required if current market rates of interest are materially different from the rate of interest earned by the note. If no payments on the note are being received by the business (as is often the case with notes receivable from the owners of the business), the appraiser may need to consider materially lowering the value of the note to the business.
- Notes payable. As with notes receivable, it may be necessary to adjust a business's notes payable if the rate(s) of interest being paid on the notes are materially different from current interest rates.
- Deferred income taxes. Deferred income taxes are often found on a business's balance sheet. In general, most appraisers remove the liability if, in their opinion, the liability is not "immediate and specific." The liability is usually left unadjusted if the appraiser is of the opinion that the business will begin to pay the deferred income tax liability in the near future. If the liability is not removed, many appraisers adjust it to an estimate of its present value.

Excess Earnings Method

The excess earnings method is a combination of an asset approach and an income approach. An asset approach is used to estimate the value of the business's tangible assets; an income approach is used to quantify the value of the intangible assets. The entity's total value is determined by summing the tangible and intangible components. The excess earnings method is the most widely used and abused methodology in existence today. Although much maligned by many in the business valuation community, it is a valuation method that, partly due to its simplicity and partly due to its "real world" applicability, continues to be used by appraisers of small businesses for purposes of a divorce. The Internal Revenue Service, in Revenue Ruling 68-609 termed the excess earnings method as a method of last resort. With the exception of very small, usually one man businesses, other methods may be more appropriate. The capitalization of excess earnings method requires estimates of

- The business's tangible assets' adjusted book value
- The business's "excess earnings"
- A capitalization rate applicable to the calculated excess earnings

Determining the Tangible Assets' Adjusted Book Value

The first step in valuing a business using the excess earnings method usually is to adjust the tangible assets to their estimated fair market value. This part of the analysis is similar to using the net asset method. After the tangible assets have been adjusted to their estimated fair market values, it is necessary to determine the value of the business's intangible assets, which is normally accomplished by determining the business's excess earnings stream and capitalizing this stream into value.

Estimating the Value of the Business's Intangible Assets

The three basic steps in determining intangible asset value using an excess earnings method are

1. Calculate an ongoing earnings base for the business.
2. Subtract a market return on the business's tangible assets from the previously calculated ongoing earnings base to calculate excess earnings.
3. Capitalize the excess earnings into intangible asset value.

The ongoing earnings base is usually adjusted to remove nonoperating and nonrecurring revenues and expenses, excess owners' compensation, and other discretionary expenses (such as charitable contributions or excess travel and entertainment). The goal is to restate the business's income statements as if the business were operated by a professional management team for the benefit of nonmanager owners. Therefore, only those costs that would be necessary to compensate the professional management team are appropriately included in the restated financial statements.

The excess earnings method assumes that the owner(s) of the business should receive a market rate of return for the tangible assets invested in the business and that any return over and above the market rate of return is a return on the intangible assets of the entity. The value of the intangible is added to the net asset value to determine the overall value of the entity. The theory is based on the opportunity cost the owners are incurring by investing in their business's tangible assets and forgoing the income that could be earned by investing a like amount in other securities. For example, if a business owner has $100,000 equity invested in her business's tangible assets and rates of return on similar assets are 10 percent, the business owner has forgone $10,000 of income by investing the $100,000 in the tangible assets of her business. In determining the excess earnings being generated by her business, this $10,000 of forgone income would be deducted from the calculated ongoing earnings base.

Determining the appropriate capitalization rate to apply to a business's excess earnings depends on many subjective factors. In general, the capitalization rate to apply to the pretax excess earnings of most small businesses range between 20 percent and 100 percent (multiple of 1× to 5×). Businesses that are highly transferable (such as a dry cleaning business) tend to sell at the higher end of the multiplier range while businesses that are not easily transferred to another owner (such as an attorney's practice) tend to sell at the lower end of the multiplier range. This 1x to 5x earnings is a rule of thumb. This is a major weakness of the excess earnings method—developing the appropriate rate. There is no easy answer; the rate needs to be justified. We prefer that the appropriate capitalization rate be developed using a more recognized methodology such as the build up method or the Capital Asset Pricing Model.

Income Approach

An income approach values a closely held company by discounting or capitalizing an expected ongoing benefit stream by a risk-adjusted discount or capitalization rate. The American Society of Appraisers defines income approach in the Business Valuation Standards as

> A general way of determining a value indication of a business, business ownership interest, or security using one or more methods wherein a value is determined by converting anticipated benefits.

In general, the three steps involved in using an income approach are

1. Estimate the business's benefit stream (using either single-period or multiperiod models).
2. Determine the appropriate risk-adjusted rate of return to apply to the benefit stream.
3. Discount or capitalize the benefit stream into estimated fair market value using the risk-adjusted discount/capitalization rate.

Depending upon the benefit stream used, the resulting value is either a marketable minority interest value or a controlling interest value.

Estimating Benefit Stream

A partial list of possible benefit streams that an analyst can calculate for a subject business includes the following:

- Net income
- Earnings before interest, taxes, depreciation, and amortization (EBITDA)
- Earnings before interest and taxes (EBIT)
- Net free cash flow

All of these benefit streams can be calculated on a single-period or multiperiod basis. It is important that the appraiser match the selected benefit stream to the appropriate discount or capitalization rate. For example, it would be incorrect to use a capitalization rate based on after-tax returns with a pretax benefit stream without adjusting either the capitalization rate or the benefit stream so that they are on the same basis.

A common method of calculating a single-period benefit stream is to adjust a business's historical income statements for nonoperating and/or nonrecurring revenues and expenses, apply weights to the adjusted benefit streams, multiply each year's benefit stream by the selected weight, sum the weighted benefit streams, and divide by the sum of the weights. The calculated weighted-average benefit stream is then divided by an appropriate capitalization rate to calculate an indicated value. Again, note that in marital litigation, many courts do not allow the use of future period projections in determining the value of the business entity due to the impact of future nonmarital efforts and investment.

A common method of calculating a multiperiod benefit stream is to first estimate a base income statement and then project the business's revenues and expenses for up to five to ten years past the date of valuation. The present value of the selected benefit stream (e.g., net income, EBITDA, net cash flow) is calculated by discounting each year at a risk-adjusted discount rate. When using a multiperiod income approach, it is usually necessary to calculate a "terminal" value of the business at the end of the projection period before discounting it to its present value as of the date of valuation. The business's terminal value is normally calculated using a single-period income approach.

Determining the Cost of Capital

Although there are many accepted methods for determining the appropriate cost of capital (discount rate), two methods, the *build-up* method and *CAPM* (capital asset pricing model) method, are primarily used by business appraisers when valuing closely held businesses. Both methods derive a risk-adjusted discount/capitalization rate by identifying and quantifying the discreet components that, summed together, comprise total return. The difference between the two methods is that the CAPM method uses a market-based beta statistic while the build-up method assumes a beta statistic of one (1).

The CAPM requires the following risk/return components to be identified and quantified:

- Risk-free rate. The risk-free rate of return is the first component of a business's required rate of return. In general, investors require higher rates of return for assuming higher levels of risk. The rate of return for long-term government bonds is commonly used as the risk-free component of the discount/capitalization rate. Common sources for the risk-free rate of return include the *Wall Street Journal,* the *Federal Reserve Bulletin,* and the *Federal Reserve Statistical Release.*
- + Equity risk premium. This component of total return is the historical premium of the total returns earned by the equity securities of large publicly traded companies versus the historical income returns of long-term government securities. A common source for the equity risk return is *Stocks, Bonds, Bills, and*

Inflation (*SBBI*) published by the Chicago-based financial research firm of Ibbotson Associates.

- × Beta factor. Beta is a statistic that measures the degree to which the returns for a specific investment move with the market. A beta of 1.0 indicates that the returns for a specific investment move in tandem with the market. A beta of 2.0 indicates that the investment's returns move with the market but at a factor of two. The beta factor is multiplied by the equity risk premium to calculate the market risk premium (which is the rate of return in excess of the risk-free rate of return). Common sources for betas include the *Cost of Capital Quarterly* (*CCQ*) published by Ibbotson Associates and the *Value Line Investment Survey.*
- + Risk adjustment for size. Studies have shown that, in general, the historical total returns of smaller capitalized companies are greater than the total returns of larger capitalized companies. The most common source for this statistic is Ibbotson Associates' *SBBI.*
- + Company-specific premium. Summing the foregoing risk components will derive a discount rate that is industry and size specific but not company specific. Because the appraiser's assignment is to value a specific closely held business, additional risk factors that are specific to the business being valued must normally be included in the total returns calculation. This component of risk involves large amounts of judgment and subjectivity by the appraiser. A partial list of the factors that an appraiser considers in determining this risk component includes the strength and depth of management, the financial outlook and risk associated with the business's industry, and the business's financial risks (such as interest coverage, amount of leverage, or profitability). Note that this could be a positive or negative number.

Summing the foregoing rate of return components results in a risk-adjusted discount rate appropriate for calculating the present values of a multiperiod benefit stream. In order to calculate a capitalization rate for use in a single-period model, an estimate of the business's long-term growth rate in its benefit stream is subtracted from the risk-adjusted discount rate.

- − Expected Long-Term Growth Rate. The long-term growth rate is based on the appraiser's judgment of the business's ability to penetrate the market, the growth potential for the market, and expected price increases.

Summing all of the foregoing components results in a risk-adjusted capitalization rate used to convert a single-period benefit stream into an indicated value.

Market Approach

A market approach is based on comparing market transactions involving comparable guideline companies and using the information on those market transactions to estimate the value of the subject business. Common pricing ratios obtained from guideline companies which are applied to the subject business include:

- Price to Earnings (P/E) Ratio
- Price to Book (P/B) Ratio
- Price to Revenues Ratio

The market approach requires estimates of (1) a pricing multiple (such as a P/E ratio) derived from publicly traded or privately held guideline companies and (2) the subject company's benefit stream (such as net earnings), which is applied to the pricing ratio to determine an indicated value. (We suggest that the reader review Shannon Pratt's *Cost of Capital* listed in Appendix A.)

Search for Guideline Companies

Guideline companies are companies that provide a reasonable basis for comparison to the relevant investment characteristics of the subject business being valued. Prices paid for shares of stock in guideline companies are used as a basis to develop valuation conclusions of the subject business under the presumption that a similar market exists for the subject business as exists for the guideline companies.

Ideal guideline companies are in the same industry as the business being valued. However, if there is insufficient transaction evidence in the same industry, it may be necessary to consider companies with an underlying similarity of relevant investment characteristics such as markets, products, growth, cyclical variability, and other salient factors. Chapter 6 discusses the various sources of publicly traded and privately held guideline companies.

The following steps should be used when performing a market approach:

- Identify the industry in which the subject business operates.
- Identify the Standard Industrial Classification (SIC) Code for the industry in which the subject business operates.
- Using Internet search tools such as FreeEdgar, search filings with the Securities and Exchange Commission (SEC) for businesses that are similar to the subject business. In addition to the Internet, other sources of guideline companies such as Standard & Poor's Corporation's Stock Guide, Bizcomps, Pratt's Stats, and Done Deals can be used to search for guideline companies.
- Screen the initial group of guideline companies to eliminate those obviously not comparable to the subject business. Reasons for excluding companies might include negative earnings, the company is in bankruptcy proceeding, revenues are too large, and too much diversification.
- Review in detail the financial and operational aspects of the remaining potential guideline companies eliminating those companies whose products and/or services differ substantially from the subject business.

A common error in using the guideline company method occurs when the appraiser blindly takes the guideline company information and applies it to the subject company. The appraiser must allow for the difference between the guideline companies and the subject company. When calculating pricing ratios derived from publicly traded guideline companies to apply to a closely held business, the appraiser should consider the following differences between publicly traded and private, closely held businesses:

- Anticipated growth. Pricing ratios derived from publicly traded companies generally reflect significantly higher anticipated growth rates as compared to a typical privately held business. To the extent that a difference in anticipated growth between the group of publicly traded companies and the subject business exist, the pricing ratios derived from the publicly traded companies should be adjusted to reflect the difference.
- Size. Most publicly traded companies are larger than the closely held businesses being appraised for purposes of a divorce. As previously written, smaller capitalized companies generally earn a higher rate of return than larger capitalized companies. Higher rates of return translate into smaller pricing ratios. Therefore, it is generally necessary to adjust the pricing multiples derived from publicly traded guideline companies downward to account for the difference in size between them and the privately held subject business.
- Financial stability. Most guideline companies have greater access to the equity and credit markets than the closely held business. Ratio analysis between the guideline companies and the subject company is very important in order to assess the magnitude of the differences. Leverage is also very important to this mix. If the debt/equity ratio of the guideline companies is 1:1, and the subject company is 4:1, there is an obvious difference in the financial stability of the entities and the appraiser must take this difference into consideration.
- Risk. Most closely held entities are inherently more risky than the guideline companies that you locate. This risk can be due to various factors such as depth of management, a small group of key customers, dependence on a single supplier, lack of diversification in products or services offered. Again, all of those factors need to be considered when using the guideline company methodology.

Once the pricing multiple has been derived and adjusted, an indicated value for the subject business is calculated by multiplying the ratio by the appropriate base (earnings, revenues, book value, etc.). The premise of value derived (i.e., control or minority interest) is based on the source of the guideline pricing ratio(s). Ratios derived from shares of publicly traded companies yield a minority interest value while ratios derived from merger and acquisition sources yield a control interest value. We suggest that the appraiser review many of the pricing multiples in order to get a clear indication of value. Where specific pricing multiples are not used, the reasons for not using those multiples should be discussed in the valuation report.

SUMMARY

Knowing both the standard of value and the appropriate premise of value is critical to the proper determination of the value to be presented in a marital litigation matter. It is incumbent on the business valuation expert to be conversant with all of the appropriate standards of value as well as the generally accepted valuation methodologies. The business valuation expert must also demonstrate the application of those standards and methodologies.

Chapter 3

Engagement Acceptance and Administration

Engagement acceptance procedures are very important to building a successful practice in the marital dissolution arena. It has been said that you can make more money from the cases that you do not accept. The larger your firm, the more complex these engagement acceptance procedures become. Yet we tend to dismiss the administrative side of the practice, concerning ourselves with charge hours and the fun part of the practice. Unfortunately, the administrative side of the practice is as important, if not more important, than valuing the business, calculating the tax impact of proposed transactions, developing a marital balance sheet, or writing the report. Proper administration avoids many problems associated with the ultimate satisfaction of the client and the attorney that you are working with as well as the collection of your fee. Mistakes in the area of conflicts can be fatal to your continued practice. This chapter has a significant discussion regarding the importance of conflict checks. The very issue of whether you should accept the engagement is critical to good administration. There are times when it is in your best interest to not accept the engagement. Engagement letters are a must. It is foolish to begin any engagement without a signed engagement letter. As we discuss later in this chapter, the engagement contract sets the terms and conditions for your engagement, and it is critical that this information be conveyed to both the attorney and the party to the dissolution.

PREENGAGEMENT PROCEDURES

Before agreeing to perform any service in a marital dissolution, certain Preengagement procedures should be performed by the person responsible for the engagement.

These procedures are necessary to ensure that the following factors have been considered before the assignment is accepted:

- Whether you can produce an objective, independent opinion of value or other required report
- Whether you have the required expertise to perform the engagement
- Whether the assignment can be competently completed within the required time frame
- Whether the engagement will be profitable
- Whether there is a reasonable expectation that the generated fees will be collected
- Whether you have staff who are available to work on the assignment
- Whether you have adequate library resources to competently perform the engagement

CONFLICTS OF INTEREST

The first step in the process is to determine that you and your firm are free from all real and perceived conflicts of interest between you and the parties to the litigation. Many years ago, Frederick Nietzsche wrote "To be independent is the business of a few only, it is the privilege of the strong." This is an interesting concept in the marital litigation arena. Ultimate independence requires that you as the expert must be ready at any time to exercise your ability to decline an engagement or to resign from an engagement that you have previously accepted. This responsibility is ongoing and continues throughout the engagement.

The American Institute of Certified Public Accountants (AICPA) has issued Rule 102, which provides the practitioner with the following guidance: "**In the performance of any professional service, a member shall maintain objectivity and integrity, shall be free of conflict of interest, and shall not knowingly misrepresent facts or subordinate his or her judgment to others.**" Let us examine this rule in detail.

- "**In the performance of any professional service**"—Clearly, business valuation and litigation services engagements are professional services performed by CPAs. Performing these and other services carries over into the area of marital dissolutions. Therefore, it is clear that Rule 102 applies to any practitioner who is providing services for marital litigation.
- "**a member shall maintain objectivity and integrity**"—Our integrity must be beyond reproach, and we have a duty to our client to maintain our objectivity. We are expected to provide independent information in these matters. Where we are asked to provide opinions, those opinions must reflect our objectivity and integrity. We must maintain our professional approach to the overall engagement.

- **"shall be free of conflict of interest"**—This phrase includes not just obvious direct conflicts, but also the appearance of conflicts. This line is much finer than it may at first appear, and is discussed in detail in this chapter.
- **"and shall not knowingly misrepresent facts or subordinate his or her judgment to others"**—Misrepresentation is an absolute error in marital litigation matters. The expert who knowingly misrepresents information is an expert doomed to extinction. Just as important is the concept of subordinating judgment to others. Your role is to maintain your objectivity and integrity, and at all times be certain that your opinions and conclusions are based on your workproduct and judgment and are not the opinions or conclusions requested by another party in the litigation.

We are all well aware of the common direct conflicts of interest: Where we have a financial interest in the transaction or the entity; where we have a contingent fee for an engagement; where we have family relationships that rise to the level of a conflict; issues where we are being asked to perform services against a former client. But let us review some potential conflicts that arise in marital litigation.

- "Who is the client?"—Let us look at a typical scenario for many accounting firms. Your client owns a mid-sized manufacturing entity. Your firm has provided certified audits over the last 10 years. Your firm also handles the corporate and individual tax issues and has performed many consulting engagements over the years. You are the client partner, and although you are not personally responsible for the audit or tax work, you primarily work with the client on the consulting side. Since your firm performs certified audits it is clear you and your firm are "independent" as that term applies to the attest function. Your client calls you and informs you that divorce papers have been filed and that the client's attorney wants you to be the business valuation expert witness in the matter on behalf of your client's side of the case. You have never met the client's spouse. The question is, Can your firm accept this engagement? On the surface it may seem that this decision is easy. Why would you not want to continue with the long-term relationship that you have with this client? In fact, you may have a conflict of interest. After all, did not your firm prepare the personal tax returns for the parties, and therefore would it not be true that both the client and spouse are clients of the firm? You must understand the client relationships that have existed in the past and determine how they impact your potential resolution of a conflict. Where both parties are former clients of your firm, you may be precluded from working on the engagement without the permission of both of your clients.
- Fees and their impact on the appearance of lack of independence—Consider the previous scenario, with the exception being that your firm has never performed any personal tax services for the couple. In addition, assume that the corporate stock to be valued is nonmarital property acquired prior to the current marriage. Also assume that your annual fees from this client are approximately $50,000 annually, which makes this client not the largest client of your firm, but certainly a

major client. Again the client asks that you accept an engagement to be the business valuation expert in the pending marital dissolution. Again on the surface, this appears to be a simple matter where you can accept the engagement as just another service that you are providing to a long-standing client. But this long-standing, material relationship may be detrimental to your overall credibility as an expert in the case. Imagine the line of questioning during your cross-examination. The questions will focus on the amount of fees that your firm receives from your continuing engagements. Follow-up questions may even imply that you would not want to harm this long-term relationship. These questions are constructed to show that you may not be independent as it relates to your work for the client's marital litigation. Certainly, opposing counsel will raise issues regarding objectivity and overall credibility. It is usually not in your or your client's best interest for your firm to be the expert witness on a litigation matter that involves that client.

- Pandora's box—Another reason that the current client might not be well served by you is the very basis of the long-term relationship that exists between you and the client. As the long-term accountant, you may have information in your files and other documents that may or may not be otherwise discoverable. Yet if you become the expert for the client, that information and documentation may be more readily discoverable by opposing counsel.

In summary, rarely is it in your existing client's best interest for you to be retained as an expert in marital litigation matters.

There are two additional ways in which you may have a conflict of interest and thus be precluded from accepting a business valuation engagement. The first way to be conflicted is by being retained by the opposing counsel. The second way to be conflicted is by not being able to perform the engagement in an *independent* manner.

If one party to the marital dissolution has retained you or your firm to provide professional services as part of that marital dissolution, you or your firm cannot perform the same or similar service for the other spouse. An exception to the previous statement would be if both parties agree, in advance and in writing, to the use of the same appraiser. When your marital litigation practice is small, it is fairly easy to keep track of your assignments; they are probably all in your head. However, as your marital litigation practice grows, and different staff members perform much of the preliminary work, you may find that you may not know all of your marital litigation assignments by name. Should this be the case, it is possible that an attorney may call you inquiring about the possibility of retaining you or your firm, when in fact, the opposing counsel has already retained your firm. To avoid this type of conflict of interest, the following procedures should be maintained by all personnel involved with accepting marital litigation engagements:

- Keep a current list of all marital litigation engagements. The list should include the names of the petitioner, the respondent, and the names of their attorneys. Clearly mark who has retained you or your firm. When an attorney calls about a possible valuation engagement, refer to this list before discussing the case.

- In general, be wary of detailed discussions regarding a possible valuation engagement with an attorney before you have been retained. If, for some reason, an attorney does not want to hire you but also does not want to oppose you, he or she may conflict you out of the case by divulging to you sensitive materials regarding the dissolution.
- After you have satisfied yourself that you do not have a conflict, make sure that you know the name of the opposing expert (if there is one and his or her name is known). This ensures that you are not on the opposite side of a case with another member of your firm.

In order to ensure you and your firm's independence with regard to marital litigation engagements, the following points should be observed in the preengagement process:

- Fees that are contingent upon the outcome of the court proceedings or on the appraiser's opinion of value are not to be accepted. Marital litigation engagements should be billed on an hourly rate.
- The appraiser should have no financial interest in the business being appraised.
- If the appraisal is for an existing client, the individual responsible for the marital litigation engagement and the individual in charge of the client should review the matter for possible independence problems. If the business that is to be appraised is marital property, the "existing client" may be both parties, therefore creating a possible conflict of interest situation.
- You should put in place a mechanism that makes one individual in your firm the ultimate decision maker as to whether a marital dissolution engagement is accepted. This person should be consulted prior to the acceptance of any marital dissolution engagement.

EXPERTISE, COMPETENCE, AND TIME COMMITMENT

Before your acceptance of the engagement you must be certain that you have both the technical competence, and the time to complete the engagement within the parameters set by your client. Obviously, if you are not an expert in the area of divorce taxation, you do not want to accept an engagement to prepare tax projections and perhaps testify as to the tax impact of certain transactions. Conversely, based on your business valuation experience and training, there may be many engagements that you may not be competent to complete. Your overall success as an expert is dependent on only accepting engagements that you are competent to perform. You should have significant training and experience that allow you to successfully complete the engagement. Also consider the issue of timing and your availability to complete the engagement within the parameters set forth by your client. If you have a large audit or tax practice, and you have a heavy time commitment during busy season, do you have the time to accept an engagement that might require an additional 100+ hours of time over six to eight weeks during that busy season? Be aware of the potential engagement where you are contacted by a client to request that you issue a report in a very short period of time. Rarely can you complete a business valuation engagement in less than 40 hours. Unreasonable time frames are a road to potential disaster for the expert witness.

Some of the issues you need to address in determining your professional competence include

- Possessing a business valuation credential from a recognized professional association. The specific designations are discussed in Chapter 15.
- Possessing a graduate degree, such as an MBA or a Master in Taxation, from an accredited university or college
- Having or having access to an understanding of the industry (including what drives value and how businesses in the industry are bought and sold) in which the subject business operates
- Taking courses on business valuation from professional associations, universities, and so forth
- Engaging in a home study program

Consider the other resources available in your office prior to accepting the engagement. Do you have adequate research materials and skills to complete the engagement? What about staff?

After you have satisfied yourself that you can competently perform the marital dissolution engagement, the following questions should be answered to be sure that the assignment could be completed within the attorney's required time frame:

- Is a written report required? If so, are schedules and numbers expected at a prior date?
- When are the appropriate reports required to be delivered?
- What is the date of the trial?
- How complex is the business to be valued?
- When can receipt of required documents be expected?
- Is a site interview/inspection required? (Almost always)
- Is there available staff to handle the lower billing aspects of the engagement?
- Can you fit the engagement into your present workload?

If, given the attorney's time constraints, you determine that there is not enough time to perform the engagement competently, it is probably better to decline the assignment than to accept it and risk either performing a substandard job or allowing other project deadlines to slip.

PROFITABLE ENGAGEMENTS

In order to perform the valuation engagement profitably, you must accurately determine the time required to perform the engagement. Your quoted fee must be both profitable to you and competitive in the marketplace. Fees for depositions or trial testimony are in addition to the quoted fee. Obviously, the more complex the engagement, the larger the expected fees in the matter. If the engagement includes a business valuation, some of the following items need to be considered in determining the fee quote:

- Research of publicly traded guideline companies (usually not required when performing a simple valuation)
- Poor or incomplete financial records
- Unique types of businesses where basic rules of thumb or private transaction data are difficult or impossible to obtain
- Corporations that own multiple assets (for example, a corporation that owns a restaurant, the building from which the restaurant operates, and large amounts of nonoperating assets)
- Minority interest holdings. It may cost more to value a minority interest than an entire business because the appraiser may have to determine minority interest discounts or discounts for lack of marketability. Also, in some minority interest situations, you may not have adequate access to financial information of the overall entity, which can greatly increase the required hours that you must put into the engagement.
- Businesses with multiple sites that must be inspected
- Start-up businesses

When determining the fee, be certain that you carefully consider all of the expected tasks to be included in the engagement. Will you be providing a business valuation? Will you be reviewing and critiquing your opposing expert's report? What services are included in your fee quote, and what services are over and above your basic fee quote and are going to be billed on a strict hourly basis.

Usually, it is best to quote a fee range. Should the attorney initially balk at the quoted appraisal fee you have three choices. The first choice is to lower the fee and perform the same level of service. This may be the appropriate action to take for a "good" client or when you want to use price as an incentive to be hired. The second choice is to lower the fee but also lower the level of service (e.g., reduce the scope of your engagement). The third choice is, of course, to simply decline to perform the engagement for a lower fee. If you decline the engagement, you should state to the attorney, in writing, your reasons for declining the engagement and why you cannot professionally perform the appraisal for less than your quoted fee. The engagement requires a minimum number of professional hours. Be cognizant that a very low fee may signal an inadequate amount of work on the engagement.

ENGAGEMENT LETTER

Every engagement starts with a signed engagement letter. (Appendix B contains a sample engagement letter) This engagement letter needs, as a minimum, the following elements:

- Who is your client? Are you being retained by the attorney, by a business entity, or by one of the parties to the marital dissolution? The importance of who your client is may vary from jurisdiction to jurisdiction. This drives many other decisions in the engagement including who the responsible party is for the payment of your fees.
- The specific assignment. What are you being retained to accomplish? What is the overall scope of the engagement? Is the engagement being accepted in phases, with future work dependent on earlier work or review of information? What type of reports will you be required to provide to your client? What are the deadlines or other time constraints that you will be working under? Are you expected to critique the opposing expert's report? Will you be required to provide deposition or trial testimony? What is the standard of value for your engagement?
- Terms and conditions of the engagement. Are there any issues that you will not consider as part of your work such as environmental issues or Y2K issues? When do you require the underlying information from the client so that you can meet the deadlines?
- Retainer and fee agreements. It is critical in the engagement letter to make very clear the financial arrangements of the engagement. What is the required retainer? Is it refundable? When do you apply the retainer, to your final billing or to your initial billings? What are your hourly rates, or is this a fixed-fee engagement? If you have quoted a fixed fee, what is included in that fixed fee, and what services are not included in that fee quote. Do you include travel time in your billings? What about time that you are sitting at the courthouse waiting to testify. What are your billing and collection procedures? Will you discontinue the engagement if you have outstanding accounts receivable?

As the engagement changes, so must the engagement letter. It is not uncommon to issue several engagement letters during the course of the divorce action, with each revised engagement letter setting forth the changes in the assignment. Even though you may think that this is just another administrative headache, it is critical that this record be made so that your tasks and fees are clear to all parties. Just as it is important for the attorney to understand clearly what you are doing, it is also important that you clearly explain what you are *not* doing. You do not want to be in the position of having the attorney and/or the underlying client holding a set of expectations that you cannot meet. This includes not just services, but potential outcomes. The attorney and/or client cannot dictate your ultimate conclusions. You must make it clear that your conclusions are your conclusions, and not the joint workproduct of the attorney, client, and you.

RETAINER AND BILLING

When performing marital dissolution services, it is highly recommended that you receive approximately one-half of the high end of the quoted fee as a retainer. At a minimum, we recommend that the retainer be at least equal to what you expect your billings to be over the first 60 days of the engagement. This 60-day period allows you to complete a billing cycle and will give you some comfort of the payment habits of your client. However, this rule of thumb can vary depending upon what is happening in the market area where you practice. The custom of collecting a retainer, or the size of the retainer, may not be the same in rural Colorado as it is in Chicago. No matter what the geographic differences are, it is still very important to create some process for protecting yourself and your firm from uncollected fees.

As with any professional service, the perceived value of the rendered service diminishes with the passage of time. Therefore, in order to maximize collections, it is imperative to regularly bill the client, to collect a retainer fee (if allowable), and to send a final bill as soon as the engagement is completed. Also, a client's accounts receivable balance should be substantially paid up prior to providing testimony in a deposition or a trial. Large accounts receivable balances may cause a perceived lack of independence by the expert (i.e., the expert may have a financial incentive to give the client a number he or she wants, or may be perceived to be handling the matter on a contingent fee basis). By not carrying a large accounts receivable balance, the expert is perceived to have no financial interest in the outcome of the trial. You must be prepared to refuse to testify if you have significant outstanding receivables, just to protect yourself from these perceptions.

SUMMARY

Proper procedures are necessary to ensure that prior to accepting an engagement you meet the criteria set for CPAs. The AICPA Rule 102 is a cornerstone of the services that you will be providing in marital litigation engagements. The CPA must take all necessary steps to ensure that objectivity and integrity are maintained during the engagement. The ultimate success and credibility of your testimony rests on those foundations.

FURTHER READING

The following items are listed in Appendix A and are sources of additional information and background regarding the information contained in this chapter. Those publications may provide an in-depth discussion of basic issues.

- *Guide to Business Valuations,* Fishman et al., Practitioners Publishing Company.
- *Guide to Divorce Engagements,* Pratt et al., Practitioners Publishing Company.

Chapter 4

The Engagement Process

There is a basic truism in providing divorce services: "The case you initially accept is rarely the same case that you take to trial." Litigation engagements are dynamic and fluid. Initially, the information you receive is the information from your underlying client, and that party has filtered that information. As you continue working on the engagement, you find out the "facts" according to the opposing side. Both sides have provided you with information that includes their bias. As you go forward, you will find that the "facts" are not necessarily what you were originally told, nor are they the "facts" that you have heard from either party during the engagement. Part of your very difficult job is to filter through these biases and come to the truth. However, the engagement does have a defined process. The better you understand this process, the easier it will be for you to provide valuation or other services in marital litigation matters.

The successful engagement requires that the CPA and the attorney completely understand what is expected of each other. This understanding comes from a good working relationship and communication. This relationship must start at the beginning of the engagement, prior even to signing the engagement letter. Both of you need to be on the same page, working toward the same goal, providing a competent, well-reasoned valuation report or other marital services, and then presenting that information to the court. This is true whether this is the first time you have worked together or if you have worked together on several engagements. Each engagement is different and unique and therefore requires a specialized plan structured for that specific engagement.

IN THE BEGINNING

Many questions need to be addressed prior to the engagement acceptance.

- What is the scope of the engagement?
- Do I have the expertise to handle the engagement?

- Can I complete the engagement on a timely basis?
- Do I have any conflicts related to this engagement?

These critical questions must be answered before you review your first document in the matter. What exactly are you being asked to do? Value a business? Income reconstruction? Develop a marital balance sheet? Review the tax implications of the divorce? Determine life style? Each of these services requires different skills and education. Just because you can provide one of the activities does not mean that you are competent to provide all of them. Do you have the time and other resources to handle the matter? When is your report due? What are the potential deposition and court dates?

DEFINING THE SCOPE OF THE ENGAGEMENT

As we discussed in Chapter 3, your engagement letter must clearly spell out exactly what services you are being asked to provide. Although marital litigation engagements are very fluid and seem to change almost on a daily basis, we need to constantly keep in mind a clear view of what we are trying to accomplish. Also keep in mind that you may be asked to present your conclusions and opinions both in the form of a written report and to testify at the trial court level. You must also keep in mind that everything that you do is most likely discoverable by opposing counsel. Because of this, the authors are not in favor of standard checklists or generic work programs. These one-size-fits-all type of checklists and work programs provide a fertile field for potential cross-examination.

Defining Your Role

There are two basic roles that you can play in a typical divorce engagement, the consulting expert or the testifying expert. Each has very distinct roles and responsibilities. The consulting expert is usually not discoverable and plays a major role in the formation and execution of the case. The consulting expert is normally not allowed to testify at trial. The consulting expert is usually involved in areas of the litigation that clearly would be attorney workproduct. The consulting expert may assist the attorney in a number of areas, such as

- Trial strategy and planning. It is not uncommon in complex marital litigation for the attorney to retain a CPA to assist him or her with the complex accounting, tax, or business valuation issues inherent in these matters. The consulting expert might not have any responsibility for creating original information that will be used in the trial, but rather will help to define issues and determine what issues will be given to the testifying expert. The consulting expert may even be involved in the ultimate selection and supervision of the various testifying experts.

- Detailed discovery issues. The consulting expert may have responsibility for the financial discovery areas of the matter. This discovery would include assisting the attorney in determining what documents should exist and reviewing documents after they are received to determine if the discovery complies with the information requested, as well as whether the information provided indicates that additional information is needed to proceed with the matter.
- Witness preparation. It is not uncommon for the consulting expert to be directly involved with the preparation of both the testifying financial expert's testimony, but also any lay witness that may be providing financial information as part of the case. This preparation includes much of the information discussed in Chapter 12.

The testifying expert is expected to testify at trial and in most jurisdictions is fully discoverable by the opposing party. This discovery can include all workpapers, communications, prior reports, and testimony. These issues are covered later in this chapter.

Is it possible to begin the engagement as a consulting expert and later in the engagement change to a testifying expert? Although the answer is yes, the danger of this conversion is that all of the workproduct that was completed while a consulting expert may be fully discoverable when the conversion is made. To the extent that you have been involved with what would otherwise be attorney workproduct, not subject to discovery, your conversion to a testifying expert may remove that privilege. These issues should be discussed with the attorney at the very beginning of the engagement. However, it is not uncommon for you to be initially engaged as a "consulting expert" until you have had the opportunity to look at specific information and render an informal opinion of the issues to the attorney. If your view of the case is opposite of that of the attorney and/or the client, you may be asked to resign from the matter. Because you were engaged as a consulting expert, your workproduct continues to be not discoverable. Remember that if this conversion is made, you need to change your engagement letter to reflect the change in your engagement responsibilities and the other terms of your retention.

Defining Expectations

Many times, at the very beginning of the engagement, the attorney and/or the underlying client will want you to provide an off the cuff idea as to the value of the business interest or other issues you are being asked to look at. Providing an answer prior to having reviewed any of the information is an enormous pitfall. Once you have provided a number, that number will always be a benchmark for the conclusions and opinions that you ultimately arrive at. If your final opinion is substantially different from the off the cuff opinion, you will have a difficult time in explaining why there is a difference, especially if the difference is a negative to the underlying client that you are representing. In a perfect world, the expert would never have to give an off the cuff number, but then we do not live in a perfect world. The attorney usually needs a working number for purposes of settlement discussions and also to evaluate the case as a whole. Our suggestion is that this preliminary number not be given out until you have at least had the time to analyze the financial statements of the subject company, and then when the number is provided, that it be in a range with a plus or minus 25 percent on either side. This number will usually satisfy the attorney and the client and allow them to proceed with the settlement discussions while you are finalizing your valuation.

A part of expectations are what the attorney expects of you as an expert witness. These are basic expectations and should not be a problem for any competent expert to follow. In fact, failure to follow these expectations can lead to numerous problems, both in the current engagement and future engagements. These goals are:

- Provide an honest evaluation of the issues you are responsible for. Some people think that attorneys want to be told what we think they want to hear. Nothing could be further from the truth. The experienced marital attorney wants the expert to be very blunt and frank when it comes time to discuss the issues in the case. If there are significant problems with those issues, the attorney can determine how to handle them as part of his or her representation of the client.
- An independent analysis. Do not ask the attorney what he or she thinks the answers are in the matter. The attorney is asking you to make those determinations; that is why you have been retained as the expert. Good attorneys encourage your analysis and assistance on an independent basis.
- Well-reasoned, credible opinions. There is an expectation that the work you do will culminate in an opinion that can stand intense scrutiny. Therefore you must be able to document the methodologies used and show that your assumptions are reasonable. Your overall opinion as well as your workproduct must be credible.
- A believable presentation of your conclusions. Both your written report and your direct testimony must be believable and reasonable. At the same time, your presentations must be understood by lay people. Remember, it is a rare situation where the judge and the attorneys have significant business valuation experience. You will be asking the judge to accept your opinions, based on your assumptions and the research and other work that you completed in the matter.

SETTING THE PLAN

Planning is an integral part of a successful engagement. Hopefully, you have been retained very early in the litigation process. Early retention is a big advantage to the successful engagement. In many instances, it is more cost effective for the client and the attorney to hire the expert early in the engagement. Remember that the plan is a fluid document that will most likely change during the course of the engagement. The plan should contain, at a minimum, the following elements:

- A clear definition of the objective of your engagement as well as the elements of that engagement. Specifically what is it that you intend to accomplish and what documents do you need to create in order to convey your conclusions and opinions?
- Identification of the documents you require to complete your assignment. This listing should include financial as well as other business records. This listing needs to be fairly detailed. A sample document request checklist is included in Appendix B.
- Who you need to interview, the purpose of the interview, and the information that you believe will be forthcoming from that interview. Obviously, you would like to interview both parties to the marital litigation. If you are providing a business valuation, you may need to interview other individuals who hold key positions in the organization that you are valuing. You may also need to interview competitors or other individuals in the specific industry. Again, this listing needs to be fairly detailed. Remember that interviews take time and may be difficult to schedule. In some cases, the attorney may need to schedule a deposition in order to get the information. You must work closely with the attorney to make that determination early in the litigation.
- Any site visits or other inspections of property or business interest premises that are necessary for you to meet the objectives of your engagement. Site visits are an essential element of a business valuation. Where your client is the operator of the business, site visits and interviews are usually easier to arrange. However, when your client is the spouse who does not have an operating interest in the business, these site visits are sometimes more difficult to arrange. Be sure that you know what you intend to accomplish during the site visit, and estimate how much time is necessary at the site.
- What specific information or documentation you need from sources other than the parties to the marital litigation. Are there key individuals (other than the parties) who have essential information that you need as part of your engagement? Examples might be the entities' key employees, the outside accountant, the banker, or other financial advisors.
- What industry-specific information you need to value this specific business. Where do you expect to obtain that information? Some of this information can be found by determining if the subject company belongs to an industry or trade organization, and even if the subject company participates in any data gathering performed by the trade group.
- Timetables for interim information and delivery of reports or other required documentation required to complete your engagement. You need to know when you can expect the information that you need to complete your engagement so that you can have adequate time to do your work and still meet the required due dates for your conclusions and report.
- Timetables and planned assignments for staff and your time. Who is going to do what and when? Business valuation is a process that has a beginning, middle, and

an ending. The engagement does not take place simultaneously. Some tasks need to be completed before other tasks can be started. Who is going to spread the financial statements? Who will be responsible for the analysis of the financial information? Who is responsible for the industry research? What about guideline companies? Who is writing the various parts of the report? It is important to build a timeline. A delay in the basic beginning of the process can push back other portions of the engagement, which creates potential time pressures at the completion of the engagement.

- Detail due dates for the delivery of the information and the analysis of the information. When must you have information to the attorney you are working with? Will there be interim discussions relating to your progress in the engagement? If the engagement is phased, what are the decision points and when will those decisions be made? What about the due dates for final reports that need to be filed with the court or exchanged with opposing counsel? In some instances, missing a report due date could prohibit you from testifying as an expert witness.

During the entire process you must remember that the attorney is in charge of the litigation. While you have a very important role to play, the attorney drives the marital litigation engagement. Litigation is fluid and your plan most likely will change as the litigation moves forward.

As the engagement progresses and you review the initial documents and related discovery items, it will be clear that information you received is different than your initial impressions and expectations. As these changes take place you must continue to change your plan. This is also true as you begin your analysis of information, including looking at industry data and guideline company information. What is the industry information telling you? Is your subject company under- or overperforming the industry averages? Do you know why? Do you need additional information? What did you learn during your site visit and the interviews with key personnel? How does that impact the methodologies that you are going to select? Can you readily discard certain methodologies based on the information you have received? Each of these questions may require a change in your timelines and planning.

KEEPING IN TOUCH

Part of your role as an expert in the litigation process is to be able to translate accounting terminology and practices into a language that the attorney is comfortable with. Even though we use terms like GAAP (generally accepted accounting principles), GAAS (generally accepted auditing standards), FASB (Financial Accounting Standards Board), Rev. Rul. (Revenue Ruling), cap rates, present value, and others, most attorneys are not familiar with the technical language that we use on a day-to-day basis. Some attorneys may not even know the difference between an audit and a compilation and may use the terms interchangeably. Thus, it becomes incumbent on the CPA to be able to move from the technical accounting or valuation language to a language that the attorney understands. Be certain that the attorney understands what you are saying. Communication means an exchange of ideas or understandings. There are many instances where you might be saying one thing, but the listener is hearing something different. You must be certain that there is two-way communications regarding both the technical information you are using, as well as your ultimate conclusions and opinions.

During the engagement you and the attorney need to have a continued discussion as to the progress of the case. Have issues changed? Have we received information that is not consistent with the initial view of the case? Have the parties agreed on issues that were previously in dispute? What is your preliminary analysis indicating? How is your progress compared to the attorney's expectations in the matter? Where in the range that you provided do you think the conclusion is going to fall?

It is also important that this communication be two-way. You need to be certain that the attorney understands that you need to receive copies of all pleading, answers, stipulations, and such that are produced during the course of the litigation, including any financial documents and financial affidavits of both parties. You also want to be provided with a copy of every document that is provided to the opposing expert witness. There can be a wealth of information in the various documents that are being filed with the court. Additionally, facts may be stipulated that allow you to use them without concern as to the veracity of the information.

WORKPAPERS

There is a good rule of thumb to remember when you are creating your workpapers and correspondence files. "The only information that should be committed to writing is that information which you are comfortable with allowing the opposing counsel to read." The reason for that rule is that normally, opposing counsel does in fact get the opportunity to read all of the memos, notes, and other correspondence that you create as part of the engagement. This does not mean that you should not create any workpapers, notes, or other written documents; quite the contrary, in most engagements you must create those types of documents. This rule tells you that you need to be very careful what you say. What seems funny at the moment might not seem so funny in the long run.

During the Savings and Loan (S&L) crisis, Robert E. Kleeman, Jr. was involved with a large matter, and during the course of the work, he had the need to review the U.S. House of Representatives committee hearings records. During the testimony of one of the government officials, there was reference to a letter that he had written several years earlier. The official began a letter to a colleague with a statement that was paraphrased as, "remember back in the 1970s, when we must have been smoking some bad dope," and went on to discuss the approval of the application to acquire a specific S&L. The official spent a great deal of time being questioned as to whether he, as well as other government employees, were in fact smoking dope or what was going on. It may have seemed funny at the time, but it was not very funny at the congressional hearings.

During the course of your engagement you should be continually reviewing your workpapers and files on the matter. Extraneous information, or information that you reviewed but determined was not part of your ultimate conclusions and opinions should be taken out of the file and destroyed. There is nothing devious about adopting that as a basic function of your day-to-day office procedures. It is the rare case when everything you look at is used as the basis of your conclusions and opinions. Keeping the extraneous information just clutters up your files and creates potential problems in the future.

In developing a set of working papers for the engagement, the following are standard items that should be contained in the files:

- Engagement acceptance. To include information on your conflict checks and other acceptance matters.
- Correspondence. This should contain signed copies of your engagement letter(s) and all other correspondence between you and the attorney or client. If you feel that you are in possession of privileged correspondence, it should be kept in a separate file. If the information is subject to a subpoena, then those items can be provided under seal until the attorneys resolve the legal issues surrounding the claimed privilege.
- Documents. This area should contain all of the documents that you have received through discovery or directly from the attorney or client. You may wish to further subdivide this section into three parts for
  1. Personal financial information to include financial affidavits, tax returns, personal financial statements, and so forth.
  2. Entity-specific financial information to include tax returns, annual and interim financial statements, and projections.
  3. Entity-specific information such as price lists, marketing materials, key man resumes, notes regarding your site visit, and other information about the company.
- Financial analysis. Here you maintain the workpapers related to the financial analysis of the subject company. This analysis includes the ratio analysis, as well as the comparison of the subject company with industry benchmarks.
- Research. All of your industry and guideline company research should be kept in this area of the workpapers.
- Capitalization rates, discounts, and premiums. This section of the workpapers should contain the information that you relied on in developing the capitalization or discount rate that you ultimately selected for the final valuation conclusion. In addition, this section should support the selected discounts or premiums that you applied to the final conclusion of value.

- Report. This area should contain a copy of your final report issued in the matter. In the event that you are also preparing a critique of the opposing expert's report, this is the appropriate place to file that.

If you are using a software product such as Wiley's ValuSource Pro, much of this information is included in the program and may not need to be separately created in hard copy for the files. However, under the discovery rules, you may be required to provide either a copy of a disk containing all of the information, or in some instances, a hard copy of the information.

PRIOR WORKPRODUCT

Many jurisdictions in the United States now require experts to provide information regarding prior workproduct. Typically, in order for the workproduct to be discoverable, it must have been provided to an opposing party in a litigation matter or been the subject of a deposition or direct examination at the trial court level. Obviously, if the matter is subject to confidentiality or other protective order, the information is usually not disclosed. If you have taken a prior position that is inconsistent with the position you are taking on the current matter, you need to inform the attorney you are working with, and hopefully, you can provide a cogent discussion of why the positions appear to be inconsistent but are not. For example, the facts and circumstances may be different in each case. Be prepared to be asked about these apparent inconsistencies at both your deposition and the trial.

SUMMARY

Although each engagement is unique, each basically requires the same process. You need to understand the expectations that are put on you by the attorney and the underlying client. After defining the engagement, you must develop a plan for that engagement, including determining timetable, assigning staff, and planning the workload. The plan will continue to change as you receive documents through discovery. You and the attorney need to maintain communications as the matter moves forward. Your workproduct is discoverable and should contain adequate documentation to support the tasks that you completed and the final conclusions and opinion of value.

Chapter 5

Data Collection and Analysis

DOCUMENT REQUEST LETTER

After a valuation engagement has been accepted, it is necessary to request certain documents from the client so that the valuation can begin. Most of the documents required to appraise a closely held business are financial (financial statements, accounts receivable aging reports, etc.). However, in order to fully understand the business that is the subject of the valuation, it is important to request certain nonfinancial information as well as financial information. Nonfinancial documents such as company brochures, organizational charts, stockholder lists, marketing materials, customer lists, and supplier lists can assist the appraiser in his or her understanding of the business and the industry in which it operates.

A word of caution regarding the language used in the document request letter. Usually, because the appraiser does not know what documents exist, he or she will request a long list of documents. Usually, receipt of certain documents is critical to valuing the business (e.g., prior period income statements or projected financial statements). Other documents, while helpful to the appraiser, are not critical in the valuation process (e.g., company brochures, company benefit plan binders). In a divorce setting, problems with the opposing counsel can arise if the document request letter contains language that implies that receipt of all of the requested documents is *critical* to deriving an opinion of fair market value. Therefore, in the drafting of the document request letter, make sure that critical documents are labeled as such but that noncritical documents are not.

PREMISE INSPECTION AND CLIENT INTERVIEW

Whenever possible, the appraiser should perform a premise inspection. During the premise inspection, the appraiser, under normal circumstances, has the opportunity to view the business's facilities and interview the business's management and other key employees.

As a general rule, the premise inspection should take place after the appraiser has received the requested documents. By reviewing the documents and, possibly, performing a number of analyses, the appraiser should have a good understanding of the subject business and, thus, the premise inspection should be more efficient and provide more usable information.

During the premise inspection, the appraiser's primary objectives are to physically see the business's operations, gain additional insight into the business's history, products or services, competitors, industry, marketing efforts, management, and employees. In addition, the premise inspection is an excellent opportunity to review the financial statements with the subject business's management and to ask them questions regarding the financials.

In a divorce situation, the appraiser for one spouse may not be granted access to the business and/or its management. We cannot emphasize strongly enough the need for a site visit. The site visit is an integral part of every valuation. There may be reasons why a site visit is not needed, and those reasons should be documented in the workpapers. In those exceptions, in order to show the court your performance of due diligence, the appraiser should carefully document all written correspondence and oral communications that show his or her attempts to conduct a premises inspection. The appraiser should also document the reason(s) why he or she was unable to perform a premise inspection on the subject business. To the extent that you believe that your inability to visit the premise impairs or restricts the scope of your engagement, you need to discuss this matter thoroughly with the attorney you are working with. If it does impact the scope of your engagement, you may need to amend your engagement letter to document this information. It is also very important that you discuss your lack of a premise inspection in detail in your valuation report.

If the appraiser is allowed a premise inspection, he or she should be thoroughly prepared as it may be a one-shot opportunity to visit the business's facilities and to ask questions of management team.

One final point regarding a premise inspection: Should the appraiser be retained by the "out spouse" (i.e., the spouse who will not be retaining his or her interest), it is still recommended that the appraiser meet with him or her. This recommendation applies regardless of whether the selling spouse has any direct knowledge of the business or its operations. Divorce proceedings can be highly emotional, and it is important that the appraiser's client feel that he or she has had some input into the appraisal.

ANALYZING FINANCIAL DATA

After the appraiser has obtained the required financial information, the data should be organized to allow the appraiser to perform critical financial analyses. Generally, the first step in performing financial analyses on a subject business is to spread the historical balance sheets and income statements using either a spreadsheet software package such as Microsoft Excel or Lotus 1-2-3.

By spreading the financial statements, the analyst can easily note trends and apparent anomalies in the subject business's balance sheet and/or income statements. As a general rule, the analyst should first spread the financial statements "as they are" (i.e., without making any adjustments). The unadjusted financial statements act as a base from which all other analyses flow. Some business valuation software packages also calculate the rate of growth for each line item in the balance sheet or income statement. This type of analysis is extremely valuable for some line items (e.g., the rate of growth in total revenues) and almost useless for other line items (e.g., the rate of growth in prepaid expenses).

The second step in analyzing a subject business's financial statements is to convert the balance sheet and income statement "spreads" to a common size basis. A common size balance sheet presents all assets and liabilities as a percentage of total assets while a common size income statement presents all revenues and expenses as a percentage of total revenues.

An advantage of presenting a business's financial statements in a percentage format is the ability to note relative changes in line items. For example, it is easier to note changes in a business's cost of goods sold by reviewing a common size income statement. A significant change in its percentage alerts the appraiser to perform additional analysis and/or ask additional questions of management regarding the expense. If operating expenses for one year varied materially from other years, the analyst may need to break down the category into its individual expenses in order to ascertain the reason for the abnormal fluctuation.

What the appraiser is specifically looking for in the financial spreads and common size statements are possible adjustments to either the date of valuation balance sheet or revenues or expenses in the income statements. Also, as previously mentioned, by analyzing the financial statements on a percentage basis, the analyst may note areas that require further investigation by reviewing additional documents or asking questions of management.

The third basic financial analysis step is to calculate various financial ratios for the subject business's adjusted information and to compare the ratios to industry standards. Industry standard ratios may come from trade association publications, the Internal Revenue Service, brokerage house financial analyst reports, and various publications. Financial ratio analysis is generally divided into liquidity ratios, coverage ratios, leverage ratios, and operating ratios.

Liquidity ratios measure the adequacy of current assets to meet current obligations as they become due. Common measures of a business's liquidity include the current ratio, the quick ratio, the receivables turnover ratio, the inventory turnover ratio, and the payables turnover ratio. The current and quick ratios are similar in that they both are measures of the amount of current assets available to meet current obligations. The difference between the two ratios is that the current ratio includes all current assets and the quick ratio generally includes only cash, cash equivalents, and receivables. The formula for the current ratio is:

$$\frac{\text{Current Assets}}{\text{Current Liabilities}}.$$

The most common formula for the quick ratio is:

$$\frac{\text{Cash + Cash Equivalents + Net Accounts Receivables}}{\text{Current Liabilities}}.$$

The accounts receivable turnover ratio measures the size of the business's accounts receivable balance relative to its sales. The higher the turnover ratio, the shorter the period between the date of sale and the date cash is realized on the sale. When using this ratio, the appraiser should take into account that seasonal fluctuations in receivables are not considered. The formula for the accounts receivable turnover ratio is:

$$\frac{\text{Net Annual Sales}}{\text{Net Accounts Receivable}}.$$

The inventory turnover ratio measures the number of times the business's inventory is turned over per year. Although, in general, a higher inventory turnover ratio implies a better cash flow, it may also be caused by the business maintaining a level of inventory that is too small for the level of sales being generated. Inventory levels that are too low may be a symptom of a business that is suffering from cash flow problems. The formula for the inventory turnover ratio is:

$$\frac{\text{Cost of Goods Sold}}{\text{Inventory}}.$$

The accounts payable turnover ratio measures how quickly a business pays its current obligations. A ratio that is increasing may be an indication that the business is experiencing cash flow problems. A business whose ratio is significantly lower than that of the industry has the ability to improve cash flow by simply slowing down payment. This ratio is calculated as follows:

$$\frac{\text{Cost of Goods Sold}}{\text{Accounts Payable}}.$$

Coverage ratios measure the ability of a business to pay the interest portion of incurred debt as well as the ability to pay the current portions of its long-term debt. The interest coverage ratio and the gross cash flow to current portion of long-term liabilities ratio are the most commonly used coverage ratios.

The interest coverage ratio measures the ability of the business to meet the interest expense on its interest-bearing debt. A high ratio is an indication that the business has not overborrowed and may be able to shift a larger percentage of its long-term capital from equity to debt. The formula for the interest coverage ratio is:

$$\frac{\text{Earnings before Interest Expense and Income Taxes}}{\text{Annual Interest Expense}}.$$

The gross cash flow to current portion of long-term debt ratio measures the ability of the business to meet current debt repayment schedules. It is also an indicator of the business's ability to assume additional long-term debt. The formula for the ratio is:

$$\frac{\text{Net Profit + Noncash Expenses}}{\text{Current Portion of Long-Term Debt}}.$$

Leverage ratios measure the amount of debt used to finance a business's operations and capital assets. These ratios vary significantly by industry so it is important that the appraiser compare the leverage ratios of the subject business to those of the industry. The two most common leverage ratios used are the *fixed assets to net worth* ratio and the *debt to net worth* ratio.

The fixed assets to net worth ratio measures the percentage of owners' equity that is invested in tangible fixed assets. This ratio would be important when valuing capital intensive businesses whose income stream is dependent upon capital machinery (such as a manufacturing plant). However, for businesses whose income is primarily dependent upon intangible assets (such as patents or copyrights), this ratio would be of little value to an appraiser. The formula for the ratio is:

$$\frac{\text{Fixed Assets (Net of Accumulated Depreciation)}}{\text{Net Worth (Excluding Intangible Assets)}}.$$

The debt to net worth ratio measures the degree to which a business's long-term capital has been financed by debt and the degree it has been financed by equity. A high ratio (indicating a high level of debt) may indicate that the business is more susceptible to economic downturns. On the other hand, too low of a ratio could cause the return on shareholders' equity to suffer. The formula for the ratio is:

$$\frac{\text{Total Liabilities}}{\text{Net Worth (Excluding Intangible Assets}}.$$

Operating ratios, such as the *return on net worth* ratio and the *return on total assets* ratio, assist the appraiser in determining how effective management has been in deploying its assets. These ratios are also highly dependent upon the industry, and therefore, should be compared to industry statistics.

The return on net worth ratio is dependent upon the business's profitability and the degree to which the assets are levered with debt. Although, in general, a high return on net worth is desirable, the appraiser should review this ratio in conjunction with the leverage ratios to ascertain whether the cause of the high returns is due to low levels of equity. Conversely, if the return on net worth for the subject business is significantly below the industry average, the appraiser should determine if the low return is due to low levels of profit, a higher-than-average percentage of equity in its capital structure, or a combination of both. The formula for the return on net worth is:

$$\frac{\text{Net Income}}{\text{Net Worth}}.$$

The return on total assets ratio measures the effectiveness in which the business's total assets are being deployed by management. This ratio can be affected by the existence of large amounts of nonoperating assets on the subject business's balance sheet. For example, if the business holds significantly larger amounts of cash than is required to operate the business, the return on total assets may appear low when compared to the industry average. However, if the appraiser recalculates the return on total assets after adjusting out the "excess" cash, the ratio may, in fact, be in line with that of the industry. The formula for the return on assets ratio is:

$$\frac{\text{Total Revenues}}{\text{Total Assets}}.$$

The authors need to note that there are general formulas which may differ slightly in other presentations.

VALUATION SOFTWARE

Over the past five years, there has been a proliferation of software developed to assist business appraisers in valuing closely held businesses. The most commonly used stand-alone business valuation software is ValuSource Pro and Value Express published by John Wiley & Sons, Inc. and Valuation Master published by the National Association of Certified Valuation Analysts. The PPC Business Valuation Companion, published by Practitioners Publishing Company, contains valuation templates that are used in conjunction with Microsoft Excel or Lotus spreadsheets.

There has been debate within the business valuation community over the propriety of using software in the valuation of closely held businesses. One side of the debate argues that business valuations require the judgment, experience, and opinions of business appraisers and that "canned" software cannot replicate the cognitive processes that go into a business appraisal. They further argue that software, with its rigid schedules, is not flexible enough to take into account the many subtle nuances that differentiate one business appraisal from another. A third negative comment offered by those professionals who oppose using business valuation software is that, historically, the software systems contained miscalculations and incorrect methodology. And, finally, it is argued that business valuation software in the hands of untrained individuals results in business appraisals that are not based on sound judgment and are often incompetent. In short, "garbage in, garbage out."

Those who favor using business valuation software would agree with most of the points mentioned in the previous paragraph. However, the argument for using software is that when used as a tool to *assist* the experienced appraiser, software can be a benefit. Software can ease some of the more time consuming and mundane aspects of performing a business appraisal. For example with most business valuation software, once the historical financial statements have been entered (or "spread"), the user can quickly view or print out common size financial statements, ratio analyses, trend analyses, and so forth. The time saved from automating some aspects of the valuation process can allow the appraiser to focus more time and analysis on those aspects of the appraisal that require judgment or empirical research (such as determining an appropriate discount rate).

Although no consensus exists regarding the use of business valuation software, most, if not all, professional appraisers agree that the software should be used only as a tool by those individuals who have the necessary training and experience to perform business valuations. There is almost universal agreement that software is not a substitute for training and experience. Software does not enhance the appraiser's knowledge, but can enhance his ability to perform the valuation.

SUMMARY

The most critical part of many business valuation engagements is the collection and analysis of the underlying data for the subject company. Analysis allows the business valuation expert to make informed judgments as to the value of the company. Your ultimate conclusion is only as good as the financial information that you used and the depth of analysis you performed.

Chapter 6

Industry Information—Where to Find It and How to Use It

As indicated in Chapter 5, in the valuation of a closely held company, it is important to analyze the company's strengths and weaknesses. One step in this process is to assess the company's performance relative to the industry it operates in. Two general types of industry information can be obtained. The first type is financial benchmarks to assist in performing a direct comparison. The second type is general economic data outlining economic conditions affecting the subject company.

FINANCIAL BENCHMARKING SOURCES

Important in the valuation process is an analysis of the performance of the subject company relative to an industry benchmark. The appraiser can perform comparable ratio analysis looking at various ratios of the subject company along with an industry-based guideline group. An example of an industry comparable ratio analysis is shown in Exhibit 6.1.

By comparing the subject business to its industry peers, the appraiser can determine the subject business's strengths and weaknesses. In addition, industry ratio comparison may assist in making adjustments to the financial statements. For example, assume the subject business's sales to working capital ratio is significantly lower than that of the industry. After valuing the subject business, the appraiser may have to consider lowering the value by an estimate of the amount of working capital that a hypothetical buyer would have to inject into the business upon the purchase of the business.

There are a number of sources for industry information. Some sources are more appropriate than others in certain situations. It is important that the appraiser understand the source of the underlying data for each of these providers. It is also important to understand the proper use of the information provided by each source.

Exhibit 6.1 Industry Comparable Ratio Analysis

		Subject Business Year Ended		
	Industry	12/31/97	12/31/96	12/31/95
Current Ratio	2.00	3.20	3.10	2.80
Quick Ratio	1.20	2.20	1.70	1.50
Sales/Receivables	8.80	10.20	6.50	9.30
COS/Inventory	8.00	8.50	7.40	9.20
Sales/Working Capital	12.30	10.30	10.00	11.50
EBIT/Interest Expenses	2.60	4.50	3.90	3.80
Fixed Assets/Net Worth	0.40	1.00	1.20	1.10
Total Debt/Net Worth	1.50	0.70	0.90	1.50
Return on Equity	10.9%	12.5%	9.9%	13.5%
Return on Assets	4.2%	6.6%	2.2%	7.5%
Fixed Asset Turnover	20.20	11.00	15.40	13.30

Notes: COS = cost of sales; EBIT = earnings before interest and taxes

Robert Morris Associates

Probably the most widely used source of financial ratios in the valuation field is *Annual Statement Studies* published by Robert Morris Associates (RMA). RMA is an association of lending and credit risk professionals. Currently, RMA has approximately 3,000 member banks. Each year, RMA publishes its *Annual Statement Studies,* which is a percentage composition of financial statements submitted by credit-seeking businesses to RMA member banks. The *Annual Statement Studies* publication is divided into approximately 500 SIC (standard industry classification) codes. For each SIC code, the financial statements are presented on a percentage basis and 16 ratios are calculated. The data is stratified by size (by the amount of assets and revenues) so that the appraiser can compare his or her subject business to businesses of comparable size.

Although, RMA's data is by far the most widely used data for industry comparison purposes, the appraiser should be aware of its limitations. RMA itself recommends that the data be regarded only as "general guidelines and not used as absolute industry norms." The data presented in the *Annual Statement Studies* may not be statistically valid for the following reasons:

- The financial statements used in the composition of the publication are not randomly selected; nor are they selected by any statistically reliable manner. Rather, any RMA member bank may submit as many financial statements as they wish. There are no limitations imposed by RMA as to size or verifiable accuracy of the financial statements.

- RMA presents the data by SIC code. Although many companies whose financial statements are submitted to RMA have multiple product or service lines and would have several SIC codes, RMA categorizes the company by its primary SIC code only.
- Some of the sample sizes are small compared to the number of businesses in the industry. Small sample sizes increase the chances that results will not be statistically representative of the entire industry.
- Extreme statements are not filtered out and therefore can cause the composite figures to misrepresent the industry.
- Different companies within the same industry may have different accounting methods, different labor markets, different terms of financing, and so forth. All of these differences would be reflected in their respective financial statements.

In addition to the foregoing RMA disclaimers, most (if not all) of the companies who submit financial statements to RMA member banks have debt on their books. Therefore, if the subject business has no debt, an appraiser should most likely look for other sources of industry statistics.

One final note on the use of RMA statistics: Be careful when using them to derive the "fair" compensation for the subject business's officers. There is no definition in the *Annual Statement Studies* as to what constitutes officers' compensation. For some businesses, it may entail one person, for others there may be fifty.

The *Almanac of Business and Industrial Financial Ratios*

Another popular source for industry ratios is *Troy's Almanac of Business and Industrial Financial Ratios* (published by Prentice-Hall). The information in the almanac is taken from corporate tax returns printed in the IRS's *Corporate Source Book of Statistics of Income* (SOI). There are approximately 60 major industry categories in which the data is broken down into. The information contains data from approximately 100 million companies and tends to lag current data by about two years.

An additional source based on the SOI data is the *IRS Corporate Ratios* (published in electronic form by Wiley-ValuSource). Because the *IRS Corporate Ratios* is in electronic format, customizing, working with, and downloading the data may be easier. Other firms also provide data in this format.

Financial Studies of Small Business

The *Financial Studies of Small Business* is published by Financial Research Associates. The studies focus on smaller firms (under $1 million in value). The financial makeup of smaller firms can differ significantly from large ones. The information is submitted by more than 1,500 independent CPA firms geographically dispersed throughout the country. The 1997 data had approximately 70 categories under the following major headings:

- Retail
- Wholesalers
- Services
- Contractors
- Professional services
- Manufacturers

Other Financial Benchmarking Sources

There are many other financial benchmarking tools, many of which are valuable for analyzing details in the financial statements. Specifically, information about officers' compensation can be obtained based on more pertinent industry-specific categories.

The *1997 Survey of Law Firm Economics* is conducted by Altman Weil Pensa, Inc. It contains benchmarking financial data based on approximately 23,000 individuals including 5,000 associates, 6,500 partners/shareholders, 350 active counsel, 3,100 paralegal employees, and 8,500 staff working in 400 U.S. law firms. The data is separated by region, population, firm size, practice area, and type of firm. The survey is designed to provide information to management of law firms to evaluate performance relative to other law firms.

Socioeconomic Characteristics of Medical Practices is available from the American Medical Association (AMA). The study contains detailed analysis on hours worked, visits, fees, expenses, and physician's compensation broken down by specialty, geographic location, type of practice, employment status, and physician's age.

An alternate study for medical practices is the *Physician Compensation and Production Study* published by the Medical Group Management Association (MGMA). The study provides summary and detailed statistics on both physicians and mid-level providers for compensation and production. The study has been conducted since 1987 and since 1997 is available in CD-ROM format.

The *Survey of Dental Practices* focuses on practice characteristics such as number and frequency of patient visits, work schedules, auxiliary employment, wages, expenses, and income. The survey has been conducted by the American Dental Association since the early 1950s and analyzes the incomes of private practitioners.

Officer Compensation Report, published by Aspen Publisher, Inc., surveys more than 1,000 small to medium-sized businesses. It contains base salary, bonus, and total direct compensation sorted by size and geographic location. The study also analyzes stock ownership by executives by industry. The report is broken down into eight industry groupings:

1. Basic materials
2. Heavy equipment and transportation

3. Electrical and electronics
4. Nondurable goods
5. Fabricated metals and wood products
6. Technological services
7. Business services
8. High-tech industry

SOURCES OF ECONOMIC DATA

Industry economic analysis is also an important part in assessing the subject company's performance. General economic analysis involves researching national and regional economic conditions. The objective of obtaining this information is to understand external conditions that affect the operation of the subject entity.

WEFA

WEFA Industrial Monitor, available in book form or CD-ROM, discusses the current events and provides general outlooks for approximately 30 distinct industry sector classifications. The *Monitor* provides information on seasonal variations and cycles, new technologies, rising/declining industries, major firms within specific industries, regulatory effects, and other aspects of the economy that have a material influence on the industry sectors. The CD-ROM version of the database is available through Wiley-ValuSource and is compatible with Microsoft Word.

U.S. Trade and Industry Outlook

The *U.S. Industry & Trade Outlook* is produced by the U.S. Department of Commerce and published by McGraw-Hill. It contains an industry-by-industry overview of the U.S. economy. The *Outlook* is broken down into fifty separate industry sectors. Like *WEFA Industrial Monitor*, the information is available in book or CD-ROM format (Adobe Acrobat).

National Economic Review

The *National Economic Review* is available quarterly from Mercer Capital. The reviews are available for quarters dating back to 1992 and contain a discussion of the current and expected performance of the national economy, interest rates, employment, inflation, the stock and bond markets, and construction, housing, and real estate. It consists of four to eight pages of text and two pages of exhibits (annual/quarterly economic indicators and investment trends).

Other Data Sources

Many industries have trade groups that are active in promoting and reporting on statistics relating to that specific industry. This potential source of information should not be overlooked. During your management interviews, one of the questions that you will want to ask is, What are the trade groups for the specific industry that the subject company operates in? As an alternative, reference sources provide listings and detailed information about all of the trade associations in the United States. If you are able to find an appropriate trade organization, these groups usually have information on the past statistics on the industry, and many also provide industry-specific economic analysis.

SUMMARY

Both comparative ratio analysis and industry and national economic review are important steps in the valuation process. There are many sources for obtaining data for assisting in this task. All sources have advantages and disadvantages in using them. The appraiser must understand the foundation in which the data is derived and displayed to optimize the source's value. When analyzed and applied properly, the data can suggest possible adjustments to be made to the subject company's financials and suggest current and future market conditions in which the company operates.

Chapter 7

Are There Really Comparable Companies?

In the not too recent past, many individuals who valued smaller closely held businesses felt that you could not use the guideline company methodology because there really are not comparable companies to these smaller organizations. In addition, there was very little data on actual transactions of closely held entities. That is not true anymore. More and more closely held transactional data is available to the appraiser. Knowing where to look and what the information means can allow the appraiser to use the guideline company method more often.

There is some comfort to using this method because we can review empirical evidence of actual transactions between willing buyers and sellers. These indicators can be applied to the subject company to give us one more method to assist us in arriving at our opinion of value.

When valuing a business, a common technique to use is to observe pricing multiples of guideline or comparable companies in the marketplace and to apply those multiples to the subject business. In general, there are two separate and distinct sources for marketplace pricing multiples: multiples derived from the stock trading prices of publicly traded companies (often referred to as guideline multiples) and multiples derived from the sales of privately held businesses (often referred to merger and acquisition multiples). The most common multiple used when valuing a business based upon guideline company data is the price to earnings ratio (P/E). Other common pricing multiples used include the price to book value ratio (P/B) and price to total assets ratio (P/A).

Additionally, invested capital multiples may be used. Invested capital is defined as total equity plus long-term debt. Because the value of invested capital is the aggregate of long-term debt and equity, the benefit stream used to derive the multiple must be the benefit prior to debt financing. Some of the more common invested capital multiples used when valuing a business based upon guideline company data are

- Market value of invested capital to earnings before interest and taxes ratio (MVIC/EBIT)

- Market value of invested capital to earnings before interest, taxes, depreciation, and amortization ratio (MVIC/EBITDA)
- Market value of invested capital to earnings before interest ratio (MVIC/EBI)

PUBLICLY TRADED ANALYSIS GUIDELINES FOR COMPARABLE COMPANIES

Revenue Ruling 59-60 states "The market prices of stock of corporations engaged in the same or a similar line of business having their stocks actively traded in a free and open market, either on an exchange or over-the-counter" should be carefully considered in the valuation of closely held stock. The applicability of this factor of Revenue Ruling 59-60 has frequently been skipped over in the past because of the perceived incomparability of companies that are publicly traded and closely held businesses. Currently several thousand domestic stocks are actively traded in a free and open market, and with the number of IPOs (initial public offerings) occurring, this number is growing rapidly. While it used to be that publicly traded companies were, in sheer size alone, dissimilar to any closely held company, this is no longer the case. There is a wide range of market capitalization sizes and industries to select from.

Following is an overview of the steps to perform a publicly traded company analysis:

- Define the criteria to be used in selecting guideline companies.
- Perform a search for guideline companies.
- Obtain financial data of the guideline companies.
- Review and narrow the guideline company search.
- Analyze and adjust the guideline company data.
- Derive pricing multiples from the data.
- Adjust the pricing multiples to be applicable to valuing a closely held business.

Define the Selection Criteria

The theoretical basis for utilizing a guideline company pricing multiple is the principle of substitution. The price of a stock is impacted by potential investors' perceived risk in purchasing the stock. The comparability of a publicly traded guideline company and the subject company should be from a risk and investment perspective. If a specific industry exhibits a unique investment characteristic, a selection criterion commonly used is the Standard Industrial Classification (SIC). The SIC identifies the industry in which the company operates.

Other criteria commonly used are:

- Similar markets the company services
- Market share the company controls
- Geographic location

Perform a Search for Guideline Companies

There are numerous sources for locating possible publicly traded guideline companies. Since there are Securities and Exchange Commission (SEC) filing requirements for all publicly-traded entities, this is often a good place to start. The Department of Commerce publishes a book annually, *Directory of Companies Required to File Annual Reports With the SEC* that lists, sorted by SIC code, all companies that have filed reports. An on-line source for public companies is from EDGAR (Electronic Data Gathering Analysis and Retrieval). Various sites allow free and easy access to EDGAR filings. The following is a few of them:

- http://www.freeedgar.com
- http://www.sec.gov
- http://www.edgar-online.com

Other sources include proprietary compact disc (CD) and on-line databases. Standards & Poor's (S&P) Corporate Descriptions contains financial and business information on more than 11,000 publicly traded companies. S&P's CompuStat contains annual and quarterly financial information and stock and dividend data on more than 9,000 publicly traded companies. Moody's Corporate Profiles gives business information on more than 10,000 publicly traded companies. Disclosure contains financial statement information for more than 12,500 publicly traded companies and Media General gives annual and quarterly financial information on more than 10,000 publicly traded companies. Other companies providing information on publicly traded companies are Morningstar, Reuters, and Hoovers.

Obtain Financial Data of the Guideline Companies

Forms 10K (annual) and 10Q (quarterly) filed with the SEC (and available from EDGAR since 1996) are the primary sources for financial information. Many of the proprietary databases utilize the 10K and 10Q filings as a source for their financial data. Some of the services provide the data "as reported" while others give a more standardized presentation format. The sites that provide a customized view of the data are easier to download and manipulate, however the information may be prone to more errors.

Depending upon the approach, different financial statements should be obtained. For asset-based multiples, the balance sheet and income statements must be obtained. For income-based multiples, the income statement and/or cash flow statement must be obtained.

For publicly traded guideline projected earnings, the Institutional Broker's Estimate System (I/B/E/S) provides earnings estimates for approximately 5,000 publicly traded U.S. companies and Zack's Investment Research estimates earnings on more than 4,000 stocks. There are many other sources available to the valuator.

Review and Narrow the Guideline Companies

Once the financial statements of the guideline companies have been obtained, analysis must be performed to assess the comparability of the possible guideline companies on an operating level. Negative earnings (or close to no earnings), sources of earnings, and differing capital structures and size are some of the possible reasons for removing a guideline company from your ultimate selection. Sheer size does not automatically eliminate a guideline company from your analysis. Some commentators have said that the guideline company can be as much as 50 times larger than the subject. We tend to believe that a range of 20 to 30 times, depending on the size of the subject company, is a more appropriate size qualification.

Analyze and Adjust Guideline Company Data

In applying data from guideline companies, adjustments may be necessary to make the guideline company more comparable to the subject company. Such adjustments could include:

- Removing nonrecurring and extraordinary items
- Discontinued operations
- Last in, first out and first in, first out (LIFO, FIFO) adjustments
- Nonoperating assets/liabilities (and related income/expenses)

Derive Pricing Multiples

Many different pricing multiples can be derived. The trading price used to determine market capitalization (share price times number of shares) should be as of the date of valuation, but the value base can be from any period available. However, the calculated multiple must be applied to the proper value base for the subject company. If an average of three years of pretax earnings for the guideline companies is used, the same must be calculated for the subject company.

Adjust the Pricing Multiples

In the selection of the appropriate multiple to apply to the subject company, adjustments may be necessary. The adjustments fall into two general categories: quantitative and qualitative adjustments. Quantitative adjustments are based on differences in anticipated growth, return on sales/assets, and other financial risk variables. Qualitative adjustments account for such items like size, management depth, product line and geographic diversification, supplier and customer reliance, and lack of capital markets.

The indication of value derived from the guideline company method is less reliable when more adjustments are identified.

PRIVATELY HELD MERGER AND ACQUISITION DATA

When appraising a small business or professional practice, the use of transactional data derived from the sale of closely held businesses can be helpful in developing a range of reasonable values for the subject business. Until recently, it was difficult to obtain pricing data on the sales of privately held businesses due to the absence of public reporting requirements. However, within the last three to five years, the market has responded with a number of products that report data related to the sale of privately held businesses and professional practices. By observing or analyzing this data, the appraiser can often directly value the subject business or professional practice or use it as a "smell test" to check the reasonableness of the value derived using a different valuation method. We would note that it is important to understand the terms of the transaction in order to understand the value of the transaction. To the extent that a database does not provide terms—it may be difficult to determine the FMV of the transaction.

Widely Used Databases

- Pratt's Stats. Pratt's Stats is the newest entry in the private transaction database market. Dr. Shannon Pratt is a well-known business appraiser and author of several business valuation books (*Valuing a Business* and *Valuing Small Businesses and Professional Practices*). For each transaction record, Pratt's Stats provides the following information:
    - Condensed income statement for the most recent fiscal year
    - Condensed balance sheet
    - Date of the sale
    - Selling price

- State of the sale
- Company type (C or S Corp., L.L.C. (limited liability company), etc.)
- Whether the transaction was a stock or asset sale
- Information on employment or consulting agreements
- Eight valuation rates for each transaction

From the data available in Pratt's Stats, price/revenues, price/earnings, price/assets and other valuation multiples can be calculated. Because Pratt's Stats selects one transaction at a time, the appraiser must make multiple searches and store the results in a spreadsheet in order to calculate composite valuation multiples. Pratt's Stats is becoming the most detail oriented database available.

- Bizcomps. Bizcomps contains transactional information on small businesses. It is an excellent source to use when appraising businesses with revenues under $1 million. Business brokers who represent either an actual buyer or seller in a transaction submit the data. Bizcomps reports the following data for each transaction:
  - Asking price
  - Actual price
  - Geographic area
  - Date of transaction
  - Amount of furniture, fixtures, and equipment
  - Amount of inventory
  - Seller's discretionary cash flow (defined as adjusted pretax income, plus all owners' compensation, interest expense, depreciation, and amortization)
  - Most recent total annual revenues

  From this data, price/revenues and price/sellers' discretionary cash flow multiples can be calculated. When using the data from the Bizcomps database, it is important to know that the value derived is for the business's furniture, fixtures, equipment, and goodwill only. In order to derive the total entity value, all other tangible assets must be added and all liabilities must be subtracted from the derived "Asset" value.
- IBA Database. The Institute of Business Appraisers' (IBA) database of transactions. The IBA has an extensive library of transactions involving the transfer of ownership of small businesses. The data is available to IBA members at no charge. This is a source of valuation multiples for small businesses (e.g., restaurants, dry cleaners, independent grocery stores, liquor stores). For each transaction in the IBA database, the following information is provided:
  - Business type description
  - Annual gross revenues
  - Annual earnings
  - Annual owners' compensation (if reported)
  - Sales price

- Date of the transaction
- Geographic location

From this data, price/revenues and price/earnings are the two primary valuation multiples that can be calculated. The data from the IBA can be supplied in an Excel spreadsheet format that allows easy data manipulation such as deleting noncomparable transactions, calculating regression lines, or graphing. A problem with the IBA database is that there is a widespread time frame for the data. In addition, many key ratios are not provided.

Other Sources of Transactional Data

- Done Deals (or Midmarket Comps) is similar to Bizcomps with the exception that it primarily contains transactional data on companies with annual revenues between $1 million and $100 million (with over 50% of the data between $1 million and $10 million in revenues). Done Deals (CD ROM subscription) reports the following data for each transaction in the database:
  - Total assets
  - Total book value
  - Revenue
  - Income

  From this data, price/assets, price/book value, price/revenues, and price/earnings multiples can be calculated. The values derived using the Done Deals database are equity (i.e., stock) values.
- The Goodwill Registry reports on the prices paid or valuations made for the intangible assets of medical and dental practices. When valuing a medical or a dental practice for the purpose of a marital dissolution, this publication could be a valuable source. The database is divided into primary care and surgical specialties as well as the year of the transactions. For each transaction, the following information is provided:
  - State in which the practice is located
  - Location of the practice (urban, suburban, or rural)
  - The valuation reason (divorce, entry/pay out, sale of practice, etc.)
  - The primary valuation method used in the appraisal of the practice's intangible assets
  - Gross revenues
  - Overhead percent
  - Price paid for the practice
  - Price paid for the practice's intangible assets (i.e., goodwill)

The one important statistic that can be derived from the foregoing data is the intangible asset price to total revenues. By adding all of the practice's tangible assets and subtracting the liabilities, the total value of the subject practice can be derived. Unfortunately, the transactions submitted may be duplicative, with each side putting its own spin on the deal. We would recommend that the Goodwill Registry be used as a supplemental, rather than primary, source.

Preparing the Data

Information about mergers and acquisitions is less abundant than stock trading prices in an open market. For this reason, the appraiser does not have the ability to always obtain the sale price as of the exact date of valuation. Prices are affected by time so how close to the date of valuation the merger or acquisition occurred may be a critical factor as to the applicability of the approach.

Multiples derived from merger and acquisition data should also be applied carefully. Many different databases define variables differently and the same definition for the variables must be applied to the subject company to obtain an accurate estimate from the data. In addition, unless you know the terms of the deal, it may be difficult to ascertain the actual cash or cash equivalent price at which the transaction took place.

Analyzing and Applying the Data

Once proper adjustments have been made to the subject company's financial data, the market derived multiple can be directly applied to the subject's value base. Depending upon the database used, the resulting value may be an estimate of total assets, equity, fixed assets and intangibles, or some other combination. It is important that you understand what the market multiple tells you and what value you arrive at when you use that multiple. If you do not understand what value you derive from each market multiple, you may arrive at an incorrect valuation opinion.

SUMMARY

No two companies are exactly comparable. But, since both the publicly traded guideline company and merger and acquisition methods are based on actual transactions, the results from applying these methods are a very direct indication of value. The appraiser must identify and adjust for differences between the subject company and the comparables for either method to be applicable. It is important to understand not only the source of the data, but also how the data was calculated. No longer can the valuator routinely dismiss the guideline company method as being inapplicable to small closely held business entities and by using the excuse that there are no comparable companies.

Chapter 8

Discounts and Premiums

VALUATION METHODOLOGY AND APPLICATION OF DISCOUNTS AND PREMIUMS

The base for applying any discounts is the equity value of the subject interest. The equity value is determined by consideration of the three approaches to value and the application of the appropriate methods of valuation to determine a value of the total equity of an enterprise. This is the value, prior to any discounts, which is the base upon which the discounts are applied. It is important that the valuator and the user understand what value is being used as the starting point for application of discounts.

The required types of premiums and discounts are usually determined based on three factors:

1. The characteristics of the weighted average value estimate previously determined
2. The standard of value that the valuator is trying to determine
3. Ownership characteristics of the subject interest that are different from the characteristics inherent in the approaches and methods used in the valuation

The starting point in determining the types of discounts to use depends on which methods or approaches were used in the valuation. The valuator needs to know and understand the type of value estimate that each of the methods or approaches provides to understand what types of discounts or premiums are appropriate.

The proper application of discounts and premiums requires the valuator to understand the impact of such discounts and premiums. Some discounts and premiums are multiplicative, while others are additive. For example, suppose the valuator is applying a minority discount of 20 percent and a discount for lack of marketability of

25 percent. One would think that the combined discount is 45 percent. This is not the case. The combined discount is actually 40 percent, which is found by subtracting each discount from one (1 − .20 and 1 − .25) and then multiplying them together (.80 × .75). This number is then subtracted from one (1 − .60) to arrive at 40 percent.

Values derived from certain methods usually result in the same types of ownership interest. For example values derived from the capitalized or discounted returns methods usually provide freely tradable minority interests primarily because the cap or discount rate is based on information about minority interests in public companies.

Values derived from the comparative companies methods usually provide freely tradable minority interest values if the numerator of the value multiple represents the share price of a comparative public company and the denominator has not been adjusted for excess compensation or similar adjustments. On the other hand, these methods may provide a control value if the numerator represents a comparative company's total price based on a purchase/sale transaction and the denominator has been adjusted for excess compensation or similar adjustments.

Values derived from the underlying assets methods are usually control interest values. These methods should be used to value minority interests only if those interests can cause the company to sell its assets or if the company is the type of company whose stock should normally be valued primarily on an asset basis.

Values derived from the Excess Earnings Method and the Multiple of Discretionary Earnings Method usually result in control interest values.

CONTROL PREMIUM

A control premium is the additional value inherent in the control interest, as contrasted to a minority interest that reflects its power of control. An investor will generally pay more (a premium) for the rights that are part of a controlling interest. These rights of a controlling interest were defined by Shannon Pratt in his earlier writings. These rights that help to assess the size of a premium include the right to:

- Declare dividends
- Register the stock for an initial public offering (IPO)
- Sell or acquire Treasury stock
- Appoint management
- Set business policy
- Change the articles of incorporation or bylaws of the corporation
- Elect the board of directors
- Determine compensation and perquisites
- Acquire or liquidate assets
- Make acquisition or divestitures

The control premium is the opposite of the minority discount (discussed in the next section). The control premium is applied to the freely traded minority value of a closely held company to determine its control value.

In some instances, the control premium may be appropriate for an interest that is less than 100 percent. The size of the premium in this case depends on a variety of factors that relate to the amount of control available to the controlling interest. These factors include:

- Cumulative versus noncumulative voting rights
- State statutes
- The distribution of ownership
- Contractual restrictions
- Financial condition of the business

Double counting is a common error when using a control premium. If the value determined is already on a control value, then a control premium is not appropriate. In other words, if the 100 percent control value of a company is $1 million, then no value in excess of $1 million would be paid for that 100 percent interest. Thus a control premium would not apply.

One question that does arise in a situation like this is what if the purchaser is acquiring 51 percent ownership as opposed to 100 percent? The only rationale that can be put forward to suggest that more than a pro rata share of the $1 million (i.e., more than $510,000) would be paid is where the new control shareholder could unjustly enrich him- or herself at the expense of the minority shareholder(s). Many would question the efficacy of such an assumption. Others would say that the ability to set compensation, pay dividends, and have the other attributes of control would justify a premium in excess of $510,000. The courts have danced around this issue.

MINORITY INTEREST DISCOUNT

A minority interest discount is the reduction from the value of the entire business to reflect the absence of the power of control. Minority interests are therefore usually worth less than a proportionate share of the value of the total entity. The size of the discount depends on the size of the interest being valued, the amount of control, and other factors.

The opposite of the control premium, the minority interest discount is intended to determine a noncontrolling interest when a control value is the starting point, whereas the control premium is intended to determine a controlling interest when a minority value is the starting point.

To distinguish between a control premium and a minority discount, the valuator must consider the shareholder's ability to exercise any or all of the rights discussed in the previous section.

Minority owners may enjoy some significant rights through their ability to cast important swing votes. Therefore, several factors need to be considered that affect the degree of control. These factors are cumulative versus noncumulative voting, contractual restrictions, state statutes, distribution of ownership, and the financial condition of the business.

Many companies have noncumulative voting provisions, which means that the majority shareholders have the ability to elect the entire board of directors, which cannot be blocked by minority shareholders. Other companies, however, have cumulative voting systems in which all shareholders are given votes as based on their percentage of ownership. It is left to the shareholder's discretion to distribute the votes for one candidate or to a variety of candidates.

In some instances, companies give up some rights of control through contract provisions. Some of the most common restrictions include the payment of dividends, acquisition of other companies, the liquidation of assets, or changes in the direction of the business. Regulations at the federal and state levels often affect the degree of control enjoyed by owners. Many of these regulations prevent certain acquisitions and limit other areas of operation.

The amount of ownership in relation to other shareholders is very important in determining control. Equal individual interests are usually worth less than a pro rata portion of what an entire company is worth. The sum of the values of the individual owners is therefore less than what the total company would be sold for to a single buyer.

The following list shows how each of the factors affect the degree of control.

- Factors that may increase the minority interest discount or control premium
  - The presence of nonvoting stock
  - A lack of consideration for the minority shareholder's interests by the company's management, board of directors, and/or majority owners
- Factors that may decrease the minority interest discount or control premium
  - The presence of enough minority interest votes to have meaningful input on electing one or more directors in a company with cumulative voting
  - The presence of enough minority interest votes to block certain actions
  - The presence of state statutes granting minority stockholder rights
- Factors that may increase or decrease the minority interest discount or control premium
  - The distribution of other shares

There is little disagreement that a minority interest is of less value than a control interest. There is disagreement, however, as to what constitutes a minority interest in a tax-related valuation. Over the years, the Internal Revenue Service (IRS) had been soundly and routinely beaten in the courts on the issue of whether a family relationship converted what was "legally" a minority interest into a control interest. It was the IRS's contention that all family members' holdings should be aggregated to determine whether the interest being valued was a control or a minority interest. In Revenue Ruling 93-12, the IRS finally gave up and declared that minority interest discounts are appropriate in family relationship situations.

DISCOUNTS FOR LACK OF MARKETABILITY

The discount for a lack of marketability is widely recognized and accepted by courts, valuation experts, and the IRS as the "cost" of the lack of liquidity inherent in stock of companies for which there is no ready market for the shares. Although this discount is widely accepted, the issue in each valuation is determining how large a marketability discount to apply.

The discount for lack of marketability is used to compensate for the lack of access to a publicly traded market. Publicly traded stocks have an element of liquidity that closely held shares do not. Ownership interests in closely held companies are typically not readily marketable compared to similar interests in public companies. Thus, a discount for lack of marketability is taken to reflect this element.

Marketability discounts are applicable to most stocks that are not listed on a public exchange or traded in an active over-the-counter market. The size of the discount, as with the minority discount, depends on several factors. These factors can affect the marketability discount in the following ways:

- Factors that may increase the discount for lack of marketability
    - Restrictions on transfers
    - Little or no dividends or partnership payout
    - Little or no prospect of either public offering or sale of company
- Factors that may decrease the discount for lack of marketability
    - "Put" option
    - Limited market available that may be interested in purchasing shares
    - Imminent public offering or sale of company
    - High dividend or partnership payouts
- Factors that may increase or decrease the discount for lack of marketability
    - Size of block
    - Buy-sell agreement

Some of the earliest marketability studies focused on value differences between common stock and restricted stock of the same publicly traded company. Restricted or "letter" stock generally has all the attributes of regular common stock with the exception that restricted stock is prohibited from sale on the open market for a specified period of time (usually two years). Because the only difference between common stock and restricted stock is this marketability feature, price differences between the two classes of stock are believed to be a fairly accurate indicator of the discount for lack of marketability.

Two types of studies have been performed that have attempted to determine the average levels of discounts for lack of marketability: (1) restricted stock studies and (2) studies of transactions in closely held stocks prior to IPOs. (For a detailed discussion of each of these studies refer to the *Discount for Lack of Marketability Model* by Z. Christopher Mercer. See Appendix A for further details.)

The restricted stock studies attempted to find differences in the price at which letter stock transactions take place compared with the open market transactions in the same stock on the same date. The following paragraphs discuss some of the more notable studies.

The Securities and Exchange Commission (SEC) Institutional Investor Study addressed the amount of discount at which transactions in restricted stock take place, compared with the prices of otherwise identical but unrestricted stock on the open market. This study examined restricted stock of 398 publicly traded companies and determined that the mean and median discount for trades of restricted shares was approximately 26 percent. The SEC study also isolated nonreporting over-the-counter (OTC) companies (companies most likely to resemble closely held companies) and found a mean and median discount of approximately 33 percent. This study concluded that the discounts were lower for those stocks that would be tradable on the New York Stock Exchange than those that could be traded over-the-counter when the restrictions expired.

The Moroney Study examined restricted stock of 146 publicly traded companies and found a mean discount of 36 percent and a median discount of 33 percent.

The Silber study, performed by William L. Silber, was done to develop a statistical model to explain the differences between securities that differ in resale provisions. He concluded that the discount on restricted stock varies directly with the size of the block of restricted stock relative to the amount of publicly traded stock issued by the company.

These studies, along with several more, have attempted to quantify the discount taken against the freely traded price of minority shares in the public market. Studies have also been done to determine the lack of marketability discount through the use of closely held companies that underwent an IPO. The most notable study of this type is the Robert W. Baird & Co. study performed by John Emory. As opposed to analyzing restricted stock, Mr. Emory used the ingenious approach of examining transaction values of company stock prior to the IPO with the actual offering price at the IPO. For example, if a shareholder disposes of company stock at $6 per share and the stock is then brought public at $10 per share, Mr. Emory would calculate a marketability discount of 40 percent. Pre-IPO stock transactions are limited to the five-month period preceding the IPO, implying that most buyers and sellers are aware of the impending IPO and the potential marketability of the company stock.

In six separate studies conducted over 18-month periods since 1980, Mr. Emory examined 173 companies and found an average discount of 47 percent and a median discount of 46 percent between the pre-IPO trades and the actual IPO price.

After examining the data, it would appear simple to apply a marketability discount to the closely held shares being valued. However, a straight application of a marketability discount may not be the proper route once various data and company-specific factors are considered. It is only through a consideration of the totality of company, market, the distribution of ownership, and a variety of other factors that the appropriate marketability discount can be determined.

Additionally, case law, IRS revenue rulings, and other complicating factors can affect how various elements interplay to impact the appropriate discount. Therefore, blind use of marketability discount study data is dangerous, particularly when no discount may actually be warranted, or conversely, where the facts warrant a higher discount. Finally, there are limitations in the studies themselves that must be considered.

When the studies are considered by the valuator, he or she must then select a discount to apply. The range of discounts are quite wide in the studies and the average or median discount varies from study to study. The selection of an appropriate discount for lack of marketability involves judgment on the part of the valuator. This judgment should involve or be based on a set of factors, including those factors described earlier in this chapter that may increase or decrease the discount.

The courts and the IRS have been receptive to the studies that assist in quantifying discounts for lack of marketability. In one case in particular, Mandelbaum, the U.S. Tax Court recognized both the restricted stock studies and the IPO studies as average starting bases to which to apply the company specific factors. The court also set forth the following factors that may also increase or decrease the discount for lack of marketability:

- Financial statement analysis. Specific items mentioned in this factor include the results of annual operations, status at year-end as determined by the balance sheet, relevant footnotes, the opinion of an independent CPA, the soundness of the company's capitalization, the ratio of the company's assets to liabilities, net worth, future earnings power, quality of earnings, and the company's goodwill.
- Dividend policy. Critical to this factor is whether the investor will receive a fair return on his or her investment. The fact that a company pays little or no dividends may not always affect the company's marketability, as an investor may aim for capital appreciation instead of dividend income.
- Nature of the company, its history, its position in the industry, and its economic outlook. Obviously the position of a company in its industry and the factors needed for success in the industry need to be considered when determining the value of a company. The stock of a market leader is usually determined to be more valuable than that of a market follower.
- Costs associated with an IPO. An above average discount may be warranted if the buyer completely bears the cost of registering a private stock. The discount is lessened if the buyer can minimize his or her registration costs.
- Company's redemption policy. Whether a company has the right to purchase its stock before it is sold to an outsider is another factor to consider when

determining the value of a company. This may be particularly critical if the redemption agreement sets a price on the stock.

- Holding period for the stock. An investment is less marketable if an investor must hold it for an extended period of time in order to reap a sufficient profit. Market risk increases and marketability decreases as the holding period gets longer.
- Restrictions on the transferability of the stock. Shareholders' agreements, as enforceable legal documents, are a factor in determining the worth of a company's stock. Whether an agreement specifies a transfer price or a formula for determining a transfer price are important factors for consideration.
- Amount of control in the transferred shares. Control reflects a shareholder's ability to direct a corporation in its daily operations. Control of a closely held corporation represents an element of value that justifies a higher value for a controlling block of stock.
- Company's management. Strength of company management is a factor to consider when determining the worth of a company's stock. A proven and experienced management team may positively affect a company's value.

From the starting bases of the restricted stock studies and the IPO studies, these factors along with the factors mentioned earlier, can be applied to help the valuator arrive at a reasonable discount.

Lack of marketability discounts for control interests are as different as day from night compared to the same discounts for minority interests. Both measure the same thing, the illiquidity of the interest being value, but the incidents of control place the discount in an entirely different light for the control interest holder.

Some prominent valuators believe that there is no lack of marketability discount for a control interest. Their thinking is that the conclusion of value arrived at prediscount represents the "nonmarketable" value since illiquidity issues have already been considered in the determination of the market multiple (in the case of the guideline companies method) or the discount or capitalization rate (in the case of an income approach method). Others believe that the market multiples and discount and capitalization rates are arrived at in the context of a freely traded interest.

Certainly, the courts have supported the theory that an additional lack of marketability discount is appropriate for application to a control interest in many cases. There is substantial support for the application of lack of marketability discounts to control interests in the business valuation profession. Many of the tax cases discuss lack of marketability discounts in control interest situations. Other cases and situations also cover this area.

SUMMARY

The key to understanding discounts and premiums is to understand the base number that they are to be applied to. Discounts and premiums can have a material impact on the ultimate conclusion of value. Many business valuation experts make the mistake of spending 35+ pages of a report describing the financial analysis of the company, the derivation of the capitalization rate, and yet spend one paragraph discussing discounts that may exceed 40 percent of the total value. In most valuations, discounts and premiums are something that must be critically analyzed and reviewed.

Chapter 9

Goodwill in a Divorce Context

DEFINING GOODWILL

Goodwill is often defined as the amount of the purchase price for a business over and above the value of its identifiable tangible and intangible assets and net of any liabilities assumed. Goodwill is based on the earnings capacity of a business and therefore rests on the excess earnings over the fair return on the net tangible assets. This is a simplistic definition which can create significant problems in a marital setting.

Goodwill is often referred to as the most intangible of the intangibles. It is undoubtedly one of the most complex and controversial assets presented in financial statements. Goodwill is unique because it can be identified only with the business as a whole. Goodwill comprises many advantageous factors and conditions that might contribute to the value and the earning power of an enterprise:

- Superior management team
- Effective advertising
- High standing in the community
- Strategic location
- Favorable association with another company

Other factors besides earnings, such as prestige and reputation of the business, the ownership of a trade or brand name, and a record of successful operation over a prolonged period in a particular locality, may support the inclusion of intangible value. In some situations, it may not be possible to make separate appraisals of the tangible and intangible assets. Whatever intangible value there is may be measured by the amount by which the appraisal value of the entity exceeds the net book value of such assets.

UNDERSTANDING STATE INTERPRETATIONS

The high incidence of divorce has created the need for valuations in a number of property settlement situations. Because each state has its own statutes relating to family law, the valuator must be aware of the standard of value that is appropriate in performing the valuation. The courts often interpret the standard of value and it is an evolving situation. Because the vast majority of personal versus entity goodwill issues arise in the valuation of professional practices and other entities where a single individual is key, the discussion necessarily focuses on those issues.

It is imperative in each case for the attorney to let the practitioner know what law pertains in each case. Laws vary from state to state. For example, in Indiana, only marital property is subject to division while in Texas community property is subject to division. Indiana also has statutes that list specific factors to be considered in property division. In Illinois, personal goodwill is not a divisible asset, yet in Colorado it can be considered. Some states require the appraiser to determine if there is any goodwill and then to apportion that goodwill between entity goodwill and personal goodwill. Practitioners involved in providing dissolution-related services should consult with the attorney they are working with to clearly determine what the statutes applicable to the marital dissolution are.

Indiana recognizes nonmonetary contributions when dividing property between spouses. This means that the spouse's contribution cannot be disregarded because the contributions were not in monetary form. Arizona has no such nonmonetary policy. Indiana also takes into consideration the economic misconduct by a spouse when dividing property between spouses. Maine, on the other hand, does not. Indiana also has statutes relating to consideration of spousal contribution to education when dividing property, while Iowa does not.

In Indiana, the courts have evolved to a position of allowing goodwill to become part of the value of a physician's practice for purposes of determining the value of the marital estate in a divorce, yet that is not allowed in Illinois. The Indiana courts do not require goodwill to be included in the fair market value (FMV) of the practice, but it can be determined as an intrinsic value (the value of the practice to the physician) since the Indiana statute refers to "value."

As one can see, states vary on a variety of topics. That is why it is so critical that you understand the goodwill issue as it relates to the jurisdiction in which you are going to provide these services. The practitioner, as well as the attorney, must know which statutes apply and what considerations need to be taken when valuing property.

A court considers the following list of factors in making equitable distribution of property between spouses. This list was summarized in "Property Division and Alimony Awards: A Survey of Statutory Limitations on Judicial Discretion" by Mary Jane Connell, *50 Fordham Law Review,* 415, 439–440 (1981).

- Economic circumstances of the parties at the time of the division, especially the amount and sources of income

- Contributions of each party to the acquisition of marital property
- Length of the marriage
- Parties' age and health, including their physical and emotional conditions
- Desirability of awarding the marital home to the spouse receiving custody of the children
- Parties' respective occupational and vocational skills
- Their employability and employment history
- The opportunity of each for future acquisition of capital assets and income
- Whether the property division replaces or supplements the maintenance award
- Parties' debts and liabilities
- Value of their separate property
- Parties' station in life and standard of living
- Estates of the parties
- Conduct of the parties especially as it relates to the dissipation of the property
- Previous marriages and obligations arising therefrom
- Agreements of the parties, whether entered into before, during, or after the marriage
- Tax consequence
- Custody of the children
- Contribution of each party to the acquisition, preservation, or appreciation in value of the respective estates
- Retirement and pension benefits
- One spouse's contribution to the other's education, training, or increased earning power
- The parties' income and property at the time of the marriage
- Other "just and equitable factors"—(unspecified) factors
- Whether the property was acquired by gift, bequest, devise, or descent
- Education of the parties
- Absence from the job market
- Time needed for education and training
- Increases or decreases in the value of separate property during the marriage
- Cause of the divorce
- Depletion of separate property for marital purposes
- Loss of inheritance and pension rights
- Liquid or nonliquid character of the marital assets
- Difficulty of evaluating a component asset or an interest in business
- Respective merits of the parties
- Burdens imposed on the property for the benefit of either party or the children

- Nature and extent of the community property
- Nature and extent of the separate property
- Party through whom the property was acquired

PERSONAL VERSUS ENTITY GOODWILL

Personal goodwill (also called professional goodwill) is the goodwill associated primarily with the individual practitioner. Entity goodwill (also called practice goodwill) the goodwill associated primarily with the entity. Personal goodwill exists based on the fact that clients or customers come to the individual because of the practitioner's skills, knowledge, reputation, personality, and other factors. There is an implied assumption that if the individual practitioner left to go to another practice, the clients would follow him or her.

This does not mean that personal goodwill cannot be transferred to a new owner. However, it generally requires effort on the part of the selling practitioner. The transfer of client trust and respect from seller to buyer requires cooperation from both parties. The transfer would include efforts of sending a letter of announcement to current clients from the seller informing them that the buyer is taking over and has the skills and expertise to handle their needs. In this way the seller can make a smooth transition of his or her goodwill to the buyer.

Entity goodwill exists based on the fact that clients come to the entity itself as opposed to the individual practitioner because of the location of the facilities, the staff, the reputation, and other factors. There is an implied assumption that if the individual practitioner left, the clients would stay with the existing entity.

There is also the concept of celebrity goodwill, which is based on the premise that the enhanced earnings capacity of a celebrity is marital property. There have only been a handful of cases involving this type of goodwill and the courts have ruled that a career in the performing arts and its accompanying celebrity status constituted a marital asset.

This issue of personal versus entity goodwill arises most often during the valuation of professional practices in marital dissolution cases, although some states have extended the concept to any type of business entity. Some courts have leaned toward the stance that sole practitioners in any profession can only have personal goodwill since the clients single them out exclusively.

The definition of value regarding goodwill varies depending on the state where the divorce is tried. The attorney should let the practitioner know at the outset of the case which definition of value to apply. Also, the attorney should explain in detail the legal precedents in the state regarding a business's goodwill as a marital asset.

In most states, courts have ruled that goodwill is indeed a part of the marital estate of a professional practitioner in divorce cases. In many states, professional goodwill is a part of the marital property value even if it is not transferable. In such cases, the definition of value is more of the nature of investment value, or the value to a particular owner, but is not fair market value. In a few states, notably Texas, courts have taken the position that professional goodwill is not a marital asset subject to division, but practice goodwill is.

The most widely cited case that details what factors should be considered when valuing professional goodwill is *Lopez v. Lopez* [In re Marriage of Lopez, 113 Cal. Rptr. 58 (38 Cal. App. 3d 1044 (1974))]. The factors listed in this case were:

- The age and health of the professional
- The professional's demonstrated past earning power
- The professional's reputation in the community for judgment, skill, and knowledge
- The professional's comparative professional success
- The nature and duration of the professional's practice, either as a sole proprietor or as a contributing member of a partnership or professional corporation

Separating personal goodwill from entity goodwill is very difficult. Several dominant factors help to determine the existence and value of entity and personal goodwill for professional practices. The following paragraphs explain these factors.

The marketability of the practice is one factor that can help determine the existence of entity and personal goodwill. Demand for the practice determines marketability, but often this demand is not for the practice itself. If there is a group of attorneys wanting to purchase law firms, then the demand for law firms is going to rise, and thus, the practice goodwill will increase as well. Along with that, if the profession is easy to enter, the practice goodwill will be lower. All these factors should be considered regarding the marketability of the practice.

The employees of the practice should also be considered. When a professional practice sells to a new buyer, repeat customers want to see the familiar faces of the support staff. The valuator should consider the number of employees, the job titles and job descriptions, the pay scale, and the length of time of employment. Another important issue is the nonowner professionals who are involved in the practice. These professionals may actually hold the goodwill of some clients. This is important to consider because if the professional were to leave the practice, the clients may go with him or her.

The location of the practice plays a vital role in goodwill determination. Some locations are more desirable than others. If a practice is located within a short travel distance for clients, it will have higher practice goodwill than a practice located an hour away. The demographics of the area where the practice is located are important as well. The people who live in the area, the health of those people, and the quality of life of the area are all important factors.

Another factor to consider is the fee schedule of the practice. How does the practice charge its clients? Does it charge by procedure performed or by amount of time spent on each client? Other considerations should include the impact of the increase or decrease of fees on the practice. Would clients leave or stay if the fees were changed?

The work habits of the practitioner are also important to consider. How many hours a week does the practitioner work? Does the practitioner spend a lot of time with each patient or does he or she work on several patients at once? A practitioner who spends more personal time with patients is likely to increase his or her personal goodwill, but the practice goodwill may decrease due to the time spent on each patient as opposed to other patients.

The types of patients and clients also play a role in the valuation of goodwill. How does each patient pay for services? Do most use some form of insurance? Are some of the patients involved in Medicare or Medicaid? Also, does the patient have family or friends who are involved in the practice? All these issues could play a part in the valuation of personal and entity goodwill.

The referral base is one of the most important considerations in the valuation of goodwill. Referrals keep new business coming in for the practice. If the referrals of the practice are coming from a large number of the current clients, the practice will generally have more practice goodwill than one that relies on referrals from a small client base or from other professionals.

The level of competition for the practice is also very important to consider. Some of the issues in this area include the other professionals who practice in the area, the reputation of the competition, and the number of patients seen by the competitor as compared to the practice. Competition also brings up issues regarding the purchase of the competitor's practice or the combination thereof.

The final factor is the expected future earnings. Generally, the higher the earnings, the higher the goodwill. The earnings of the practice are the result of other factors. These factors include the hours worked, the skills of the professional, the reputation of the professional, and the efficiency of the professional.

The factors outlined in the previous nine paragraphs are the dominant factors that should be considered that help to determine the existence and value of personal goodwill and entity goodwill. These factors should be considered by the valuator as well as the factors specific to divorce situations. These factors include the age and health of the practitioner, the demonstrated past earning power, the reputation for judgment, skill, and knowledge, comparative professional success, and the nature and duration of practice.

The age and health of the practitioner are important issues in the determination of goodwill in divorce situations. A practitioner close to retirement will have low personal goodwill because the expected future earnings cannot continue into the future very far. Health is another important consideration because the practitioner may have a health problem that can hamper his or her performance and thus lower the goodwill.

The demonstrated past earning power is important to consider because past earnings are in fact indicative of future earnings. Future earnings are important because goodwill value is merely an expression of the value of expected future income.

The reputation for judgment, skill, and knowledge is vital due to their impact on new or repeat business. The practitioner should have a qualified background and education and should possess the skills and judgment to perform as a professional. These qualities are what keep customers coming back and referring to new customers.

Comparative professional success is a very important factor in the value of professional goodwill. The success is usually measured by earnings of the practice, but other factors such as hours worked, patients seen, and community standards of living also play a role. The comparison of the professional to other professionals is the ideal comparative test. Surveys of earnings should also be considered, but comparison of professionals is usually the better method.

The nature and the duration of the practice are important to consider as well. The length of time the practice has been in operation has an effect on the goodwill because goodwill is built over time. The following factors can be relevant in determining goodwill:

- Type of service offered
- Type of client served
- Length of time at the current location
- Length of time remaining on the lease
- How the fees are billed
- Source of new clients
- The individual practitioner's amount of production
- The number of employees and their length of service
- Economic and demographic information on the community where the practice is located
- The number of other professionals in the community offering the same service or specialty

California has more reported case law on the issue of valuation of professional practices in divorces than any other state. When family courts in other states cannot find a precedent on some issue of professional practice valuation, they often look to California cases. Some courts in other states have also followed some cases in Texas as well.

A practitioner engaged to perform a valuation of a professional practice should seek advice of the client's attorney on the appropriate state law and how the courts stand on the issue. Some of the more relevant cases in this area of goodwill include:

- *Beasley v. Beasley,* 518 A.2d 545 (Pa. Super. 1986). The Pennsylvania superior court ruled that the sole proprietorship law practice cannot have goodwill since goodwill constitutes the present value of future earnings, which stem from the future postmarital efforts of the attorney spouse.
- *Dugan v. Dugan,* 92 N.J. 423 (1983). The supreme court of New Jersey decided that an individual's law practice can have goodwill that is transferable.

- *Sorenson v. Sorensen,* Utah Sup. Ct., No. 890145. The Utah supreme court reversed the lower court's ruling that the dental practice does not have goodwill. The court reasoned that unless there is an actual transaction concomitant with the divorce wherein the doctor realized the goodwill, then the goodwill is the same as a professional degree, which is not divisible since it only enhances future earnings.

THE VALUATOR'S GOAL

Only since the 1980s have business valuations become common in the divorce property settlement area. This is due, in part, to the risk of malpractice suits against an attorney who recommends a settlement in a divorce without an independent valuation of a closely held business interest that is part of the marital estate. In most situations, each party hires a valuation expert and the judge must decide the appropriate value based on their testimony. In some cases, the parties agree to hire a single valuator and agree to rely on his value for purposes of the property settlement. However, this latter situation is the exception rather than the rule since emotions of divorce and family businesses do not often allow the use of a single valuator.

The practitioner is really trying to perform a valuation that will help in some way for the sides to reach an agreement. Sometimes only one valuator is used to determine the value of the subject company. At other times, both sides each appoint their own valuator. If a compromise cannot be reached, a third valuator might be appointed and the value determined by him or her may be binding. If a third valuator is not appointed and the sides are still at disagreement, a trial is held and the court determines the value after hearing expert witness testimony presented by each valuator.

The American Institute of Certified Public Accountants (AICPA) Code of Professional Conduct requires a practitioner to be objective and free of conflicts of interest. Upon entering an engagement, it should be specified whether the practitioner's role is to determine an objective, independent value or to assist the client in negotiating the best deal.

SUMMARY

The issue of personal versus entity goodwill is a rapidly evolving area and is not consistent across the country. Even states that use the same "name" for the goodwill may have defined the concept differently. The practitioner has to monitor this issue very closely in order to be certain that the work being performed is consistent with the most recent case law on the issue.

Chapter 10

Arriving at a Conclusion of Value

SELECTING THE VALUATION APPROACH

The final step in the valuation process is to arrive at a conclusion of value. The conclusion should be in line with the analyses and computations completed in previous steps.

Often more than one method is selected for consideration of final value. Also, there are often several computations of value within a method. For example, computations such as price/earnings, price/dividends, and price/cash flow, among others, might be made within the guideline companies method.

The valuator must use precise judgment to determine whether to use one method for the valuation conclusion or to use a conclusion which incorporates several methods. In general, on an intuitive selection of a value from among several methods, the various methods deemed appropriate to value the company should reasonably result in values that are close in amount to each other. If they do not, then the valuator should investigate and determine the reasons for the difference.

There is no precise guideline or quantitative formula for selecting the approach or approaches most applicable under a specific business valuation situation. However, a valuator should consider some important factors when selecting among different valuation approaches, including

- Amount and source of data. How much data is provided and where the data came from are both crucial considerations in a valuation. The valuator must have enough data to perform the valuation and the data must also have come from a reliable source. Certain information may provide a better indication of a company's value than other information. However, when information has been found, the valuator should still assess its quality.

- Restrictions on data. In certain situations, the valuator may find that access to some company data, company management, and so forth may be restricted in some manner. Thus, in determining which valuation approach is most applicable, the valuator must keep in mind the unavailable data and what impact it could have on the conclusion of value.
- Industry data. Today, Industry-related data is more abundant than ever before. New publications and resources are coming out each year that provide such data. When determining which method is appropriate, the valuator will probably select the market-based approach when this industry data is substantial. However, if there is not enough data to rely on, the valuator will probably rely on other valuation approaches. Even when a number of comparative transactions can be found, the valuator should still carefully determine its worth in the process.
- Business-related considerations. Certain rules of thumb for certain industries are used as a guide to determine a quick estimate of value of a business within that industry. These industry rules of thumb may provide the valuator with a decent idea of the approximate value for the business, but can never be totally relied upon. The nature of the assets of the business being valuated should also be considered, thus different valuation approaches may be applicable.
- Valuation of the whole business versus part of the business. The valuator must also keep in mind that some valuation approaches are more appropriate for overall business valuations whereas other approaches may be appropriate for interests in the business. The valuation of a control, marketable interest in a business is far different than a minority, nonmarketable interest.
- Special considerations. Special type business valuations, such as an employee stock ownership plan (ESOP), have certain approaches that are required and certain approaches that are prohibited. Certainly, the valuator must be aware of this issue. The Internal Revenue Service (IRS) has published valuation procedures for special type valuations. The valuator needs to be aware of such specific requirements and prohibitions.
- The valuation audience. Some considerations regarding the valuation audience have to be considered by the valuator in selecting the appropriate approaches. The level of sophistication of the valuation audience and the familiarity of the valuation audience with the valuation process are two critical considerations the valuator must think about.
- The valuator's purpose and objective for performing the valuation. The purpose and objective of the valuation also plays a part in the determination of valuation approaches. Several objectives of the valuator include the description of the business interest being valued, the standard of value applied, the premise of value applied, and the date of valuation. The valuator's purpose includes the audience for the valuation and any related decisions to be influenced by the valuation. The purpose of the valuation often dictates the most appropriate methods and standard of value to use.

- The judgment, expertise, and common sense of the valuator. This final factor affecting the selection of the appropriate valuation approach to be used is the most important: The judgment, expertise, and common sense of the valuator. The valuator must ensure that all relevant factors have been considered. Knowing this, the valuator should feel comfortable with the conclusion because it is based on his or her professionalism.

When weighting the appropriate valuation approaches, there are two ways that the valuator may consider. The first is subjective weighting, which allows the valuator to arrive at a single conclusion based on more than one method. The determination of the single conclusion is just simply supported by a narrative description of how and why this figure was selected.

The other way to weight the selected approaches is by mathematical weighting. In this process, each value and its related method are listed and then a weighting is applied to each and shown to the valuation audience. Allowing the audience to see the weighting schedule shows which method was deemed most appropriate (i.e., most appropriate weighted highest). The weakness associated with this weighting method is that the valuator is responsible for the weights. There are known guidelines as to which method should receive a certain weight. The methods are weighted based purely on the judgment of the valuator. The good point in all of this is that it forces the valuator to present the conclusion in quantified terms. In other words, the audience can clearly follow the valuator's thought process by following the weighting process.

Revenue Ruling 59-60 provides the following evidence regarding the mathematical weighting technique:

> Because valuations cannot be made on the basis of a prescribed formula, there is no means whereby the various applicable factors in a particular case can be assigned mathematical weights in deriving the fair market value. For this reason, no useful purpose is served by taking an average of several factors (for example, book value, capitalized earnings, and capitalized dividends) and basing the valuation on the result. Such a process excludes active consideration of other pertinent factors, and the end result cannot be supported by a realistic application of the significant facts in the case except by mere chance.

As one can see, the IRS is not a big supporter of the mathematical technique. However, this technique can be very helpful and is used quite often.

When the mathematical technique is used, some disclosures should be made regarding the weightings that were made. The disclosures should state that the weightings are not intended to be precise and that they may change over time.

So, which technique should be used and when? Even though Revenue Ruling 59-60 appears not to accept the mathematical technique, it is often used and accepted by courts and others. However, the wider the range in the individual values, the less useful the mathematical technique will be.

RANGES VERSUS SPECIFICITY

The best situation to encounter is where the valuator concludes using two or more approaches and methods with each method providing the same conclusions. Obviously, this never happens. When several conclusions of value are used, the valuator might conclude a range of those conclusions. However, in marital litigation matters, it is more common to arrive at a single valuation number.

Most situations result in conclusions that differ by only a small amount. In this situation, the valuator can pick out a reasonable range to conclude on. When the range of values differs only by a small amount, the valuator has evidence that the final conclusion is within that range.

There are other times when the range of conclusions differ by only a small amount with the exception of one value. In this situation, three alternatives are available to the valuator. The first alternative is for the valuator to investigate and determine the reason for such an odd value. During this process, the valuator should rethink the quantitative and qualitative conclusions that were made. The second alternative is to keep the odd value, but assign a small weight to it in the weighting process. The reason for this alternative is that even if the value looks odd, the methodology is correct and the value determined should be given some consideration in the conclusion. The third and final alternative is to simply discard the odd value because the value simply does not fit given the facts and circumstances surrounding the valuation.

ESTIMATES OF VALUE

To arrive at an estimate(s) of value for the ownership interest being valued, the valuator should have applied one or more of the valuation methods and then applied the weighting techniques, or picked a number within the range of information. The next step, for some valuators, is to apply what is called *sanity checks.* Sanity checks are designed to test the reasonableness of the estimate of value. Some of the most common tests are described in the following paragraphs.

During the final phase of the valuation, the valuator should always review the logic and math used during the valuation process. Some common mistakes usually discovered when the valuator rechecks the logic and math are the incorrect commingling of before-tax amounts and rates with after-tax amounts and rates, using an incorrect discount or capitalization rate, using unrealistic earnings, cash flows, or other amount, and failing to apply premiums and/or discounts. Such mistakes could materially alter a conclusion of value.

Another highly effective test is the comparison of some of the subject company's ratios with those of other comparative companies. This test should be performed on the operating value of the company to provide an overall picture of how the company is really performing. Comparing it to companies that operate within the same industry can show the subject company's true colors.

A well-accepted way to test the reasonableness of a proposed value is by examining the value from a buyer's point of view. The payback period computation is a common aspect of this test. That is, will the income that will be produced from this investment recover the purchase price as well as a reasonable return on the investment over a reasonable period of time?

The final test often used is the testing of the reasonableness of a value estimate from an adversary's point of view. This test is appropriate in circumstances where the value may have to be defended in court. The goal of this test is to have the valuator, acting as the adversary, challenge every aspect of the methodology used to establish the conclusion of value.

DOCUMENTING THE CONCLUSION

The conclusion of value should always be documented clearly to the user of the valuation. The method, value, and any applicable discounts should all be presented in the documentation of the conclusion. If the conclusion of value is on a control, marketable basis, then it should be presented as such. If there are discounts taken, the amount of the discount should also be documented.

The Written Report

A valuation is useful only if the valuator provides a report as to the valuation conclusion. Such a report is essential to help the user determine the purpose, intended use, standard of value, and other aspects of the valuation process. The report should include all of the elements necessary to adequately inform the audience. An incomplete report can mislead the audience.

Full Versus Basic Reports

Deciding which type of report is a crucial step in the valuation process. The two types of reports are full and basic reports. A full report is the highest level report that a valuator can provide to the audience. Full reports are usually a minimum of forty pages and can have as many pages as necessary. A full report usually includes the following elements:

- Introductory section that includes a description of the assignment and the item being valued
- The background and history of the subject company
- Economic and industry data
- Detailed financial analysis of the subject company, including presentation of financial statements and ratio analysis

- Comparative company search, and to the extent that a guideline company methodology was adopted, presentation of the financial information of the guideline companies selected
- The methods of valuation considered and applied

Basic reports are the most requested and are perfectly acceptable in situations in which the audience is informed that the detailed information is excluded from the report. These reports contain substantially less information than the formal reports; they usually contain the valuation with a small amount of narrative. These reports should state that the same process that would be undertaken for a valuation in which a full report is issued is also going to be followed, but the report is summarized as opposed to detailed.

Basic reports are issued for a variety of reasons. One reason might be the cost: A basic report requires less time than is normally needed to issue a full report. Another reason a basic report would be issued as opposed to a full report is that the audience may already understand the valuation process. The valuator should determine, under each circumstance, which report would best suit the client.

Elements of a Good Report

The first major understanding that a valuator must come to is that a good report must be written well. If a report is issued with all of the necessary information included but the writing is sketchy, the report will not be highly regarded. A good report also must meet certain engagement requirements as well as professional standards. The report should be very detailed, it should be well supported, it should discuss negative and positive factors, it should flow smoothly, and, most of all, it should be readable. A goal of the report should be to give another reasonably competent business valuation expert enough information that he or she could replicate the conclusions reached in your report.

There are common elements contained in well-prepared, full reports. Each of these elements is discussed in detail.

The *introduction* is simply a summary of the valuation engagement and conclusions. This section usually presents several matters that were present in the valuation: company and ownership interests that are being valued, any classes of stock and distribution to owners, and the valuation date. A description of the company being valued should be present giving such information as to the operations, industry, legal form, and state of incorporation. The standard of value used in the valuation and the purpose of the valuation should be stated. The purpose places the valuation in the proper context. Finally, the methods and conclusion should be stated to give the audience a starting point as to what the report is concluding on.

Sources of data used in the determination of value for a subject company should be disclosed within the report. These sources allow the audience of the report to see how the valuator arrived at the conclusion. If the source of the financial data is from the individual or firm that is preparing the valuation report, then the level of service provided on those financials (audit, review, or compilation) should be addressed in this section. If the financial data is not prepared by the person(s) involved with the business valuation, it is appropriate to provide a statement to that effect.

Assumptions or limiting conditions should be presented in the report to help the audience understand some of the conditions that the valuator had to work around in arriving at a conclusion of a value. Were there limitations on what the valuation expert could do on the engagement, for example, was he unable to visit the plant? What was the impact of this limitation on the overall report and conclusions as to value? Additionally, this area may include assumptions that the valuator accepts all information from the client as valid or that information used in this report was pulled from sources that are considered reliable. This section of the report is considered one of the most important.

Economic and industry data should be presented to help the audience understand the conditions present at the time of the valuation. National, regional, and local economic data are all relevant and should be considered in the report. This information allows the reader to understand the economic environment that you expect the subject company to operate in over the near term. The industry data is also vital because the audience will more than likely not know much about the industry in which the subject company operates. Industry trends can be correlated with subject company trends to demonstrate the subject company's ability to operate in the environment.

The *background and history of the subject company* should cover any nonfinancial information important in the valuation. Some common points usually presented in this section are the history, preferably since inception, of the subject company, the operations, the management, stock ownership, and strengths and weaknesses of the subject company.

The *financial analysis* of the subject company includes the financial condition it is currently in, the profitability and earnings capacity, the dividend-paying capacity, the value of goodwill and other intangible assets, and any transactions in the subject company's stock. This section should also discuss any adjustments that were made to the financial statements for valuation purposes, the prior historical financial information, the outlook for the subject company, and any negative and positive factors that may affect the conclusion.

A *search for guideline companies* should also be performed and presented in the valuation report. There are two types of comparatives. One type is comparative public companies and the other is mergers and acquisitions involving comparative companies. Such information as the sources of this data, the reasons for using this data, and the results of this data should be presented in this section. Some reports even go as far as to list the comparative companies that were rejected and give reasons why each was not used.

The *valuation methods* that were considered should be described in the report. The methods that are used in the formation of a conclusion of value should be described in detail as to the steps that were involved. The methods not used in the formation of a conclusion of value should be presented in the report, but should include a brief discussion of why they were not utilized.

Some common errors have been found that cause the reports to not be considered good reports. Some of these errors include the failure to consider comparative companies method, insufficient support, inadequate data, the failure to follow the standard of value, and internal inconsistencies in the report.

A comparative companies method should always be considered, and if guideline companies are located, this method should be presented as part of the report. If a search for guideline companies is conducted, the results of the search should be included in the report along with any sources that were used in connection with the results. Insufficient support is an imperative part of a valuation report. Not including support for conclusions does not help the audience of the report to understand what was actually done. Inadequate data is a concept that determines whether a valuation can be completed. Without the required data, the valuator cannot perform a valuation.

Failing to follow the standard of value is the most common valuation error. The standard of value not only helps to determine which methods of valuation should be used, but also how those methods should be applied. The valuator should carefully consider the standard of value and how it affects the valuation. The inclusion of inconsistencies in a valuation report can easily mislead the audience. Some common inconsistencies include the application of multiples to the wrong benefit stream and failing to match the capitalization or discount rates to the proper benefit stream.

WHAT IS USPAP?

During 1986 and 1987, the ad hoc committee on uniform standards established by the Appraisal Foundation developed and copyrighted the first Uniform Standards of Professional Appraisal Practice (USPAP). This was the first successful attempt to bring a set of rules [similar to GAAP (generally accepted accounting principles) or GAAS (generally accepted auditing standards)] to appraisal practice. Before establishment of the Appraisal Standards Board of the Appraisal Foundation in 1989, USPAP had been adopted by the regular member organizations of The Appraisal Foundation and were recognized throughout the United States as the generally accepted standards of appraisal practice.

The introductory section of USPAP includes an ethics provision, a competency provision, and a departure provision. Standards 1 through 6 deal with the appraisal of real estate. Standard 3 deals with reviewing an appraisal. Standards 7 and 8 deal with personal property appraisal. Standard 9 deals with business appraisals and standard 10 deals with reporting the business appraisals.

The Appraisal Foundation appointed a five-person task force to recommend changes to USPAP. As of this writing, USPAP is under review and an exposure draft is expected to be released late in 1999.

Why Does USPAP Apply to Divorce Engagements?

Although there may not be any specific state statutes that require the use of USPAP in a marital litigation engagement, it is important for the business valuation expert to know and understand USPAP. Certainly, if the business valuation expert is a member of a professional organization that has embraced USPAP, then that individual must conform with USPAP. Even though the USPAP do not specifically address their application in marital litigation, the application of USPAP is not denied to the business valuation expert. USPAP standard 9 provides the business valuation expert with guidance to the issues that may need to be addressed in completing the business valuation report. Standard 9 requires that the valuator:

- Be competent to perform the valuation and not make an error of omission or commission, nor be negligent in the conduct of the appraisal
- Adequately identify the business enterprise or assets being valued and define the standard of value being considered
- Consider whether liquidation value is higher than going concern value if the value is a majority interest
- Use an appropriate method or technique
- Collect and analyze relevant data
- Must not withhold pertinent information from the user of the valuation
- Select one or more approaches that apply to the specific appraisal assignments and consider and reconcile the quality and quantity of data available for analysis within the applicable approaches.

Standard 10 also provides guidance to the reporting requirement of a good business valuation report.

The legal profession is aware of USPAP, and in many cases, you might be cross examined about your knowledge of USPAP and why you did or did not apply those standards to your workproduct.

USPAP Guidance

Standard 10 of the Uniform Standards of Professional Appraisal Practice (USPAP) contains reporting guidelines and related rules. This standard deals with the content and format of the report the valuator is required to issue as a result of the conduct of a business valuation. The preamble to this standard states the overall objective of communicating the conclusions of the valuator in a manner that is clear and not misleading. The significant issues covered by this standard are:

- Each written or oral business appraisal report must not be misleading, must contain sufficient information to be understood by the user, and must disclose extraordinary assumptions or limiting conditions.

- Each written report must identify the enterprise or property being valued, state the purpose of the appraisal, define the value to be estimated, indicate the effective date of the appraisal and the effective date of the report, describe the scope of the appraisal, indicate assumptions and limiting conditions that affect the conclusions of the valuator, indicate the information considered, the procedures followed, and the reasoning that supports the conclusions, indicate other information which is appropriate to show compliance with or departures from Standard 9 (Business Appraisal), include a certification as required by Standard Rule 10-3, and include a transmittal signed by the person accepting technical responsibility for the valuation.
- Each written report must include a certification similar to the following (directly quoted from Standard Rule 10-3):

> I certify that, to the best of my knowledge and belief:
>
> The statements of fact contained in this report are true and correct.
>
> The reported analyses, opinion, and conclusions are limited only by the reported assumption and limiting conditions, and is my personal, unbiased professional analyses, opinions, and conclusions.
>
> I have no (or the specified) present or prospective interest in the property that is the subject of this report, and I have no (or the specified) personal interest or bias with respect to the parties involved.
>
> My (our) compensation is not contingent on an action or even resulting from the analyses, opinions, or conclusions in, or the use of, this report.
>
> My analyses, opinions, and conclusions were developed, and this report has been prepared, in conformity with the Uniform Standards of Professional Appraisal Practice.
>
> No one provided significant professional assistance to the person signing this report. (If there are exceptions, the name of each individual providing significant professional assistance must be stated.)

To the extent possible and appropriate, an oral report should set forth the other requirements of this standard.

An appraiser who signs a report, even as a reviewer, must accept full responsibility for its contents.

The standard does allow for an oral report to be issued in a business valuation. This shows the understanding of the Appraisal Standards Board of the litigation process, which often requires only an oral report to allow the effective presentation of the case. The oral report, however, is not limited to litigation situations, but is apparently allowed whenever the valuator deems it to be appropriate for the situation.

OTHER PROFESSIONAL STANDARDS

In addition to the Uniform Standards of Professional Appraisal Practice, other standards may need to be followed during the valuation process. These are the standards of the American Institute of Certified Public Accountants (AICPA), the American Society of Appraisers (ASA), the Institute of Business Appraisers (IBA), and the National Association of Certified Valuation Analysts (NACVA).

American Institute of Certified Public Accountants

The standards set forth by the AICPA do not specifically address business valuation reports but provide guidance that may affect the reports. The three standards are:

1. Statement on Standards for Consulting Services (SSCS)
2. Standards relating to the historical financial statement (SSARS, GAAS)
3. Standards relating to prospective financial information

Other professional standards of the institute apply to these engagements such as Rule 102, which was discussed in Chapter 3. These standards are binding on CPAs who are members of the institute.

American Society of Appraisers

Section 8 of the ASA's Principles of Appraisal Practice and Code of Ethics provides guidance regarding appraisal reports. After the USPAP set the tone and provided a framework for the professional conduct of a business valuation, the ASA believed that a series of more detailed and specific business valuation standards would be helpful to the business valuator and to the engagers and user of business valuations in ensuring compliance with the requirements of USPAP. These standards are required to be used by all members of ASA whether they are candidates, accredited members (AM), accredited senior appraisers (ASA), or fellows (FASA). According to the guidelines set forth by the ASA, appraisal reports should include the following:

- Complete description of the property being appraised
- Statement of the objective of the appraisal engagement
- Explanation of the type of value used in the appraisal
- Statement of the date to which the value estimate applies
- Analysis of the highest and best use of property, when appropriate
- A summary of any statements, information, or data obtained by the appraiser that may affect the appraisal findings
- Description of the method used in the appraisal
- Statement that the appraiser has no present or planned future interest in the property being valued or any property that might prevent the appraiser from making an unbiased appraisal

- Signatures of the person(s) who supervised the appraisal and any collaborating appraisers
- Signed reports from any collaborating appraiser who disagreed with the findings in the appraisal report, if applicable
- Appropriate labeling if it is a hypothetical, partial interest, or preliminary appraisal

Institute of Business Appraisers

The IBA is an organization geared toward the valuation of smaller closely held businesses. The standards used by the IBA are quite similar to those used by The Appraisal Foundation. For members of IBA, the following standards should be considered when preparing a valuation report:

- Standard 2, Oral Appraisal Reports
- Standard 4, Letter From Written Appraisal Reports
- Standard 5, Formal Written Appraisal Reports
- Standard 6, Preliminary Reports

National Association of Certified Valuation Analysts

This organization is also geared toward the valuation of small businesses and is comprised almost exclusively of CPAs. The standards set forth by the NACVA require members to comply with the AICPA's SSCS standard and contain standards defining the key components of each of the following four report formats:

- Full written reports
- Short-form written reports
- Oral (verbal) reports
- Limited scope reports

SUMMARY

The report is your ultimate deliverable and is the only tangible product that your client and the attorney will see. It is very important that the report be of the highest quality and comply with all applicable standards. A well-versed, competent expert uses the report to explain to the reader all of the complexities involved with arriving at an opinion of value. It also clearly advises the reader of the assumptions used, the data referred to, and the general economics in place at the time of the valuation. A well-written report is an excellent tool to make your direct testimony more effective.

Chapter 11

The Deposition

The deposition is most likely the first opportunity for opposing counsel to have the opportunity to discuss with you the engagement objectives, the methodologies that you used, the assumptions that you made, and your ultimate conclusions and opinions. It may also be your first opportunity to meet opposing counsel.

The deposition is a formal legal proceeding, held in the presence of a court reporter who transcribes your testimony during the deposition. There are some very simple rules for the deposition. The attorney taking your deposition must ask you cogent questions, and you must provide factual answers to the questions asked. The deposition is not a time to be coy or to attempt to mislead the opposing attorney. Remember that everything that you say is recorded by the reporter, including flip remarks and misplaced attempts at humor.

There is also another truism as it relates to your deposition: "You will not win the case during the deposition, but you can lose it." Think about that statement. If you participate in a perfect deposition, you can be sure that opposing counsel will not take it out of the briefcase at trial and tell the judge to read the deposition because it is so good. However, if you do a poor job at the deposition, it is much more likely that the deposition will be brought out to demonstrate your incompetence and inconsistencies.

Some expert witnesses do not treat the deposition with the respect that it is due. Just because the procedure takes place in a conference room rather than a courtroom does not make the procedure any less formal or important. You must respect the deposition for what it is, a discovery tool for opposing counsel—a tool that may be used against you during your cross-examination at the trial. The deposition can also be a time for you to learn. As we discuss, there are many things that you can learn from the deposition.

THREE RULES FOR SUCCESSFUL DEPOSITIONS

The expert witness needs to understand three very simple rules to assist in the deposition and cross-examination. We have found these three rules to be very beneficial in our own practice and expert testimony.

1. Listen to the question.
2. Answer only what has been asked.
3. Never anticipate the next question or volunteer information.

These three simple rules are a lot harder to follow than you might think. Quite frankly, humans do not communicate this way. When we first started to communicate, we learned to be helpful and to convey information when we are questioned. It takes patience and focus in order to consistently follow the rules, but let us discuss why each of these rules is so important for you as an expert witness.

- Listen to the Question. It is very important that you listen to the question so that you can understand what exactly has been asked of you. If you do not understand what has been asked, how can you possibly provide an appropriate answer? Be certain that you completely understand what the question means before you begin to answer. Make certain that what you are being asked is a single question, rather than multiple questions in the same sentence.
- Answer only what has been asked. Assuming that you have listened carefully to the question, you want to provide an answer only to that specific question. It is to your benefit to keep your answers as short as possible while still answering the question. Ideally, every answer would be a yes or no answer. If you cannot answer with a yes or no, try to keep your answer to 10 words or less. If you need to use more than 10 words to answer the question, perhaps you need to carefully think about the answer you are about to provide. Is that lengthy answer consistent with these three goals?
- Never anticipate the next question or volunteer information. You do not want to be thinking about the next question while you are answering the current question. Again, in our day-to-day life we generally anticipate where the conversation is going. When we have discussions with clients, we listen to what they are asking us, and then we attempt to solve the problem as we perceive it. This is different from your responsibility in a deposition. It is not your job to anticipate what the attorney will ask you so that you can shorten the deposition time by providing answers to unasked questions. The attorney may or may not know what the next question is, so you do not need to assist in determining what should be asked. The same is true as to volunteering information. If the attorney who retained you wants you to volunteer information during the deposition, you will be so instructed. Otherwise, only concern yourself with the question asked.

THE OPPOSING ATTORNEY'S GOALS IN THE DEPOSITION

In order to properly prepare for your deposition, you must understand the purpose and the goal of the deposition. The deposition is the primary opportunity for the opposing attorney to evaluate you as a potential witness. During the deposition, the attorney will be looking at four goals as they relate to you.

1. Evaluating you as the expert witness. During the course of the deposition the opposing attorney will try to evaluate your strengths and weaknesses in the following areas:

- Qualifications
    - What is your background, education, training, and how well do those attributes fit in with the matter under litigation. What prior experiences have you had, and are they all the same, or are they opposite positions you are taking in this matter?
    - Do you have any special qualifications and strengths or any obvious weakness in your qualifications that will be important to bring out during trial?
    - Do you demonstrate a working knowledge of the technical issues present in the case?
- Communication skills
    - Are you able to convey your information and opinions in a cogent, understandable, effective manner?
    - Can you discuss technical concepts simply and clearly in lay terms?
- Temperament, demeanor, personality
    - What kind of presence will you have on the witness stand? Do you have a stage presence or are you nervous and unsure of yourself?
    - Are there hot buttons that can be pressed that will cause you to lose your temper, become combative, or otherwise set you off?
    - How do you respond to pressure?
    - How strong is your personality and your belief in what you are saying?
- Biases and other prejudices
    - What biases do you bring to the stand with you?
    - Do you only testify for wives, or for husbands?
    - Have you been personally involved in a matter that has similar issues to this case?
    - How often do you work for the attorney who has retained you in this matter? Is that a significant amount of money as it relates to your practice? What about as a percentage of your marital litigation work?

2. Establishing the limitations of your testimony. The old saying that a good trial attorney never asks a question that he does not know the answer to is true in the trial setting. In the deposition, the attorney can find out what the answer is to the questions that will be asked at trial.

The deposition allows the opposing attorney the opportunity to establish the limitations of your trial testimony. The deposition allows him or her to assess such issues as:

- What exactly are the positions that you are taking? How do those positions contrast with the positions taken by the opposing expert? Can you reconcile the differences? Are there any other problems that you believe are contained in the opposing expert's report?
- What are the boundaries of your testimony? What issues have you been asked to address? Are there issues not contained in your report that you intend to testify to at trial?
- What documents did you rely on? Were there documents that you wanted that you did not receive? What was the source of your research?
- What information did you review and then discard as not being pertinent to your opinions? Is any of that information included in the opposing expert's report?
- What treatises do you regard as authoritative? What about methodologies?

All of these questions enable the opposing attorney to confine your potential testimony to the structure of your deposition. Opposing counsel will attempt to use your deposition testimony to limit and direct your testimony during cross-examination, as well as potentially for your direct examination.

3. Identifying possible sources of information for your impeachment at trial. This is a trap only expert witnesses can set for themselves. Certainly opposing counsel is going to be interested if you are saying something in this matter that is inconsistent with prior matters that you have worked on. Have you previously testified that a sole practitioner in a professional practice has no goodwill, but in this matter, you are saying that goodwill exists? There may be reasons for the inconsistent testimony, but if none exists, this testimony will be used to impeach you. Are the procedures that you used generally accepted in the business valuation community? Did you define terms consistent with the literature that exists? Are you taking positions contrary to other recognized experts procedures?

4. Education. Your deposition provides an opportunity for the opposing attorney to educate him- or herself at your expense and build a more effective cross-examination. Therefore, you must remember you are at the deposition to answer only the questions that are asked. You are not at the deposition to be helpful and to volunteer information. If opposing counsel is skilled and understands the issues in the matter, counsel will be able to elicit the answers that they need.

YOUR GOALS DURING THE DEPOSITION

Just as the opposing counsel is using the deposition to learn as much as possible about you, you can also use the deposition to learn as much about opposing counsel as possible. A number of items may be important to you.

- What are the tactics of opposing counsel? Is counsel friendly and helpful? Is counsel a bully and pushy?
- What type of questions are you being asked? Are they compound? Are they clear and unambiguous? Do they seem designed to confuse you or mislead you?
- How much technical expertise is displayed by opposing counsel? However, just because opposing counsel does not appear to be sophisticated and technically oriented during the deposition, do not assume that this will be the same at trial.

DEPOSITION STRATEGIES

Preparing for your deposition with your attorney is almost as important as preparing for your direct testimony. The first thing that you need to determine is how the attorney wants you to present the information.

In all situations, your role is to truthfully respond to the questions being asked by opposing counsel. In most instances, your answers should be limited to the exact question asked, without gratuitous comments and lengthy answers.

It is crucial that you understand how the attorney who retained you approaches the deposition. Will counsel object for the purpose of offering you guidance, or is the objection purely for the record? Or does counsel remain fairly passive during the whole process.

One of the hardest things to remember about the deposition is that all of your comments are being reduced to writing. If the information is ultimately put into the record at trial, it will be without eye-to-eye contact or body language. Therefore, it is important that you learn to speak for the written word.

This means that not only must you communicate, but that communication must be simple and clear without dependence on the nuances of your physical presence. You must also speak clearly and carefully, using proper grammar and vocabulary, and avoiding slang and other habits of speech that distract from your testimony's credibility.

Reviewing Your Deposition

In most jurisdictions, you, as the deponent, have the right to review your deposition and make corrections prior to signing the document. At the completion of many depositions, you may be asked to waive signature. If you do waive signature, you have no right to later review the deposition. In our opinion, it is not appropriate for an expert witness to waive signature. A prudent expert reviews the entire transcript prior to signing off on the correctness of the written document. Remember that one of the purposes of the depositions is to attempt to impeach you. Therefore, it is important for you to review your testimony before you accept the transcript as correct.

Attendance at the Opposing Expert's Deposition

A key role that you can play in the overall discovery in the marital litigation matter is to attend the deposition of your opposing expert. What are the tasks that you should be performing as part of that service?

- Providing technical expertise at the deposition. Unless the attorney that you are working with considers himself very fluent in business valuation, you may be a critical part of the deposition process. You may be requested to prepare an outline of issues to be discussed with the opposing expert, along with expected answers.
- Providing follow-up for responses that the opposing expert has given to deposition questions. As the opposing expert responds to the deposition questions, you will think of other follow-up questions. To the extent that the opposing expert cites specific business valuation standards or generally accepted accounting principles, it is your responsibility to be certain that they were correctly discussed and applied in the engagement.
- Observing the behavior of the opposing expert. You can observe the reactions of the expert to the questions being posed. In addition, you can help to measure the technical expertise of the expert and her ability to explain the various concepts involved in the business valuation process.

SUMMARY

The deposition is an important part of the discovery process. As an expert it is critical that you be well prepared for your own deposition. This is your opportunity to show the opposing counsel that you in fact adequately understand the issues to have reached the conclusions and opinions contained in your report. Your assistance at the opposing expert's deposition is also an important service that you can provide to the attorney with whom you are working.

Chapter 12

Preparing for the Trial

PREPARATION, PREPARATION, PREPARATION

It has been said in real estate that the three most important criteria for creating value in a piece of property are location, location, and location. Your success as an expert witness also has three very important criteria. Preparation, preparation, and more preparation. You will find that successful trial presentations are the result of not just good technical valuation work, but also of your demonstration of that knowledge and expertise. You may have already put countless hours into the engagement, developing the financial analysis and arriving at your ultimate conclusions of value. However, your overall success as an expert witness is directly attributable to your ability to present your valuation conclusions in the trial court. Much of that success depends a great deal on the preparation between you and the attorney who engaged you. As we discuss in Chapter 13, your direct testimony is your only opportunity to convince the court of the information you have obtained, the work that you have done, and the reasonableness of your expert opinion.

Preparing for direct examination is much the same as preparing for a presentation of Abbott and Costello's great comedy sketch "Who's on First." This sketch comes off only because of the timing of each of the presenters, and the knowledge of what each is going to say and when. A great direct examination is, in fact, a presentation by two parties, the attorney asking the questions and the expert providing the answers. In order to make this a good presentation, the two of you must prepare and work together.

It is imperative that you spend adequate time with the attorney you are working with in order for both you and the attorney to properly prepare for your direct testimony. This session is a joint session. The attorney should be preparing you for the nuances of courtroom procedure and trial testimony. In addition, this preparation time allows the two of you to get comfortable about each other's methods of providing testimony. During this preparation period, you need to be certain that the attorney understands the various concepts and technical terms that you will need to use as part of your direct examination, including the proper pronunciation and usage so that the attorney you are working with can incorporate the proper usage into the questions that will be asked of you.

Another reason to discuss the technical issues is so that you and the attorney can determine how technical your presentation should be. The best suggestion is to avoid making the presentation technical. In most marital dissolution matters, it is key that the expert simplify the valuation issues. This decision may also be greatly driven by the experience of the judge who is hearing the case. But as we discuss later in Chapter 13, your job is to take the complex business valuation issues and turn them into a simple presentation that can be easily understood by someone who does not have your technical expertise.

Scripts Versus Outlines

Good preparation does not mean scripting a presentation. Preparing a script is a sure recipe for disaster during your direct examination. The problem with scripting is that both of you have to memorize the script and be certain that it is carried out exactly as planned. You certainly do not want to have a script on the stand during your direct examination. That could be a great blow to your credibility. There is really no room for ad libs in the script. Add to that the fact that most of us do not have acting skills that would help us play the part called for in the script. Scripting your direct testimony almost always results in a poor direct examination, and in fact, could prove embarrassing if the script gets changed or you lose your place.

Just because you should not script out your direct examination does not mean that you should not prepare an outline of your expected direct testimony. In most matters that we testify in, we prepare an outline of our testimony and give that outline to the attorney at the time that we are preparing for the trial. We do not keep a copy of the outline for our own use. Since we like to follow the format of our report during direct examination, the outline provided is usually an expanded outline of our report in the matter. Whatever your preference, the outline should be structured so that your presentation flows smoothly, allowing you to tell the story of your conclusions and opinions.

Also understand that the outline is a very fluid document. The attorney may choose to change questions based on the reactions of the court. You and the attorney may have planned for your direct examination to take longer than the time that the court is willing to allow you. All of these issues must be worked out in advance so that there are no surprises in the courtroom. Remember that your goal is a smooth, understandable presentation of your conclusions and opinions.

Prepare to Handle the Inherent Weaknesses in the Case

Nobody has ever taken the perfect case to the trial court. If everything were perfect, the case would have settled a long time ago. Every business valuation engagement has at least one weakness. During our work we have had to make assumptions, we have made subjective analysis of financial and nonfinancial information, and we have had to apply our common sense, informed judgment, and reasonableness to our ultimate conclusions. We normally do not have the ability to test our conclusions through an actual transaction. It is very rare that the business that you value for a marital litigation matter is actually sold during the litigation. True, we may have used a guideline company methodology, and we may have significant empirical data to support our conclusions and opinions. We may also have passed every sanity check put forward during our review. However, as we can recall from the definition of fair market value, a completed transaction is assumed to be the best indicator of value.

Some individuals believe that it is best not to raise these weaknesses during direct examination. Instead they believe that the weaknesses will probably be ignored by the other side, justifying this decision with the knowledge that if the other side does raise the issues, they can be addressed on redirect. This is another recipe for disaster. If the attorney that you are working with holds this belief, you must persuade him or her to change that belief. It is very important that the weaknesses be addressed during the direct examination for several reasons:

- The attorney and you control your testimony while you are presenting the direct testimony. The attorney and you can discuss in detail how you wish to address the presentation of this information and therefore can put the discussion in the best possible light.
- As the expert witness, you will have the opportunity to discuss the impact of the so-called weakness. You can explain that there are assumptions and judgmental items inherent in every valuation engagement. While on direct, you can discuss the impact of those items on your ultimate conclusions and opinions, making certain that you explain that these issues do not render your conclusions and opinions unsound.
- You have the opportunity to demonstrate your credibility and independence. After all, you are discussing with the court not only the parts of the opinion that are solid, but pointing out the areas where your professional expertise and judgment were exercised.
- Why would you want these issues to be raised on cross-examination? During cross, opposing counsel is in complete control of the questioning. The questions most likely will be structured so that you are limited to yes or no answers, which can severely inhibit your ability to explain the reasons behind those judgmental issues.

Review the Events Leading up to Trial

This is the opportunity for you and the attorney to review all of the events that have taken place since you have been retained.

- What documentation has been received that changed the initial assessment of the case?
- What issues have been stipulated to?
- In reviewing the opposing expert's report, what issues do you agree on, and where are the areas of disagreement?
- What other witnesses are testifying and what are they expected to say?

It is important to review these issues so that you can better plan and prepare your direct testimony. Prior to going to trial, the expert must be fully aware of all of the activities that surround the case. Part of this review is also to be certain that the underlying facts that were relied on in the expert report are in fact the same facts that will be presented at trial. On the stand is not the time to find out that there are discrepancies in the underlying testimony of witnesses that you are relying upon. It might be important to know that the real estate appraiser has changed his opinion of value since the initial discussions that you had. This information may or may not have any bearing on your ultimate opinion, but again, this information is important.

This is a good time also to review your deposition in the matter. What did you say at that time? Is your planned direct testimony consistent with the testimony that you provided in the deposition? What issues were raised at your deposition? Were there areas of clear conflict? Discuss the information that you have from the opposing expert. Assuming the opposing expert has issued a written report on the matter, discuss in detail the issues that may be germane for direct testimony. If the opposing expert has issued a rebuttal report, you may need to determine what areas of the rebuttal report you want to address during your direct examination, rather than hold that discussion for redirect. Some of these issues are dependent on whether you are the expert for the petitioner or the respondent. However, these are all issues that need to be addressed during your preparation for your direct examination.

LEARN ABOUT THE TRIER OF FACT

Knowing about the judge in the trial is a great advantage to a well-prepared expert witness. In most situations, the marital dispute is heard by a judge. (As of this writing, only three states have divorce litigation heard by a jury.) Since the judge is the ultimate decision maker in the matter, we as experts need to aim our presentation to that decision maker. To the extent that we understand background information on the ultimate decision maker, we can focus our presentation to that background. Several issues immediately come to mind:

- What is the level of business valuation sophistication of the judge? Based on the judge's level of knowledge on business valuation issues, we may choose to either simplify or upgrade our presentation of the business valuation information.
- Will the judge follow along with exhibits? To the extent that the judge follows exhibits, we may choose to put more demonstrative evidence in our testimony. When you know that a judge follows exhibits, you should make it a point to emphasize key exhibits during your testimony.
- Will the judge ask questions from the bench? This is more an issue of surprise than anything else. Having questions come from the bench allows you to get a feel for what information the judge is interested in. When a judge asks a question from the bench, it is very important that you do everything to answer that question clearly and concisely.
- How does the judge control his courtroom? Is testimony allowed in on a narrative basis, or is a strict question and answer format required? Are there any rules specific to that courtroom that you as the expert need to be aware of?

REVIEW EXPECTED CROSS-EXAMINATION

A good expert always anticipates cross-examination and plans for it. By the time you and the attorney are meeting to prepare your direct examination, you should have copies of your opposing expert's report, and perhaps a copy of a rebuttal report. The opposing expert may also have been deposed in this matter. You need to review those documents and determine the differences between your conclusions and your opposing expert's conclusions. Common sense tells you that these are the areas of potential cross-examination. So how do you plan to handle the cross-examination? Should you be addressing these issues on your direct examination? Both you and counsel have to determine the impact of each area of potential cross-examination. This issue should not be left to chance.

In preparing for the expected cross-examination, the valuation expert should do several things prior to trial:

- Reconcile the expert's reports. A good expert can dissect both reports and prepare a schedule that clearly shows the differences between your report and that of the opposing expert. There may be a number of differences but it is very important to determine each of those differences. Some may be very fundamental, for example, the benefit stream, the capitalization rate, or the application of the various discounts or premiums. Other differences may be subtler. The purpose of making this comparison is so that you can explain to the judge why the two experts have arrived at different conclusions. Most lay people expect that two equally qualified experts should arrive at about the same conclusion. As we know, this may or may not be true in business valuation.

- Quantify the differences. Once you have determined what the differences are, it is very important to quantify the impact of each of those differences. Ultimately, you will want to be able to inform the judge what the magnitude of each of the differences is. Doing so allows the judge to prioritize the impact of different decisions.
- Explain the differences. This part of the task is the most difficult. Once you have identified the differences and quantified the dollar impact of each difference, it is your job to explain to the judge why those differences occurred and why your interpretation of the difference is the correct one to apply. Experts complain that judges just "split the difference" between the experts. But we have had discussions with judges that indicate they hate to split the baby. The judge is looking for someone to explain why the differences exist and what the impact is if he or she accepts one position versus another. The judge is requesting that the expert witness do the job. Remember, under Rule 702, an expert witness is allowed to provide opinion testimony to assist the trier of fact in determining an issue that is outside the expertise of the court.

GET COMFORTABLE WITH YOUR UPCOMING TRIAL EXPERIENCE

This may seem to be an oxymoron. How could you ever get comfortable about an experience as stressful as testifying in open court. Frankly, everyone has a different way to diffuse stress. However, you can make some specific preparation to help you in getting ready for the experience.

- Personally prepare the materials you plan to take to court. Different cases require different information. However, for each case you work on, you should be the individual who pulls together the information that you believe you need to take to the stand with you. You may not think that this is an efficient use of your time and that this task is something that should be delegated to a secretary or other clerical person, but you are the one who will have to find that information while you are sitting in the witness box. There is a great comfort in knowing where the information is because you put it there. This knowledge can keep you from panicking when you need to find a document and cannot immediately locate it.
- Review your report and make certain that you are familiar with both the layout and the underlying information. Since the report should be the basis for your direct testimony, you need to be certain that you are very familiar where information and other documentation is in your report.
- Know and understand your exhibits. Review the exhibits that you intend to use during your direct testimony. When in your testimony will you introduce the exhibit? What information does the exhibit convey? How does the exhibit tie into your report? Exactly what will your testimony be regarding the exhibit?

There are several general rules that you need to keep in mind when preparing demonstrative exhibits. The first is to forget that you are a CPA. We CPAs seem to want to create all of our exhibits from Excel. And since we are using a computer spreadsheet program to develop the exhibit, we want to have 30 columns and 150 rows of information on that spreadsheet. In fact, we have every piece of information that anyone could ever want on the spreadsheet. The second rule is that a piece of demonstrative evidence should be very simple. At best it should contain no more than three or four items of information. Lastly, limit the number of demonstrative exhibits. These exhibits should be used only for very key information, and should be used to simplify an otherwise complex issue. You don't want to have every piece of information on a demonstrative exhibit. It just provides information overload.

Relax

This must really seem like a strange thing to say to you just before you are scheduled to be in the trial court. But this is a key concept: Part of the testimonial experience is confidence. If you are properly prepared and you have done your job, you are ready to take the stand. You really do not want to be preparing for trial at 3:00 in the morning, still concerned that you have not done everything that needs to be done. Aside from being tired in the morning, you will also lack the confidence necessary to be a credible witness. Confidence is the quality that allows you to stand up to adversity, to withstand cross-examination, and to present a credible direct examination.

Be Ready to Teach

Yes, teach. An effective direct testimony is a teaching experience. Your job is to take complex business valuation concepts and explain them to the trier of fact. Your testimony will not be accepted just because you said it is right. Your testimony will be accepted if you are able to explain to the judge what you did, why it was the right thing to do, and how you arrived at your ultimate conclusions and opinions. This is an important concept to keep in mind, and we will spend a significant time discussing it in Chapter 13.

SUMMARY

Success at trial is directly related to your preparation and knowledge of the relative issues. It is critical that you meet with the attorney that retained you to make certain that you are prepared for the direct examination process. View your role as a teacher who is present to assist the trial by providing facts from your experience and expertise.

Chapter 13

Direct Examination

THE TRUTH, THE WHOLE TRUTH, AND NOTHING BUT THE TRUTH

It may seem trite, and even a little incredulous, but the truth is an important part of your direct examination. You will be asked to take an oath prior to testifying, and the oath is to be taken seriously. Throughout your entire testimony, the most important thought that you can have is your credibility, and that means that you are telling the truth—no exaggerations, no embellishments, and no partial truths. As an expert witness you must at all times have the court believing that you are providing only truthful testimony. In fact, the court must be able to totally rely on that concept. The slightest deviation from this position is almost always fatal to the expert. Remember that your testimony will be subject to an intense cross-examination. Opposing counsel will attempt to point out any misstatement or other inconsistency in your direct testimony. The main asset that an expert witness has is credibility and believability. Being less than truthful destroys that credibility, rendering the expert's opinion useless.

GETTING COMFORTABLE

Anyone who is not a little nervous prior to beginning direct examination is either dead or stupid. And in either case, that person has no business being on the witness stand. It is normal to be nervous and apprehensive, no matter how much preparation you have put in. Presenting expert testimony is very stressful. Your goal is to get by that nervousness, allowing yourself to make your presentation to the trier of fact.

Some people wonder why professional entertainers have a theme song, or why they always open their act with the same piece. It is really very simple: The entertainer knows that piece so well that he can perform it very well without any concern. Muscle memory takes over, allowing the performance. After a few minutes, the entertainer is totally at ease with the audience, and the nervousness is gone.

As the expert witness you have the same advantage. The beginning of your direct examination should be in areas where you are totally at ease, areas where you surely know the answers. The entire structure for your initial qualifying questions should be your curriculum vitae.

- Would you state your name for the record?
- What is your business address?
- Describe your educational background.
- Do you hold any professional licenses?
- Describe your business valuation education.
- Do you have any business valuation credentials?
- What is the area of your professional employment?
- Have you previously testified on business valuation matters?

After this set of qualifying questions, your initial nervousness should have subsided, and you should be gaining confidence as to the future progress of your direct examination. These questions allow you to build a rapport with the court, establish a rhythm for your testimony, and set the stage for your presentation. Remember that you have prepared with counsel your direct examination. It is based on your workproduct and your written report. During your preparation, you have discussed the questions that will be part of the examination, and you know what your answers will be to those questions. Because you have thoroughly prepared, you know your material and you can testify with confidence and professionalism.

Do not be ashamed of your accomplishments. Be certain that you present them to the court in a very professional manner. At the same time, do not oversell yourself. It is important that the court understands all of your accomplishments, but it cannot get the feeling that you are arrogant or elitist. Never intimate that you have a credential or qualification that you do not actually possess. Case law is replete with expert witnesses who have been excoriated because they implied they were a member of a certain organization or held a certain credential, and then it was shown that this was not the truth.

Do not be concerned if this is the first, second, or third time that you have testified. Not everyone in the area has testified more than 20 times. It is clear that you are capable of providing competent testimony on even the first engagement. It is not the number of times that you have testified, it is the quality of your workproduct, and your ability to communicate that workproduct both in writing and orally.

You need to take control of the direct presentation, because that will allow you to also be in control for your cross-examination. What is meant by being in control? You as the expert will determine the pace of the examination and that will allow you to keep in personal control. When you testify, you create a built-in cadence to your testimony. You should set a regular pace, and try never to vary from that pace. For instance, when you are asked a question, mentally count to three before answering the question. This gives you time to think through what the question is and what your answer needs to be. This is especially valuable on cross-examination. If you are answering all of the questions very quickly, and then on cross have to take a pause, that might indicate to the opposing counsel that you are not certain about that point. When you consistently take a little bit of time to answer every question, you are giving yourself a safe haven for the question that needs more thought.

PAINTING THE PICTURE, TELLING THE STORY

A great direct examination is much like painting a great picture. It is based on your vision. What have you seen during the course of your engagement? What information did you uncover that became a basis for your opinion? What steps did you take to finally arrive at that expert opinion? What is your expert opinion? Your job is to answer all of those questions in a dialogue with the attorney who retained you. Again, you need to go back to the initial preparation that the two of you had regarding this case. How can you verbally provide the information so that the listener clearly sees the picture that you want seen? What are the key points that you need to make? How do you intend to make those points to the trier of fact? What do you really want the court to see?

Your goal is to explain to the court the issues that you are involved with, and then to explain the steps taken and the ultimate opinion. This is done by "painting the picture" for the court. Your engagement has taken from 40 to several hundred hours. You have applied generally accepted procedures and methodologies to your work. You have made thorough and complete analyses of the information. You have drawn accurate and reasonable expert opinions. The court does not know what work you have done, does not know the issues that you have reviewed. All of these important items need to be addressed. Now is the time for you to distill all of this information into a few hours of direct examination to convince the court that your workproduct should be accepted.

Because you are telling a story, your direct examination should be structured so that it features your presentation skills. Most of the questions asked of you should not require only a yes or no answer. The questions should be open-ended. They should allow you to present information to the court. After all, in most engagements, the experts testimony is some of the most important testimony that will be given in the matter. You are the expert witness, and it is important that you be given the opportunity to display that expertise.

In a nutshell, you are making a technical presentation to nontechnical individuals, under time constraints and great stress. This is the essence of your direct examination. Being able to do this is what makes a good expert witness.

WORKING THROUGH YOUR PRESENTATION

Your direct testimony is your opportunity to demonstrate your knowledge, training, experience, and skill to the court. It is also the time for you to demonstrate your credibility, reasonableness, objectivity, and independence. This is done by both your oral testimony, the use of your exhibits, and/or demonstrative evidence. Your presentation must be logical and easy to follow. There is nothing to be gained by discussing this information at a level that only another experienced business valuation expert understands. If you choose to follow that path, you will soon lose your audience, making your presentation absolutely ineffective.

If you write your report very logically, taking the reader from start to finish, you can use it as the outline and general direction for your direct testimony. Just as your report should start at the beginning and follow a natural progression to your conclusions and opinions, so should your testimony. The testimony needs to start at the beginning and conclude with your expert opinions as to the value of the business. Along the way, your testimony should describe the process of the valuation.

- What data did you review and rely on?
- What methodologies did you review?
- Why did you choose the methods that you did, while discarding others?
- How did you develop your capitalization/discount rate?
- What discounts and premiums are applicable to this case?
- What is your final conclusion of value?

Do not allow your testimony to get bogged down with all of the nonvaluation details of the case. You are not the right person to introduce all of the tax returns, financial statements, and other financial information into the trial. That can only diminish your effectiveness during the trial. Putting that information into the record should be done by the person who prepared or caused those documents to be prepared. You relied on the documents, but you are not the author of those documents. Having you introduce all of these documents reduces your impact as an impartial, credible, expert witness.

Determine in advance which of the exhibits are important to your testimony and how they are marked. When you need to refer to the exhibit, you must know the proper exhibit number. You can ask the attorney or whoever is keeping the court's copy of the exhibits to let you review the exhibit in order to refer to the specific information. This shows your understanding of the documentation that you used to form your expert opinion.

The use of exhibits and other types of demonstrative evidence can greatly increase the effectiveness of your direct testimony. However, poorly prepared or presented exhibits are worse than no exhibits at all. CPAs tend to suffer from a disease known as "cramitis"—the tendency to put 40 different pieces of information on the same sheet. As CPAs, we are comfortable with managing hundreds of pieces of information at any given time. However, the court may not have the same interest in these vast quantities of information. The court is looking for demonstrative evidence to be simple, clear, and easily understood. Therefore, an exhibit should not try to provide more than two or three pieces of information at a time. The 10-column wide, 50-row deep spreadsheet is unintelligible in a courtroom and does not convey the narrow issues that you should be focusing on during your testimony.

Determine exactly what information you want to convey in your demonstrative evidence. These charts, graphs, or other tools are just that—tools to assist your oral presentation. Exhibits can explain and fine tune important details. They make your presentation easier to understand.

Should your exhibits be slides, overheads, or large poster boards? There really is no right answer to this question. It is a combination of personal preference, attorney's preference, and perhaps even judicial preference. It also may be determined by the physical layout of the courtroom. We have been in courtrooms where there are no power outlets available to a witness or attorney. Obviously, if you have prepared slides or overheads and you have no access to an electrical outlet, you have no way to make that presentation. We also prefer not to use demonstrative evidence where the court has to dim the lights. This tends to reduce your ability to determine how the presentation is being received by the court. We also have some concern when it comes to high-tech techniques. If you are going to make your presentation high tech, you must be certain that you have a back-up plan in the event that the high-tech equipment fails during your testimony. Finally, make certain that your conclusion has impact. Perhaps a summary is appropriate, or perhaps some other information should be presented. Whatever the case, you want the conclusion of your direct testimony to have a significant impact on the trier of fact.

TEACH, DO NOT LECTURE

The only difference between a fact witness and an expert witness is that the expert witness possesses specialized knowledge, training, education, or skills, which should assist the court in reaching its final conclusion of the matter. The best way to convey this specialized knowledge is to take the role of a teacher, rather than a lecturer. You need to involve the intellect of your intended audience, the judge or the jury, in the presentation, rather than bore them. A good teacher is always cognizant of audience reactions and adjusts the presentation based on those reactions.

If we think back to our days in college, we can recall the differences between the large lecture classes and the very personal impact of a great teacher. The lecturer stood at the podium and showered us with information. The lecturer did not try to make that information specific to any of us in the audience. The information was put forth, we took our own notes, made our own interpretations of the information, and went forward.

Contrast that with someone you consider one of the great teachers you had. That individual also provided information, but tried to see the information through the student's eyes. That individual worked with the student to make certain that the ideas being transmitted were the same ideas being received. This is our role in the direct examination process. We need to provide information to the court, yet at the same time, we must be certain that the information we are providing is the same information that is needed and being received by the court.

During direct examination the expert witness should keep four objectives in mind. These objectives help to focus the direct examination, but also keep the direct examination fluid. The courtroom experience is not a stilted, scripted setting. It is alive and vibrant. The courtroom is an interaction of a number of individuals, many with competing desires. Because of that interaction, situations change in the courtroom as the trial progresses. The expert must maintain the flexibility to meet those changes and adapt the testimony as it moves forward. The objectives for the expert witness are:

- Inform the Court, and explain your opinions. You are being asked to be a source of information for the Court, you are not being told to pontificate to the Court. In order for you to be an effective expert witness you must use your powers of persuasion. One of the most important tools that you can use to persuade someone to accept your opinion is to make certain that the individual has sufficient information to understand the basis and reasoning behind your position. The more effectively that you can explain what you did, why you did it, and why that information led you to your ultimate conclusion, the easier your ultimate job will be.
- Involve the Court in your presentation—Do not create a boring lecture. Think about your audience, in most cases, the judge. Your presentation should be vibrant and exciting. You need to involve the court, yet how do you do that? When you reach an important part of your direct examination, you might refer the judge to the appropriate page of your report so that he or she can follow along with your explanation. This can be highly effective when discussing concepts such as the Build-up method or CAPM (capital asset pricing model). By involving the court, you give the judge the opportunity to visualize the information that you are providing in an oral presentation.
- Be alert to the Court's reactions to your testimony. The expert witness must always be aware of the Court's reaction to the direct examination. It is important to know personal information about the trial judge. Does the judge take copious notes? Will the judge follow along with your exhibits? Obviously, if you have a judge who you know is a note taker, and during a portion of your direct presentation the judge stops taking notes, that would indicate that you have either lost the judge on that point or the judge has heard enough of that issue. By being alert to the court's reactions you can measure the effectiveness of your direct examination.
- Adjust your presentation to the Court's reactions. Do not just observe what reaction you are getting from the Court. React to those reactions. If you are sure that

the Court has heard enough of a certain area, move on to a new area. If the judge appears to be perplexed, then perhaps you need to find a way to restate the point you were trying to make.

As part of your overall presentation, keep in mind the idea that you want to have a conversation with the decision maker. That means that you should look at the person that you are talking to. Do not underestimate the importance of eye contact.

THE THEORY OF EFFECTIVE TEACHING

Countless studies have been done about how humans learn, yet there seems to be some common threads that come together in all of these studies. If we can harness these learning concepts as part of our direct examination, we stand a better chance of succeeding in our goals of educating the court. Four basic elements are part of the learning process, and it is critical that we incorporate those four elements into our presentation. Doing so will make our presentation much more dynamic and will ensure that the information we are sending is the same information that is being received. These four elements are as follows:

1. Primacy. As humans, we tend to have a great deal of recall for the information that we receive at the beginning of our listening. Remember the concept of making a good first impression? The listener is fresh. The listener is focused. The listener is interested in what we have to say. We have been qualified as an expert witness, and the listener now wants us to provide the technical information. It is very important that you, the expert witness, let your listener know what your opinion is at the beginning of your testimony.
2. Recency. Humans also recall the information that was most recently conveyed. As the expert witness, you must leave your listener with the most important part of your testimony, your opinion. The concluding portion of your direct examination should summarize all of your workproduct. The last statement you make on direct examination should be a restatement of your ultimate conclusion about the matter.
3. Repetition. The listener learns by repetition. We know this to be a fact in many areas, including sports. Why do we practice our golf swing or our tennis stroke? If we continue to do something repetitively, we develop muscle memory and therefore we become proficient at that specific task. The same is true with our learning and listening skills. The more often we hear the information, the more that we will retain it. During your direct testimony, you want to continue to restate and reemphasize your expert opinions to the listener.
4. Probability of human conduct. This is the theory that the listener will react in a normal and predictable method to your presentation of the information. If you approach the presentation with the attitude of "I'm the expert, you don't know

anything, so you must believe me," the listener will react poorly, perhaps even turning you off. How would you react if someone told you that it was right "because they said so"? Your initial reaction might be, "Why do I want to believe that bag of wind?" However, if you make your presentation so that you draw in the listener, working together through the understanding of the issues, and the listener believes you are attempting to inform, the listener will react more favorably toward the information you are presenting. To the extent possible, the expert needs to build a professional rapport with the trier of fact. Part of this rapport is founded in credibility and confidence. If the trier of fact finds the witness to be very credible, it is very likely that the trier of fact will adopt the conclusions and opinions of that expert.

Note that these four items are very similar to one of the first rules of presenting a speech or other presentation. In speech class, we learned that the three rules to a good presentation are:

- Tell your audience what you are going to tell them.
- Tell them.
- Tell your audience what you told them.

Think how those thoughts go hand in hand with the learning experience. The first thing that we tell the audience is part of primacy, the first thing that is presented. During our presentation we continue to make our points, which is repetition. Finally during the summary, we repeat the main thesis of our presentation, which is recency. This concept should be included in every direct examination.

DEVELOP THE LOGIC OF YOUR CONCLUSIONS

You must carefully develop the logic and reasonableness of your expert opinion so that your listener can make a reasoned differentiation between your analysis and opinion and the opinion of the opposing expert. During your preparation with the attorney, you should have discussed the types of questions that would form the basis for your direct testimony. Make certain that you are answering questions that you know the judge would like to have answered. Build on the foundational questions that were part of your qualifications. Continue to build on the basic questions about what you saw, who you talked to, what analysis you made. Answer the "why" questions for the Court. Explain *why* you looked at certain financial information. Explain *why* you felt the research that you did is appropriate. Discuss the alternative methodologies that are available and *why* you chose the methods that you did. Explain *why* you reached the ultimate conclusions and opinions. Tell the Court *why* your conclusions and opinions should be accepted by the Court.

This is also the time to present testimony that compares and contrasts your report and expert opinion with the report and opinion of the opposing expert. You should have analyzed the similarities and differences between the two experts. Your ability to teach the listener what issues the two of you agree on and what issues you disagree on is very important. Start with all of the issues that you do agree on. This adds credibility to your presentation and starts the comparison with areas of agreement rather than areas of controversy. Where there is disagreement or controversy, this is your opportunity to explain why there is a difference and why your opinion should be more credible. To the extent that you can quantify these differences, it is very helpful to do that. This gives the listener the ability to understand the significance of the differences. Again, during this explanation bring back the idea of the "why" statements. Tell the court why this difference exists. Tell the court why you believe your interpretation or number is the better information to use.

KEEP THE PRESENTATION INTERESTING

A key part of your successful direct testimony is that you must keep the presentation interesting. During your testimony it is important that you demonstrate your skill, knowledge, and experience in the subject area you are discussing by explaining the underlying principles that you are using and how those principles are applied to the subject matter. Remember that your listeners are not as skilled as you are in this area, so you must convey the information without losing them. If you can bring the listeners genuine understanding of your opinion, you will enhance the likelihood of your opinion carrying weight with the trier of fact.

KEEP IT SIMPLE, STUPID (KISS)

Keeping it simple should be a constant thought as you prepare the outline of your testimony and certainly prior to actually presenting the testimony. The KISS idea is really very simple. Your audience is not a bunch of business valuation experts. They do not have the expertise that you have. However, they really want to hear what you have to say, and, until you convince them otherwise, they want to believe in what you say. The way to keep them believing in you is to put your expertise into terms and experiences that they can understand. On the surface, it may be very hard to think that a business that has gross revenues of several million dollars could have little or no fair market value. With explanation however, this message could be conveyed.

The best rule for the KISS system is to avoid the technical and complex during your testimony. In 99 percent of the cases that you will testify in, there is no need to become overly technical and to rely only on complex discussions of the issues. Yet the other side of the coin is that you need to take the complex issues that you have been dealing with (capitalization rates, discounts, etc.) and make those issues seem simple. Sometimes we like to explain that business valuation is a very simple procedure. Because in fact, it really is. After all, what is business valuation other than determining the benefit stream from the entity, and then applying an appropriate capitalization or discount rate to that benefit stream? What could be more simple? However, as we well know, it takes a great deal of work to determine what the appropriate benefit stream should be, and then even more work and judgment to determine the appropriate multiplier.

You must remember that your job is not to turn the trier of fact into a business valuation expert. You do not have the time and the judge probably does not have the inclination to make that happen. You must make clear that you are a business valuation expert, and then it is your responsibility to make sure that your listener understands why your workproduct and opinions should be accepted. As simple as this sounds, this is the essence of a great expert witness.

BE AN ORATOR

Orating is an art that has almost been lost today. Everyone can talk, and some individuals are considered to be good speakers, but it is rare to find a true orator. What do we mean when we use the term *orator?* To be concise, we mean an individual who is a true public speaker. That is what you need to be when you are on the witness stand. What distinguishes an orator from a run-of-the-mill person who is speaking? A number of items distinguish the witness from the great expert witness, including:

- The orator speaks clearly and distinctively. This means that the presentation is understandable by all of the listeners. It means that there is no use of slang or other words that can be misconstrued. It means an unambiguous statement that clearly details the underlying foundation for your ultimate conclusions.
- An orator conveys ideas and teaches during the presentation. The true orator is a teacher. The true orator is interested in making certain that the listener is involved in the presentation and is being persuaded. Think about this question, If the presenter is bored, what is happening to the listener? The true orator is never boring and is always concerned with the listener.
- As part of your presentation, use your voice to your advantage. You can use your voice to indicate concern, importance, or any one of a number of moods. You can make your voice loud or quiet to emphasize points. Whatever you do, there are two things you must avoid. The first is being so quiet that no one can hear you. What good is your testimony if it cannot be heard? The second is to make certain that your voice has some emotion. Who wants to listen to the mechanical voice of a computer?
- Do not think that you need to enter the witness box and become a statue. It is important that you use your body and your hands to convey ideas and to keep the lis-

tener part of your presentation. We are not suggesting that you become a symphony conductor on the stand, waving your hands in wild abandon as you lead the band. Be normal in your gestures, but comfortable in using your hands and body to emphasize your points. The Court expects you to be a human, and to react that way.

SUMMARY

Direct examination is the ultimate goal of the expert witness. And in fact, your ability as a witness can determine your ultimate success as a business valuator. If you do not understand the principles of business valuation, you cannot fake it on the stand with a great direct examination. However, you can be very skilled in business valuation, but without the ability to present that information in the courtroom, you will never become a great expert.

Direct examination is the art of telling your story and of providing the judge with all of the details necessary to make a determination in the matter. The great expert witness is someone who understands the concept of teaching, because that is what your presentation is all about.

Your job is to take the complex issues you have been asked to review and to provide a simplified, understandable explanation of both the process and the ultimate value.

Chapter 14

Surviving Cross-Examination

Your goal on cross-examination is to survive. Survival means that you retain your credibility and that you do not contradict the information contained in your direct examination. The only way that you can really win on cross-examination is if the opposing attorney does not perform competently. Cross-examination is a necessary part of the litigation process. Because our court system is adversarial by design, cross-examination is the opportunity for the other side to inquire into what you did and did not do.

As discussed in Chapter 13, direct examination is a structured process where the expert and the attorney have worked together to prepare a presentation that paints the picture for the court. Under direct examination, you as the witness have a great deal of control over what is presented and how it is presented. Cross-examination is just the opposite. Certainly, you as the expert can anticipate the areas of your cross-examination, but you have no input into the areas of inquiry, nor do you assist the attorney in the structure of the questions that will be asked of you. In fact, your opposing expert probably had significant input into the preparation for your cross-examination. In addition, the opposing attorney will take every step possible to make certain that you do not take control. That attorney determines the areas of inquiry and the issues.

A skilled attorney conducting your cross-examination structures the questions so that your answers are controlled. As discussed in Chapter 11, the opposing attorney only asks you questions where your answers are already known. Most questions asked of you will require a yes or no answer, rather than an explanation. Basically, the opposing attorney is providing the information and is just asking you to confirm or deny the statement.

WHAT THE OPPOSING COUNSEL IS TRYING TO DO

Many years ago, a presentation was made at an American Institute of Certified Public Accountants (AICPA) conference regarding expert witnesses. One of the presenters, an attorney by the name of Ken Turek, discussed his thoughts on expert witnesses. To paraphrase his discussion, Mr. Turek explained that when he first sees your name on a piece of paper identifying you as an opposing expert witness in a matter, that from that day forward his only goal as it relates to you is to destroy you. Because if he does not destroy you, you will destroy him. This is a little harsh, but it makes a point. To the extent that you are successful as an expert witness, you harm the opposing attorney's case.

Basically there are four outcomes that the cross-examining attorney is hoping for. As an expert witness, it is important that you understand these four outcomes and the methods that the opposing counsel may try to use to achieve them. The four potential outcomes are:

1. To raise doubt about you and your workproduct. This may be done very subtly. The attorney may question the amount of hours that you personally have in the engagement as compared to the total time in the engagement. There may be questions regarding the methodologies that you selected. You may even be questioned regarding the validity of the underlying financial information and research that you used in arriving at your ultimate conclusion of value. As the expert, you should not become defensive over these issues. Your testimony should stay focused on the facts. If you believe that the underlying information is appropriate, you need to continue to make that point.
2. To discredit your testimony. Usually, this requires some inconsistent history on the expert's part. Questions in this area will be about methodologies that you have used on prior engagements that differ from the methods you used on the current engagement. You will be questioned as to how often you have worked for the propertied spouse versus the nonpropertied spouse. How often have you worked for the attorney involved with the current engagement? Have you ever testified in other courts where your opinion was not adopted by the court? Have you ever tried to qualify as an expert witness and not been accepted by the court? If you have any history, that alone will not disqualify you from being an expert in the current engagement. But, you need to discuss these issues with your attorney and determine whether these issues need to be addressed on direct examination, rather than allowing the issues to be brought up on cross-examination.
3. To use you as a witness for their side of the case. This happens many times when there is a significant mismatch between the credentials of the two expert witnesses and where you are the expert with the broader curriculum vitae. If the cross-examining attorney adopts this strategy, the questions will basically focus on the areas of agreement between you and the opposing expert. The attorney is using your credibility to ratify the methods or assumptions used by their expert.

The areas of disagreement are usually ignored, with the cross-examining attorney choosing to bring those issues to the court during their case in chief. If the opposing attorney chooses this strategy, there is very little that you as the expert can do about it.

4. The last outcome is not something that the attorney does, but is really something created by the expert. This outcome is referred to as "killing the witness," however that is a misnomer. Attorneys do not "kill" competent expert witnesses. The witness is "killed" because the witness has not done the work or was not competent to complete the engagement. The lesson to be learned here is that an expert who is not competent or does not do the work that needs to be done in the engagement will end up being embarrassed on the stand. That embarrassment may lead to being dismissed by the court and could end your expert witness career immediately.

HANDLING THE CROSS-EXAMINATION

During your preparation for direct examination, you worked with the attorney who engaged you to prepare and discuss your direct examination. As presented in Chapter 12, you should also have discussed the issues expected to be addressed in your cross-examination. You should also discuss how to react on cross-examination. The following story is related by Robert Kleeman. Several years ago, while preparing to testify in a trial in Oklahoma City, the attorney I was working with gave me a thought process to prepare for the cross-examination. The advice was that as the opposing counsel is about to begin my cross-examination, I should think of that attorney as my favorite nephew who is a little slow. The reason for that thought is that I would have an abundance of patience, and I would speak slowly and distinctly and use short answers, in order not to confuse my nephew. I have always remembered that advice and recall it just before I start cross-examination.

You should have some additional thoughts as you begin your cross-examination. The first suggestion is to remember the three rules of testimony discussed in Chapter 11. Those three simple rules are your life raft during cross-examination. Those rules are:

1. Listen to the question.
2. Answer only what has been asked.
3. Do not anticipate or volunteer information.

Try to answer every question in as few words as possible. The ultimate goal would be to answer every question with a yes or no. When that is not possible, try to keep your responses to 10 words or less. If you are going to use more than 10 words, carefully think through your answer prior to giving it. Another suggestion is a physical one. Many of us have nervous habits or tics, such as pulling on an ear, wiping our brow with a handkerchief, or lowering our eyes and speaking into our hand. All of these nervous habits send a signal to the cross-examining attorney that you are not comfortable with the line of questioning or the areas being explored. This is exactly what you do not want to do. It is similar to throwing chum into the water when you see the sharks; an attack is imminent.

A number of questions can be asked of you that are fraught with danger. As an expert, you need to recognize the types of questions that are being asked, and you need to know how to respond to those questions.

- Questions that contain the words "possible" or "could" should immediately alert you to the issues of speculation. As an expert witness, you need to have a good understanding of the concept of reasonable probability. You need not testify to a possibility, only a reasonable probability. If you climb on the slippery slope of speculation, you are asking for a fall.
- Hypothetical questions are used many times during cross-examination to confuse the testimony of the witness. When a hypothetical question is posed to you as the expert you must clearly restate the hypothetical nature of the question. During your answer, again clearly state that your answer is premised on the hypothetical and not based on your work or testimony. Many times the attorney will continue to ask the hypothetical question hoping that you will provide an answer without stating that it is a hypothetical answer. Keep in mind that anyone can create a hypothetical situation that results in a desired outcome.
- Another potential problem is the question that calls for a yes or no answer, but is a question that cannot be answered that way. This is similar to the question "Do you still beat your spouse?" If you say yes, it is an admission, but if you say no, it implies that at one time you did beat your spouse. If you are given a question like this, your first line of defense is to tell the court that you cannot answer that question yes or no without being misleading to the court. If the court orders that you must answer the question using either a yes or no, then you must do so. Hopefully, you and the attorney you are working with will come back to that question on redirect, and you will have an opportunity to provide an explanation then.

We end this chapter with four rules for helping you to survive cross-examination. Each of these rules is equally important and violating any one of them could be fatal to your ultimate credibility. Although these seem simple, it is very easy for you to get caught up in the matter and make one of these mistakes.

- Don't take it personally. To paraphrase a line from the movie *The Godfather:* "You killed my kid, I killed your kid. It's only business, don't take it personal." You may be subject to attack on your qualifications, or your workproduct, or any other number of issues. You must not take those attacks as personal. Rather you need to remain calm and collected and stay focused on your cross-examination.

You may have heard Bob Kleeman tell the story about his wife attending a trial he was testifying in. We share it here to demonstrate why you cannot take it personally. A number of years ago, my wife was in the courtroom during my cross-examination. The cross was somewhat strong, and it made for a very long day. As we were walking out of the courthouse, the opposing attorney was also leaving. I had known the opposing attorney for a number of years and, in fact, had been engaged by that attorney a number of times. As he turned to his car and my wife and I turned the other direction to our car, he said goodnight and inquired if he would see us at his family's Christmas party on Saturday night. I said sure, see you Saturday, and have a good night. As my wife and I walked a few steps further, she told me in no uncertain terms that we would not be going to the Christmas party. When I asked why, she told me how she had listened to that lawyer questioning my judgment, raising issues about my competence, and asking questions about my integrity. She was angry and upset and wanted to know why I was not upset. I explained to her that the cross-examination had not been very effective, and that it was the attorney's job to do what he had done. I then explained that you cannot take it personally.

- Don't pick a fight you can't win. As an expert witness in the case, you are one of the stars in the courtroom. The attorneys are not the stars. If the attorney can get you angry and goad you into a verbal fight, you may seriously damage your credibility. Remember the last time you had a fight with your significant other? Did you have the situation where you were trying to take back the words that you said in anger? Never lose your temper and begin a verbal fight with the attorney. You have nothing to gain but everything to lose.
- Don't be Dr. Jekyll and Mr. Hyde. During your cross-examination you need to treat the opposing attorney exactly the same as you treated the attorney you are working with. You can't be Mister Nice Guy to the attorney you are working with and then have an attitude on cross-examination. You are not an adversary. Remember that under Rule 702 you are being permitted to testify because you have specialized training or education, and you are there to assist the trier of fact. Your role is not that of an advocate for either party. If you treat the attorneys differently, the court will view you as an advocate, and not as the expert who is there to assist the court.
- Don't be an opponent, be a teacher. As discussed in Chapter 13, your role during direct examination is to be a teacher. To the extent possible during cross-examination you want to continue that role. Opposing counsel may not give you many opportunities to continue to teach, but when the opportunity arises, use the chance to return to your teaching role.

Cross-examination is the true test of the expert witness. It tests your patience, your verbal skills, and your knowledge of the engagement. Quite frankly, it can be the most rewarding part of your trial experience. You need not fear it, but you must respect it.

Chapter 15

Business Valuation Credentials, Organizations, and Professional Standards

Several recognized professional organizations have taken leadership roles in the business valuation profession. These organizations also have published standards that apply to business valuation engagements. Although you may or may not be required to follow the standards of any of these organizations, it is important that you know that they exist and what they say.

These standards tend to be very common sense oriented, and following the standards will improve the quality of your workproduct and reports. Note that the standards are very similar. The various business valuation groups are currently holding cooperative meetings for the purpose of developing a common glossary of business valuation terms and definitions. These groups are also cooperating on other issues that impact the business valuation professional. It is clear that these organizations are more cooperative than competitive.

The specific credentials, the related information regarding the organizations that grant the credential, and their standards have been provided in alphabetical order. We are not suggesting that any one group or credential is superior or inferior to another. Those decisions are made by the users of our services in the marketplace.

ACCREDITED IN BUSINESS VALUATION

Accredited in Business Valuation (ABV) is issued by the American Institute of Certified Public Accountants (AICPA). The credential was created after many years of debate among the profession, which included an aborted attempt to create a credential in the early 1990s. To qualify for the credential, the applicant must be a licensed CPA and a member of the AICPA. In addition, the applicant must demonstrate significant experience in a minimum of 10 business valuation engagements. This information is submitted to a credential committee that reviews the required documentation, and either rejects or accepts the application to sit for the Business Valuation Examination. There is a comprehensive, eight-hour, proctored written examination that is currently offered in November of each year.

The first examination was in November of 1997. As a result of that examination, 520 ABV credentials were issued by the AICPA. The 1998 exam was held in November with approximately 450 individuals qualified to take that examination. About 70 + percent of the individuals passed. Once individuals have received the credential, they are subject to annual continuing education requirements and face recertification every three years.

The AICPA Business Valuation and Appraisal Subcommittee of the Management Consulting Services (MCS) Committee is the organization within the AICPA that primarily focuses on emerging and day-to-day business valuation issues as they relate to AICPA members. In addition, there is an ABV Examination Committee that has the exclusive responsibility for developing and administrating the ABV credential examination. Finally, there is the ABV Credentials Committee, which determines the eligibility of candidates to sit for the ABV examination.

AICPA BUSINESS VALUATION STANDARDS

No AICPA standards have been written specifically for the business valuation practice. However, because business valuation services are considered professional services under the umbrella of the AICPA standards, a number of existing standards are applicable in the business valuation context. These standards include:

- AICPA Code of Professional Conduct
  - Rule 102—Integrity and Objectivity, as modified by Statement on Standards for Consulting Services 1.
  - Rule 201—General Standards
  - Rule 202—Compliance with Standards
  - Rule 301—Confidential Client Information
  - Rule 302—Contingent Fees
  - Rule 501—Acts Discreditable
- AICPA Statement on Standards for Consulting Services (SSCS 1)
- The AICPA can be contacted at American Institute of Certified Public Accountants, Harborside Financial Center, 201 Plaza Three, Jersey City, NJ 07311-3381. Phone (212) 596-6200 or (201) 938-3000

ACCREDITED SENIOR APPRAISER

Accredited Senior Appraiser (ASA) is issued by the American Society of Appraisers, a multidisciplinary organization that represents appraisers in many fields. Although the designation ASA does not indicate any specific area of expertise, it is awarded for a specific discipline. It is common for the holder of an ASA to note that discipline on curriculum vitae.

The credential is earned by either completing four, 30-hour courses, which each have a proctored, written examination at their completion, or by applying to challenge the examination and the successful completion of an eight-hour, written, proctored examination. In addition, prior to receiving the designation, the candidate must submit two business valuation reports for peer review. After successful completion of the written examination and a successful result from the peer review of the written reports, the candidate must demonstrate a minimum of five years of full-time business valuation experience. This experience is defined in number of hours worked directly on business valuation projects. The ASA designation requires continuing business valuation education as well as other recertification procedures. As of this writing, there are approximately 750 ASAs designated in business valuation.

There are three other levels of membership in the ASA:

1. Fellow, American Society of Appraisers (FASA). Fellowships may be bestowed on Accredited Senior Appraisers (ASAs) by the society's International Board of Governors in recognition of outstanding service to the appraisal profession or the society. Currently, there are five FASAs in business valuation.
2. Accredited Member (AM). Accredited Member is the designation given to a member who has completed all of the requirements for the ASA with the exception that the designee has attained two years of full-time business valuation experience rather than the five years required under the ASA designation. Currently, there are approximately 90 accredited members.
3. Candidate Member. Candidate Member is not a designation, but is a membership category for the organization. This membership category is not considered to carry any professional status, and is similar to the Affiliate and Affiliate Firm membership category. The category indicates that there is an intention of becoming a designated member in the future. There are certain basic qualifications, but the candidate member has not yet completed the required course of study and examinations, peer review of reports, or basic experience requirements. A candidate member may not give the impression that he or she is a credential holder. There are more than 1,600 business valuation candidate members at this writing.

The Business Valuation Committee of the American Society of Appraisers is the lead organization in the ASA regarding the promulgation of standards as well as other issues in business valuation as they relate to the membership.

ASA BUSINESS VALUATION PROFESSIONAL STANDARDS

The ASA has issued a set of business valuation standards that must be followed by all business valuation members of the organization. In addition, the ASA has adopted and endorses the Uniform Standards of Professional Appraisal Practice (USPAP), and members are expected to comply with Standards 9 and 10 for business valuation engagements.

You can contact the ASA at American Society of Appraisers, PO Box 17265, Washington, DC 20041. Phone (703) 478-2228.

American Society of Appraisers
in cooperation with
The Appraisal Foundation*

ASA Business Valuation Standards and portions of Uniform Standards of Professional Appraisal Practice (USPAP)

This brochure contains the ASA Business Valuation Standards (ASA/BVS) and for your information, portions of the Uniform Standards of Professional Appraisal Practice (USPAP) of The Appraisal Foundation.

USPAP in its entirety includes other standards as well as statements on standards and accompanying advisory opinions which are not included here. Business valuation appraisers and reviewers should be familiar with all parts of USPAP.

ASA/BVS include:

Preamble
General Requirements for Developing A Business Valuation
Financial Statement Adjustments
Asset-Based Approach to Business Valuation
Statement
Income Approach to Business Valuation
Market Approach to Business Valuation
Reaching a Conclusion of Value
Comprehensive, Written Business Valuation Report
Definitions
The Guideline Company Valuation Method

USPAP portions include:

Preamble
Ethics Provision
Competency Provision
Departure Provision
Jurisdictional Exception
Supplemental Standards

Appraisal Standard 3
Appraisal Standard 9
Appraisal Standard 10
Certain Definitions

All USPAP material is copyrighted by The Appraisal Foundation and is updated annually as of January 1. The 1995 edition of USPAP has been used in this brochure. USPAP in its entirety can be obtained for $25 from the Appraisal Foundation. Address: 1029 Vermont Ave., N. W. Suite 900, Washington, D.C. 20005-3517; Phone (202) 347-7722; Fax (202) 347-7727.

All ASA-Business Valuations Standards are copyrighted by the American Society of Appraisers, and are updated periodically to make appropriate changes and corrections, and to add new standards.

This material is printed together with the consent of the American Society of Appraisers and The Appraisal Foundation

**ASA Business Valuation Standards* and portions of *Uniform Standards of Professional Appraisal Practice,* American Society of Appraisers, © 1989, 1991, 1992, 1994. Reprinted with permission.

American Society of Appraisers

Business Valuation Standards©

This release of the approved Business Valuation Standards of the American Society of Appraisers contains all standards approved through January 23, 1994, and are to be used in conjunction with the Uniform Standards of Professional Appraisal Practice (USPAP) of The Appraisal Foundation and the Principles of Appraisal Practice Code of Ethics of the American Society of Appraisers.

It contains the following sections, with the effective approval date of each:

Item	Title	Effective Date
PREAMBLE		September 1992 Revised January 1994
BUSINESS VALUATION STANDARDS		
BVS-I	General Requirements for Developing A Business Valuation	January 1992 Revised June 1993 Revised January 1994
BVS-II	Financial Statement Adjustments	September 1992 Revised January 1994
BVS-III	Asset-Based Approach to Business Valuation	January 1992 Revised January 1994
BVS-IV	Income Approach to Business Valuation	September 1992 Revised January 1994
BVS-V	Market Approach to Business Valuation	September 1992 Revised January 1994
BVS-VI	Reaching a Conclusion of Value	September 1992 Revised January 1994
BVS-VII	Comprehensive, Written Business Valuation Report	June 1991 Revised January 1994
DEFINITIONS		January 1989 Revised September 1992 Revised June 1993 Revised January 1994
STATEMENTS ON BUSINESS VALUATIONS STANDARDS		
SBVS-I	The Guideline Company Valuation Method	January 1992 Revised January 1994

PROCEDURAL GUIDELINES AND/OR ADVISORY OPINIONS
(To be issued when appropriate)

Copyright, © 1994—American Society of Appraisers

AMERICAN SOCIETY OF APPRAISERS
Business Valuation Standards

Preamble©

Approved by the ASA Board of Governors, September 1992

I. To enhance and maintain the quality of business valuations for the benefit of the business valuation profession and users of business valuations, the American Society of Appraisers, through its Business Valuation Committee, has adopted these standards.

II. The American Society of Appraisers (in its Principles of Appraisal Practice and Code Of Ethics) and the Appraisal Foundation (in its Uniform Standards of Professional Appraisal Practice) have established authoritative principles and a code of professional ethics. These standards include these requirements, either explicitly or by reference, and are designed to clarify and proved additional requirements specifically applicable to the valuation of businesses, business ownership interests or securities.

III. These standards incorporate, where appropriate, all relevant business valuation standards adopted by the American Society of Appraisers through its Business Valuation Committee.

IV. These standards provide minimum criteria to be followed by business appraisers in the valuation of businesses, business ownership interests or securities.

V. If, in the opinion of the appraiser, circumstances of a specified business valuation assignment dictate a departure from any provisions of any Standard, such departure must be disclosed and will apply only to the specific departure.

VI. These Standards are designed to provide guidance to ASA Appraisers conducting business valuations and to provide a structure for regulating conduct of members of the ASA through Uniform Practices and Procedures. Deviations from the Standards are not designed or intended to be the basis of any civil liability; and should not create any presumption or evidence that a legal duty has been breached; or create any special relationship between the appraiser and any other person.

Copyright, © 1992, 1994—American Society of Appraisers

SOCIETY OF AMERICAN APPRAISERS
Business Valuation Standards

BVS-I General Requirements for Developing A Business Valuation ©

I. Preamble

A. This standard is required to be followed in all valuations of businesses, business ownership interests, and securities by all members of the American Society of Appraisers, be they Candidates, Accredited Members (AM), Accredited Senior Appraisers (ASA), or Fellows (FASA).

B. The purpose of this standard is to define and describe the general requirements for developing the valuation of businesses, business ownership interests, or securities.

C. This standard incorporates the general preamble to the Business Valuation Standards of the American Society of Appraisers.

II. The Valuation Assignment shall be Appropriately Defined

A. In developing a business valuation, an appraiser must identify and define the following:
   1. The business, business ownership interest, or security to be valued
   2. The effective date of the appraisal
   3. The standard of value
   4. The purpose and use of the valuation

B. The nature and scope of the assignment must be defined. Acceptable scopes of work would generally be of three types as delineated below. Other scopes of work should be explained and described.

   1. Appraisal
      a. The objective of an appraisal is to express an unambiguous opinion as to the value of the business, business ownership interest, or security, which is supported by all procedures that the appraiser deems to be relevant to the valuation.

      b. An appraisal has the following qualities:
         (1) It is expressed as a single dollar amount or as a range.
         (2) It considers all relevant information as of the appraisal date available to the appraiser at the time of performance of the valuation.
         (3) The appraiser conducts appropriate procedures to collect and analyze all information expected to be relevant to the valuation.

(4) The valuation is based upon consideration of all conceptual approaches deemed to be relevant by the appraiser.

2. Limited Appraisal
   a. The objective of a limited appraisal is to express an estimate as to the value of a business, business ownership interest, or security, which lacks the performance of additional procedures that are required in an appraisal.
   b. A limited appraisal has the following qualities:
      (1) It is expressed as a single dollar amount or as a range.
      (2) It is based upon consideration of limited relevant information
      (3) The appraiser conducts only limited procedures to collect and analyze the information which such appraiser considers necessary to support the conclusion presented
      (4) The valuation is based upon the conceptual approach(es) deemed by the appraiser to be most appropriate.
3. Calculations
   a. The objective of calculations is to provide an approximate indication of value based upon the performance of limited procedures agreed upon by the appraiser and the client.
   b. Calculations have the following qualities:
      (1) They may be expressed as a single dollar amount or as a range.
      (2) They may be based upon consideration of only limited relevant information.
      (3) The appraiser performs limited information collection and analysis procedures.
      (4) The calculations may be based upon conceptual approached as agreed upon with the client.

III. Information Collection and Analysis

The appraiser shall gather, analyze, and adjust relevant information to perform the valuation as appropriate to the scope of work. Such information shall include the following:

A. Characteristics of the business, business ownership interest, or security to be valued including rights, privileges, and conditions, quantity, factors affecting control, and agreements restricting sale or transfer.
B. Nature, history, and outlook of the business.
C. Historical financial information for the business.
D. Assets and liabilities of the business.

E. Nature and condition of the relevant industries which have an impact on the business.
F. Economic factors affecting the business.
G. Capital markets providing relevant information, e.g., available rates of return on alternative investments, relevant public stock transactions, and relevant mergers and acquisitions.
H. Prior transactions involving subject business, interest in the subject business, or its securities.
I. Other information deemed by the appraiser to be relevant.

IV. Approaches, Methods and Procedures

A. The appraiser shall select and apply appropriate valuation approaches, methods and procedures.
B. The appraiser shall develop a conclusion of value pursuant to the valuation assignments as defined, considering the relevant valuation approaches, methods, and procedures, and appropriate premiums and discounts, if any.

V. Documentation and Retention

The appraiser shall appropriately document and retain all information and workproduct that were relied on in reaching the conclusion.

VI. Reporting

The appraiser shall report to the client the conclusion of value in an appropriate written or oral format. The report must meet the requirements of Standard 10 of the Uniform Standards of Professional Appraisal Practice. In the event the assignment results in a comprehensive written report, the report shall meet the requirements of BVS-VII.

Copyright, © 1992, 1994—American Society of Appraisers

AMERICAN SOCIETY OF APPRAISERS
Business Valuation Standards

BVS-II Financial Statement Adjustments©

I. Preamble

A. This standard is required to be followed in all valuations of business, business ownership interests, and securities by all members of the American Society of Appraisers, be they Candidates, Accredited Members (AM), Accredited Senior Appraisers (ASA), or Fellows (FASA).

B. The purpose of this standard is to define and describe the requirements for making financial statement adjustments in valuation of businesses, business ownership interests, and securities.

C. This present standard is applicable to appraisals and may not necessarily be applicable to limited appraisals and calculations as defined in BVS-I, Section II.B.

D. This standard incorporates the general preamble to the Business Valuation Standards of the American Society of Appraisers.

II. Conceptual Framework

A. Financial statements should be analyzed and, if appropriate, adjusted as a procedure in the valuation process. Financial statements to be analyzed include those of the subject entity and any entities used as guideline companies.

B. Financial statement adjustments are modifications to report financial information that are relevant and significant to the appraisal process. Adjustments may be necessary in order to make the financial statements more meaningful for the appraisal process. Adjustments may be appropriate for the following reasons, among others: (1) To present financial data of the subject and guideline companies on a consistent basis; (2) To adjust from reported values current values; (3) To adjust revenues and expenses to levels which are reasonably representative of continuing results; and (4) To adjust for nonoperating assets and liabilities and the related revenue and expenses.

C. Financial statement adjustments are made for the purpose of assisting the appraiser in reaching a valuation conclusion and for no other purpose.

III. Documentation of Adjustments

Adjustments made should be fully described and supported.

Copyright, © 1992, 1994—American Society of Appraisers

AMERICAN SOCIETY OF APPRAISERS
Business Valuation Standards

BVS-III Asset-Based Approach to Business Valuation©

I. Preamble

A. This standard is required to be followed in all valuations of businesses, business ownership interests, and securities by all members of the American Society of Appraisers, be they Candidates, Accredited Members (AM), Accredited Senior Appraisers (ASA), or Fellows (FASA).

B. The purpose of this standard is to define and describe the requirements for the use of the Asset-Based Approach to business valuation and the circumstances in which it is appropriate.

C. This present standard is applicable to appraisals and may not necessarily be applicable to limited appraisals and calculations as defined in BVS-I, Section II.B.

D. This standard incorporates the general preamble to the Business Valuation Standards of the American Society of Appraisers.

II. The Asset-Based Approach

A. In business valuation the Asset-Based Approach may be analogous to the Cost Approach of other disciplines.

B. Assets, liabilities, and equity relate to a business that is an operating company, a holding company, or a combination thereof (mixed business).
   1. An operating company is a business which conducts an economical activity by generating and selling, or trading, in a product or service.
   2. A holding company is a business which derives its revenues by receiving returns on its assets which may include operating companies and/or other businesses.

C. The Asset-Based Approach should be considered in valuations conducted at the total entity level and involving the following:
   1. An investment or real estate holding company
   2. A business appraised on a basis other than as a going concern. Valuations of particular ownership interests in an entity may or may not require the use of the Asset-Based Approach.

D. The Asset-Based Approach should not be the sole appraisal approach used in assignments relating to operating companies appraised as going concerns unless it is customarily used by sellers and buyers. In such cases, the appraiser must support the selection of this approach.

Copyright, © 1992, 1994—American Society of Appraisers

AMERICAN SOCIETY OF APPRAISERS
Business Valuation Standards

BVS-IV Income Approach to Business Valuation©

I. Preamble

A. This standard is required to be followed in all valuations of businesses, business ownership interests, and securities by all members of the American Society of Appraisers, be they Candidates, Accredited Members (AM), Accredited Senior Appraisers (ASA), or Fellows (FASA).

B. The purpose of this standard is to define and describe the requirements for the use of the income approach in valuation of businesses, business ownership interests, and securities, but not the reporting therefor.

C. This present standard is applicable to appraisals and may not necessarily be applicable to limited appraisals and calculations as defined in BVS-I, Section II.B.

D. This standard incorporates the general preamble to the Business Valuation Standards of the American Society of Appraisers.

II. The Income Approach

A. The income approach is a general way of determining a value indication of a business, business ownership interest, or security using one or more methods wherein a value is determined by converting anticipated benefits.

B. Both capitalization of benefits methods and discounted future benefits methods are acceptable. In capitalization of benefits methods, a representative benefit level is divided or multiplied by a capitalization factor to convert the benefit to value. In discounted future benefits methods, benefits are estimated for each several future periods. These benefits are converted to value by the application of a discount rate using present value techniques.

III. Anticipated Benefits

A. Anticipated benefits, as used in the income approach, are expressed in monetary terms, depending on the nature of the business, business ownership interest or security being appraised and other relevant factors, anticipated benefits may be reasonably represented by such items as net cash flow, dividends, and various forms of earnings.

B. Anticipated benefits should be estimated considering such items as the nature, capital structure, and historical performance of the related business entity, expected future outlook for the business entity and relevant industries, and relevant economic factors.

IV. Conversion of Anticipated Benefit

A. Anticipated benefits are converted to value using procedures which consider the expected growth and timing of the benefits, the risk profile of the benefits stream, and the time value of money.

B. The conversion of anticipated benefits to value normally requires the determination of a capitalization rate or discount rate. In determining the appropriate rate, the appraiser should consider such factors as the level of interest rates, rate of return expected by investors on relevant investments, and the risk characteristics of the anticipated benefits.

C. In discounted future benefits methods, expected growth is considered in estimating the future stream of benefits. In capitalization of benefits methods, expected growth is incorporated in the capitalization rate.

D. The rate of return used (capitalization rate or discount rate) should be considered with the type of anticipated benefits used. For example, pre-tax rates of return should be used with pre-tax benefits; common equity rates of return should be used with common equity benefits; and net cash flow rates should be used with net cash flow benefits.

Copyright, © 1992, 1994—American Society of Appraisers

AMERICAN SOCIETY OF APPRAISERS
Business Valuation Standards

BVS-V Market Approach to Business Valuation©

I. Preamble

A. This standard is required to be followed in all valuations of businesses, business ownership interests and securities by all members of the American Society of Appraisers, be they Candidates, Accredited Members (AM), Accredited Senior Appraisers (ASA), or Fellows (FASA).

B. The Purpose of this standard is to define and describe the requirements for use of the market approach in valuation of businesses, business ownership interests, and securities, but not the reporting therefor.

C. This present standard is applicable to appraisals and may not necessarily be applicable to limited appraisals and calculations as defined in BVS-I, Section II.B.

D. This standard incorporates the general preamble to the Business Valuation Standards of the American Society of Appraisers.

II. Market Approach

A. The market approach is a general way of determining a value indication of a business, business ownership interest, or security using one or more methods that compare the subject to similar businesses, business ownership interests, and securities that have been sold.

B. Examples of market approach methods include the Guideline Company method and analysis of prior transactions in the ownership of the subject company

III. Reasonable Basis for Comparison

A. The investment used for comparison must provide a reasonable basis for the comparison.

B. Factors to be considered in judging whether a reasonable basis for comparison exists include:

1. Sufficient similarity of qualitative and quantitative investment characteristics.

2. Amount and verifiability of data known about the similar investment.
3. Whether or not the price of the similar investment was obtained in an arm's-length transaction, or a forced or distress sale.

IV. Manner of Comparison

A. The comparison must be made in a meaningful manner and must not be misleading. Such comparisons are normally made through the use of valuation ratios. The computation and use of such ratios should provide meaningful insight about the pricing of the subject considering all relevant factors. Accordingly, care should be exercised in the following:
   1. Selection of underlying data used for the ratio.
   2. Selection of the time period and/or averaging method used for the underlying data.
   3. Manner of computing and comparing the subject's underlying data.
   4. The timing of the price data used in the ratio.

B. In. general, comparisons should be made using comparable definitions of the components of the valuation ratios. However, where appropriate, valuation ratios based on components which are reasonably representative of continuing results may be used.

V. Rules of Thumb

A. Rules of thumb may provide insight on the value of a business, business ownership interest or security. However, value indications derived from the use of rules of thumb should not be given substantial weight unless supported by other valuation methods and it can be established that knowledgeable buyers and sellers place substantial reliance on them.

Copyright, © 1992, 1994—American Society of Appraisers

AMERICAN SOCIETY OF APPRAISERS
Business Valuation Standards

BVS-VI Reaching a Conclusion of Value©

I. Preamble

A. This standard is required to be followed in all valuations of businesses, business ownership interests, and securities by all members of the American Society of Appraisers, be they Candidates, Accredited Members (AM), Accredited Senior Appraisers (ASA), or Fellows (FASA).

B. The purpose of this standard is to define and describe the requirements for reaching a final conclusion of value in valuations of businesses, business ownership interests, or securities.

C. This present standard is applicable to appraisals and may not necessarily be applicable to limited appraisals and calculations as defined in BVS-I, Section II.B.

D. This standard incorporates the general preamble to the Business Valuation Standards of the American Society of Appraisers.

II. General

A. The conclusion of value reached by the appraiser shall be based upon the applicable standard of value, the purpose and intended use of the valuation, and all relevant information obtained as of the appraisal date in carrying out the scope of the assignment.

B. The conclusion of value reached by the appraiser will be based on value indications resulting from one or more methods performed under one or more appraisal approaches.

III. Selection and Weighing of Methods

A. The selection of and reliance on the appropriate method and procedures depends on the judgment of the appraiser and not on the basis of any prescribed formula. One or more approaches may not be relevant to the particular situation. More than one method under an approach may be relevant to a particular situation.

B. The appraiser must use informed judgment when determining the relative weight to be accorded to indications of value reached on the basis of various methods or whether an indication of value from a single method should dominate. The appraiser's judgment may be presented either in general terms or in terms of mathematical weighting of the indicated values reflected in the conclusion. In any case, the appraiser should provide the rationale for the selection or weighting of the method or methods relied on in reaching the conclusion.

C. In formulating a judgment about the relative weights to be accorded to indications of value determined under each method or whether an indication of value from a single method should dominate, the appraiser should consider factors such as:
   1. The applicable standard of value;
   2. The purpose and intended use of the valuation;
   3. Whether the subject is an operating company, a real estate or investment holding company, or a company with substantial nonoperating or excess assets;
   4. Quality and reliability of data underlying the indication of value;
   5. Such other factors which, in the opinion of the appraiser, are appropriate for consideration.

IV. Additional Factors to Consider

As appropriate for the valuation assignment as defined, and if not considered in the process of determining and weighting the indications of value provided by various procedures, the appraiser should separately consider the following factors in reaching a final conclusion of value:

A. Marketability, or lack thereof, considering the nature of the business, business ownership interest or security, the effect of relevant contractual and legal restrictions, and the condition of the markets.

B. Ability of the appraised interest to control the operation, sale or liquidation of the relevant business.

C. Such other factors which, in the opinion of the appraiser, are appropriate for consideration.

Copyright, © 1992, 1994—American Society of Appraisers

AMERICAN SOCIETY OF APPRAISERS
Business Valuation Standards

BVS-VII Comprehensive, Written Business Valuation Report©

I. Preamble

A. This standard is required to be followed in the preparation of comprehensive, written business valuation reports by all members of the American Society of Appraisers, be they Candidates, Accredited Members (AM), Accredited Senior Appraisers (ASA), or Fellows (FASA).

B. The purpose of this standard is to define and describe the requirements for the written communication of the results of a business valuation, analysis, or opinion, but not the conduct thereof.

C. This standard incorporates the general preamble to the Business Valuation Standards of the American Society of Appraisers.

II. Signature and Certification

A. An appraiser assumes responsibility for the statements made in the comprehensive, written report and indicates the acceptance of that responsibility by signing the report. To comply with this standard, a comprehensive, written report must be signed by the appraiser. For the purpose of this standard, the appraiser is the individual or entity undertaking the appraisal assignment under a contract with the client.

B. Clearly, at least one individual is responsible for the valuation conclusion(s) expressed in the report. A report must contain a certification, as required by Standard 10 of the Uniform Standards of Professional Appraisal Practice of The Appraisal Foundation, in which the individuals responsible for the valuation conclusion(s) must be identified.

III. Assumptions and Limiting Conditions

A. The following assumptions and/or limiting conditions must be stated:

1. Pertaining to bias—a report must contain a statement that the appraiser has no interest in the asset appraised, or other conflict, which could cause a question as to the appraiser's independence or objectivity or if such an interest or conflict exists, it must be disclosed.

2. Pertaining to data used—where appropriate, a report must indicate that an appraiser relied on data supplied by others, without further verification by the appraiser, as well as the sources which were relied on.
3. Pertaining to validity of the valuation—a report must contain a statement that a valuation is valid only for the valuation date indicated and for the purpose stated.

IV. Definition of the Valuation Assignment

The precise definition of the valuation assignment is a key aspect of communication with users of the report. The following are key components of such a definition and must be included in the report:

1. The business interest valued must be clearly defined such as "100 shares of the Class A common stock of the XYZ Corporation:" or "a 20% limited partnership interest in the ABC Limited Partnership." The existence, rights, and/or restrictions of other classes of ownership in the business appraised must also be adequately described if they are relevant to the conclusion of value.
2. The purpose and use of the valuation must be clearly stated, such as " a determination of fair market value for ESOP purposes" or "a determination of fair value for dissenter's rights purposes." If a valuation is being done pursuant to a particular statute, the particular statute must be referenced.
3. The standard of value used in the valuation must be stated and defined. The premise of value, such as a valuation on a minority interest or a control basis, must be stated.
4. The appraisal date must be clearly defined. The date of the preparation of the report must be indicated.

V. Business Description

A comprehensive, written business valuation report must include a business description which covers all relevant factual areas, such as:

1. Form of organization (corporation, partnership, etc.)
2. History
3. Products and/or services and markets and customers
4. Management
5. Major assets, both tangible and intangible
6. Outlook for the economy, industry, and company
7. Past transactional evidence of value
8. Sensitivity to seasonal or cyclical factors

9. Competition
10. Sources of information used

VI. Financial Analysis

A. An analysis and discussion of a firm's financial statements is an integral part of a business valuation and must be included. Exhibits summarizing balance sheets and income statements for a period of years sufficient to the purpose of the valuation and the nature of the subject company must be included in the valuation report.

B. Any adjustments made to the reported financial data must be fully explained.

C. If projections of balance sheets or income statements were utilized in the valuation, key assumptions underlying the projections must be included and discussed.

D. If appropriate, the company's financial results relative to those of its industry must be discussed.

VII. Valuation Methodology

A. The valuation method or methods selected, and the reasons for their selection, must be discussed. The steps followed in the application of the method or methods selected must be described and must lead to the valuation conclusion

B. The report must include an explanation of how any variables such as discount rates, capitalization rates, or valuation multiples were determined and used. The rationale and/or supporting data for any premiums or discounts must be clearly presented.

VIII. Comprehensive, Written Report Format

A. The comprehensive, written report format must provide a logical progression for clear communication of pertinent information, valuation methods, and conclusions and must incorporate the other specific requirements of this standard, including the signature and certification provisions.

IX. Confidentiality of Report

No copies of the report will be furnished to persons other than the client without the client's specific permission or direction unless ordered by a court of competent jurisdiction.

Copyright, © 1991, 1994—American Society of Appraisers

AMERICAN SOCIETY OF APPRAISERS

Business Valuation Standards

Definitions©

ADJUSTED BOOK VALUE	The book value which results after one or more asset or liability amounts are added, deleted, or changed from the respective book amounts.
APPRAISAL	The act or process of determining value. It is synonymous with valuation.
APPRAISAL APPROACH	A general way of determining value using one or more specific appraisal methods. (See Asset-Based Approach, Market Approach, and Income Approach definitions).
APPRAISAL METHOD	Within approaches, a specific way to determine value.
APPRAISAL PROCEDURE	The act, manner, and technique of performing the steps of an appraisal method.
APPRAISED VALUE	The appraiser's opinion or determination of value.
ASSET BASED APPROACH	A general way of determining a value indication of a business's assets and/or equity interest using one or more methods based directly on the value of the assets of the business less liabilities.
BOOK VALUE	1. With respect to assets, the capitalized cost of an asset less accumulated depreciation, depletion, or amortization as it appears on the books of account of the enterprise. 2. With respect to a business enterprise, the difference between total assets (net of depreciation, depletion and amortization) and total liabilities of an enterprise as they appear on the balance sheet. It is synonymous with net book value, net worth, and shareholder's equity.

BUSINESS APPRAISER	A person, who by education, training, and experience is qualified to make an appraisal of a business enterprise and/or its intangible assets.
BUSINESS ENTERPRISE	A commercial, industrial, or service organization pursuing an economic activity.
BUSINESS VALUATION	The act of process of arriving at an opinion or determination of the value of a business or enterprise or an interest therein.
CAPITALIZATION	1. The conversion of income into value. 2. The capital structure of a business enterprise. 3. The recognition of an expenditure as a capital asset rather than a period expense.
CAPITALIZATION FACTOR	Any multiple or divisor used to convert income into value.
CAPITALIZATION RATE	Any divisor (usually expressed as a percentage) that is used to convert income into value.
CAPITAL STRUCTURE	The composition of the invested capital.
CASH FLOW	Net income plus depreciation and other noncash charges.
CONTROL	The power to direct the management and policies of an enterprise.
CONTROL PREMIUM	The additional value inherent in the control interest, as contrasted to a minority interest, that reflects its power of control.
DISCOUNT FOR LACK OF	An amount or percentage deducted from a prorata.
CONTROL	Share of the value of 100 percent of an equity interest in a business, to reflect the absence of some or all of the powers of control.
DISCOUNT RATE	A rate of return used to convert a monetary sum, payable or receivable in the future, into present value.
ECONOMIC LIFE	The period over which property may be profitably used.

EFFECTIVE DATE	The date as of which the appraiser's opinion of value applies (Also referred to as Appraisal Date, Valuation Date and/or As Of Date).
ENTERPRISE	See BUSINESS ENTERPRISE
EQUITY	The owner's interest in property after deduction of all liability.
FAIR MARKET VALUE	The amount at which property would change hands between a willing seller and a willing buyer when neither is under compulsion and when both have reasonable knowledge of the relevant facts.
GOING CONCERN	An operating business enterprise.
GOING CONCERN VALUE	1. The value of an enterprise, or an interest therein, as a going concern. 2. Intangible elements of value in a business enterprise resulting from factors such as: having a trained workforce; and operational plan; and the necessary licenses, systems and procedures in place.
GOODWILL	That intangible asset which arises as a result of name, reputation, customer patronage, location, products, and similar factors that have not been separately identified and/or valued but which generate economic benefits.
INCOME APPROACH	A general way of determining a value indication of a business, business ownership interest or security using one or more methods wherein a value is determined converting anticipated benefits.
INVESTED CAPITAL	The sum of the debt and equity in an enterprise on a long-term basis.
MAJORITY CONTROL	The degree of control provided by a majority position.
MAJORITY INTEREST	Ownership position greater than 50% of the voting interest in an enterprise.
MARKET APPROACH	A general way of determining a value indication of a business, business

	ownership interest, or security using one or more methods that compare the subject to similar businesses, business ownership interest, or securities that have been sold.
MARKETABILITY DISCOUNT	An amount or percentage deducted from an equity interest to reflect lack of marketability.
MINORITY INTEREST	Ownership position less than 50% of the voting interest in an enterprise.
MINORITY DISCOUNT	A Discount for Lack of Control applicable to a minority interest.
NET ASSETS	Total assets less total liabilities.
NET INCOME	Revenue less expenses, including taxes.
RATE OF RETURN	An amount of income (loss) and/or change in value realized or anticipated on an investment, expressed as a percentage of that investment.
REPLACEMENT COST NEW	The current cost of a similar new item having the nearest equivalent utility as item being appraised.
REPORT DATE	The date of the report. May be the same as or different from the APPRAISAL DATE.
REPRODUCTION COST NEW	The current cost of an identical new item.
RULE OF THUMB	A mathematical relationship between or among a number of variables based on experience, observation, hearsay, or a combination of these, usually applicable to a specific industry.
VALUATION	See APPRAISAL.
VALUATION RATIO	A factor wherein a value or price serves as the numerator and financial, operating or physical data serve as the denominator.
WORKING CAPITAL	The amount by which current assets exceed current liabilities.

Copyright, © 1989, 1994—American Society of Appraisers

AMERICAN SOCIETY OF APPRAISERS
Business Valuation Standards

SBVS-I The Guideline Company Valuation Method©

I. Preamble

A. This statement is required to be followed in all valuations of businesses, business ownership interest, and securities by all members of the American Society of Appraisers, be they Candidates, Accredited Members (AM), Accredited Senior Appraisers (ASA), or Fellows (FASA).

B. The purpose of this statement is to define and describe the requirements for the use of guideline companies in the valuation of businesses, business ownership interest, or securities.

C. This statement incorporates the general preamble of the Business Valuation Standards of the American Society of Appraisers.

II. Conceptual Framework

A. Market transactions in businesses, business ownership interests, or securities can provide objective, empirical data for developing valuation ratios to apply in business valuation.

B. The development of valuation ratios from guideline companies should be considered for use in the valuation of businesses, business ownership interests, or securities, to the extent that adequate information is available.

C. Guideline companies are companies that provide a reasonable basis for comparison to the investment characteristics of the company being valued. Ideal guideline companies are in the same industry as the company being valued; but if there is insufficient transaction evidence available in the same industry, it may be necessary to select companies with an underlying similarity of relevant investment characteristics such as markets, products, growth, cyclical variability, and other salient factors.

III. Search for and Selection of Guideline Companies

A. A thorough, objective search for guideline companies is required to establish the credibility of the valuation analysis. The procedure must include criteria for screening and selecting guideline companies.

B. Empirical data from guideline companies can be found in transactions involving either minority or controlling interest in either publicly traded or closed held companies.

IV. Financial Data of the Guideline Companies

A. It is necessary to obtain and analyze financial and operating data on the guideline companies, as available.

B. Consideration should be given to adjustments to the financial data of the subject company and the guideline companies to minimize the difference in accounting treatments when such differences are significant. Unusual or nonrecurring items should be analyzed and adjusted as appropriate.

V. Comparative Analysis of Qualitative and Quantitative Factors

A comparative analysis of qualitative and quantitative similarities and differences between guideline companies and the subject company must be made to assess the investment attributes of the guideline companies relative to the subject company.

VI. Valuation Ratios Derived From Guideline Companies

A. Price information of the guideline companies must be related to the appropriate underlying financial data of each guideline company in order to compute appropriate valuation ratios.

B. The valuation ratios for the guideline companies and comparative analysis of qualitative and quantitative factors should be used together to determine appropriate valuation ratios for application to the subject company.

C. Several valuation ratios may be selected for application to the subject company and several value indications may be obtained. The appraiser should consider the relative importance accorded to each of the value indications utilized in arriving at the valuation conclusion.

D. To the extent that adjustments for dissimilarities with respect to minority and control, or marketability, have not been made earlier, appropriate adjustment for these factors must be made, if applicable.

Copyright, © 1992, 1994—American Society of Appraisers

The Appraisal Foundation

Uniform Standards of Professional Appraisal Practice©

All USPAP material is copyrighted by The Appraisal Foundation and is updated annually as of January 1. The 1995 edition of USPAP has been used in this brochure. USPAP in its entirety can be obtained for $25 from the Appraisal Foundation. Address: 1029 Vermont Ave., N.W., Suite 900, Washington, D.C. 20005-3517; Phone (202) 347-7722, but is provided free to ASA members.

USPAP in its entirety includes other standards as well as statements on standards and accompanying advisory opinions which are not included here. Business valuation appraisers and reviewers should be familiar with all parts of USPAP.

This publication contains the following sections:

Published in the United States of America Copyright, © 1995 by The Appraisal Foundation. All rights reserved.

No parts of this publication may be reproduced, stored in a retrieval system, or transmitted in any form or by any means, electronic, mechanical, photocopy, recording or otherwise, without the prior written consent of the publisher.

UNIFORM STANDARDS OF PROFESSIONAL APPRAISAL PRACTICE

as promulgated by the Appraisal Standards Board of The Appraisal Foundation

PREAMBLE

It is essential that a professional appraiser arrive at and communicate his or her analyses, opinions, and advice in a manner that will be meaningful to the client and will not be misleading in the marketplace. These Uniform Standards of Professional Appraisal Practice reflect the current standards of the appraisal profession.

The importance of the role of the appraiser places ethical obligations on those who serve in this capacity. These standards include explanatory comments and begin with an Ethics Provision setting forth the requirements for integrity, objectivity, independent judgment, and ethical conduct. In addition, these standards include a Competency Provision which places an immediate responsibility on the appraiser prior to acceptance of an assignment. The standards contain binding requirements as well as specific guidelines to which a Departure Provision may apply under certain limited conditions. Definitions applicable to these standards are also included.

These standards deal with the procedures to be followed in performing an appraisal, review or consulting service and the manner in which an appraisal, review or consulting service is communicated. Standards 1 and 2 relate to the development and communication of a real property appraisal. Standard 3 establishes guidelines for reviewing an appraisal and reporting on that review. Standards 4 and 5 address the development and communication of various real estate or real property consulting functions by an appraiser. Standard 6 sets forth criteria for the development and reporting of mass appraisals for ad valorem tax purposes or any other universe of properties. Standard 7 and 8 establish guidelines for developing and communicating personal property appraisals. Standards 9 and 10 establish guidelines for developing and communicating business appraisals.

These Standards include Statements on Appraisal Standards issued by the Appraisal Standards Board for the purpose of clarification, interpretation, explanation, or elaboration of a Standard or Standard Rule.

These standards are for appraisers and the users of appraisal services. To maintain the highest level or professional practice, appraisers must observe these standards. The users of appraisal services should demand work performed in conformance with these standards.

Comment: Explanatory comments are an integral part of the Uniform Standards and should be viewed as extensions of the provisions, definitions, and standard rules. Comments provide interpretation from the Appraisal Standards Board concerning the background or application of certain provisions, definitions, or standards rules. There are no comments for provisions, definitions, and Standard Rules that are axiomatic or have not yet required further explanation; however, additional comments will be developed and others supplemented or revised as the need arises.

ETHICS PROVISION

Because of the fiduciary responsibilities inherent in professional appraisal practice, the appraiser must observe the highest standards of professional ethics. This Ethics Provision is divided into four sections: Conduct, Management, Confidentiality, and Record Keeping.

Comment: This provision emphasizes the personal obligations and responsibilities of the individual appraiser. However, it should also be emphasized that groups and organizations engaged in appraisal practice share the same ethical obligations.

Conduct

An appraiser must perform ethically and competently in accordance with these standards and not engage in conduct that is unlawful, unethical, or improper. An appraiser who could reasonably be perceived to act as a disinterested third party in rendering an unbiased appraisal, review or consulting service must perform assignments with impartiality, objectivity, and independence and without accommodation of personal interests.

Comment: An appraiser is required to avoid any action that could be considered misleading or fraudulent. In particular, it is unethical for an appraiser to use or communicate a misleading or fraudulent report or to knowingly permit an employee or other person to communicate a misleading or fraudulent report.[1]

The development of an appraisal, review, or consulting service based on a hypothetical condition is unethical unless: 1) the use of the hypothesis is clearly disclosed; 2) the assumption of the hypothetical condition is clearly required for legal purposes, for purposes of reasonable analysis, or for purposes of comparison and would not be misleading; and 3) the report clearly describes the rationale for this assumption, the nature of the hypothetical condition, and its effect on the result of the appraisal, review or consulting service.

[1]See Advisory Opinion G-5

An individual appraiser employed by a group or organization which conducts itself in a manner that does not conform to these standards should take steps that are appropriate under the circumstances to ensure compliance with standards.

Management

The acceptance of compensation that is contingent upon the reporting of a predetermined value or a direction in value that favors the cause of the client, the amount of the value estimate, the attainment of a stipulated result, or the occurrence of a subsequent event is unethical.

The payment of undisclosed fees, commissions, or things of value in connection with the procurement of appraisal, review or consulting assignments is unethical.

Comment: Disclosure of fees, commissions, or things of value connected to the procurement of an assignment should appear in the certification of a written report and in any transmittal letter in which conclusions are stated. In groups or organizations engaged in appraisal practice, intra-company payments to employees for business development are not considered to be unethical. Competency, rather than financial incentives, should be the primary basis for awarding an assignment.

Advertising for or soliciting appraisal assignments in a manner which is false, misleading or exaggerated is unethical.

Comment: In groups or organizations engaged in appraisal practice, decisions concerning finder or referral fees, contingent compensation, and advertising may not be the responsibility of an individual appraiser, but for a particular assignment, it is the responsibility of the individual appraiser to ascertain that there has been no breach of ethics, that the appraiser is prepared in accordance with these Standards, and that the report can be properly certified as required by Standards Rule 2-3, 3-2, 5-3, 6-8, 8-3 or 10-3.

The restriction on contingent compensation in the first paragraph of this section does not apply to consulting assignments where the appraiser is not acting in a disinterested manner and would not reasonably be perceived as performing a service that requires impartiality. This permitted contingent compensation must be properly disclosed in the report.

Comment: Assignments where the appraiser is not acting in a disinterested manner are further discussed in the General Comment to Standard 4. The preparer of the written report of such an assignment must certify that the compensation is contingent and must explain the basis for the contingency in the report (See S.R. 5-3) and in any transmittal letter in which conclusions are stated.

Confidentiality[2]

An appraiser must protect the confidential nature of the appraiser–client relationship.

Comment: An appraiser must not disclose confidential factual data obtained from a client or the results of an assignment prepared for a client to anyone other than 1) the client and persons specifically authorized by the client; 2) such third parties as may be authorized by due process of law; and 3) a duly authorized professional peer review committee. As a corollary, it is unethical for a member of a duly authorized professional peer review committee to disclose confidential information or factual data presented to the committee.

Record Keeping

An appraiser must prepare written records of appraisal, review, and consulting assignments—including oral testimony and reports—and retain such records for a period of at least five (5) years after preparation or at least two (2) years after final disposition of any judicial proceeding in which testimony was given, whichever period expires last.

Comment: Written records of assignments include true copies of written reports, written summaries of oral testimony and reports (or a transcript of testimony), all data and statements required by these standards, and other information as may be required to support the findings and conclusions of the appraiser. The term written records also includes information stored on electronic, magnetic, or other media. Such records must be made available by the appraiser when required by due process of law or by a duly authorized professional peer review committee.

COMPETENCY PROVISION

Prior to accepting an assignment or entering into an agreement to perform any assignment, an appraiser must properly identify the problem to be addressed and have the knowledge and experience to complete the assignment competently; or alternatively:

1. Disclose the lack of knowledge and/or experience to the client before accepting the assignment; and
2. Take all steps necessary or appropriate to complete the assignment competently; and
3. Describe the lack of knowledge and/or experience and the steps taken to complete the assignment competently in the report.

[2]See Statement on Appraisal Standards Number 5

<u>Comment</u>: The background and experience of appraisers varies widely and a lack of knowledge or experience can lead to inaccurate or inappropriate appraisal practice. The Competency Provision requires an appraiser to have both the knowledge and the experience required to perform a specific appraisal service competently. If an appraiser is offered the opportunity to perform an appraisal service but lacks the necessary knowledge or experience to complete it competently, the appraiser must disclose his or her lack of knowledge or experience to complete it before accepting the assignment and then take the necessary or appropriate steps to complete the appraisal service competently. This may be accomplished in various ways including, but not limited to, personal study by the appraiser; association with an appraiser reasonably believed to have the necessary knowledge or experience; or retention of others who possess the required knowledge or experience.

Although this provision requires an appraiser to identify the problem and disclose any deficiency in competence prior to accepting an assignment, facts or conditions uncovered during the course of an assignment could cause an appraiser to discover that he or she lacks the required knowledge or experience to complete the assignment competently. At the point of such discovery, the appraiser is obligated to notify the client and comply with items 2 and 3 of the provision.

The concept of competency also extends to appraisers who are requested or required to travel to geographic areas wherein they have no recent appraisal experience. An appraiser preparing an appraisal in an unfamiliar location must spend sufficient time to understand the nuances of the local market and the supply and demand factors relating to the specific property type and location involved. Such understanding will not be imparted solely from a consideration of specific data such as demographics, costs, sales, and rentals. The necessary understanding of local market conditions provides the bridge between a sale and a comparable sale or a rental and a comparable rental. If an appraiser is not in a position to spend the necessary amount of time in a market area to obtain this understanding, affiliation with a qualified local appraiser may be the appropriate response to ensure the development of a competent appraisal.

DEPARTURE PROVISION

This provision permits limited departures from sections of the Uniform Standards that are classified as specific guidelines rather than binding requirements. The burden of proof is on the appraiser to decide before accepting an assignment and invoking this provision that the result will not confuse or mislead. The burden of disclosure is also on the appraiser to report any departures from specific guidelines.

An appraiser may enter into an agreement to perform an assignment that calls for something less than, or different from, the work that would otherwise be required by the specific guidelines, provided that prior to entering into such an agreement:

1. The appraiser has determined that the appraisal or consulting process to be performed is not so limited that the resulting assignment would tend to mislead or confuse the client or the intended users of the report;
2. The appraiser has advised the client that the assignment calls for something less than, or different from, the work required by the specific guidelines and that the report will clearly identify and explain the departure(s); and
3. The client has agreed that the performance of a limited appraisal or consulting service would be appropriate.

Exceptions to the following requirements are not permitted: Standard Rules 1–1, 1–5, 2–1, 2–2, 2–3, 2–5, 3–1, 3–2, 4–1, 5–1, 5–3, 6–1, 6–3, 6–6, 6–7, 6–8, 7–1, 8–1, 8–3, 9–1, 9–3, 9–5, 10–1, 10–3, and 10–5. This restriction on departure is reiterated throughout the document with reminder comment: Departure from this binding requirement if not permitted.

Comment: For the purpose of this provision, intended users of the report might include parties such as lenders, employees of government agencies, partners of a client, and a client's attorney and accountant. In this context, the purpose and intended use of the appraisal or consulting service are critical.

If an appraiser enters into an agreement to perform an appraisal or consulting service that calls for something less than, or different from, the work that would otherwise be required by the specific appraisal guidelines, Standard Rules 2–2(a)(xi), 2–2(b)(xi), 5–2(i), 8–2(m), and 10–2(h) require that the report clearly identify and explain departure(s) from the specific guidelines.

JURISDICTIONAL EXCEPTION

If any part of these standards is contrary to the law or public policy of any jurisdiction, only that part shall be void and of no force or effect in that jurisdiction.

SUPPLEMENTAL STANDARDS

These Uniform Standards provide the common basis for all appraisal practice. Supplemental standards applicable to appraisers prepared for specific purposes or property types may be issued by public agencies and certain client groups, e.g., regulatory agencies, eminent domain authorities, asset managers, and financial institutions. Appraisers and clients must ascertain whether any supplemental standards in addition to these Uniform Standards apply to the assignment being considered.[3]

[3]See Advisory opinions G-7 and G-8.

Selected USPAP Definitions

Readers of these pages should also be familiar with the general definitions in the full body of the Uniform Standards of Professional Appraisal Practice.

APPRAISAL

> **COMPLETE APPRAISAL:** The act or process of estimating value or an estimate of value performed without invoking the Departure Provision.
>
> **LIMITED APPRAISAL:** The act or process of estimating value or an estimate of value performed under and resulting from invoking the Departure Provision.

BINDING REQUIREMENT: All or part of a standards rule of USPAP from which departure is not permitted (See DEPARTURE PROVISION).

BUSINESS ASSETS: Tangible and intangible resources that are employed by a business enterprise in its operations.

BUSINESS ENTERPRISE: A commercial, industrial, or service organization pursuing an economic activity.

BUSINESS EQUITY: The interests, benefits, and rights inherent in the ownership of a business enterprise or a part thereof in any form (including, but not necessarily limited to, capital stock, partnership interests, cooperatives, sole proprietorships, options, and warrants).

INTANGIBLE PROPERTY (INTANGIBLE ASSETS): Nonphysical assets including but not limited to franchises, trademarks, patents, copyrights, goodwill, equities, mineral rights, securities, and contracts, as distinguished from physical assets such as facilities and equipment.

REPORT: Any communication, written or oral, of an appraisal, review, or consulting service that is transmitted to the client upon completion of an assignment.

SPECIFIC GUIDELINE: All or part of a standards rule of USPAP from which departure is permitted under certain limited conditions. (See DEPARTURE PROVISION).

Appraisal Standards 3, 9 and 10

STANDARD 3 – Review appraisal and Reporting

In reviewing an appraisal and reporting the results of that review, an appraiser must form an opinion as to the adequacy and appropriateness of the report being reviewed and must clearly disclose the nature of the review process undertaken.[4]

Comment: The function of reviewing an appraisal requires the preparation of a separate report or a file memorandum by the appraiser performing the review setting forth the results of the review process. Review appraisers go beyond checking for a level of completeness and consistency in the report under review by providing comment on the content and conclusions of the report. They may or may not have first-hand knowledge of the subject property or of data in the report. The COMPETENCY PROVISION applies to the appraiser performing the review as well as the appraiser who prepared the report under review.

Reviewing is a distinctly different function from that addressed in Standards Rule 2-5. To avoid confusion in the marketplace between these two functions, review appraisers should not sign the report under review unless they intend to take the responsibility of a cosigner.

Review appraisers must take appropriate steps to indicate to third parties the precise extent of the review process. A separate report or letter is one method. Another appropriate method is a form or checklist prepared and signed by the appraiser conducting the review and attached to the report under review. It is also possible that a stamped impression on the appraisal report under review, signed or initialed by the reviewing appraiser, may be an appropriate method for separating the review function from the actual signing of the report. To be effective, however, the stamp must briefly indicate the extent of the review process and refer to a file memorandum that clearly outlines the review process conducted.

The review appraiser must exercise extreme care in clearly distinguishing between the review process and the appraisal or consulting processes. Original work by the review appraiser may be governed by STANDARD 1 or STANDARD 4 rather than this standard. A misleading or fraudulent review and/or report violates the ETHICS PROVISION.

Standards Rule 3-1

In reviewing an appraisal, an appraiser must:

(a) Identify the report under review, the real estate and real property interest being appraised, the effective date of the opinion in the report under review, and the date of the review;

[4]See Advisory Option G-6.

(b) Identify the extent of the review process to be conducted;
(c) Form an opinion as to the completeness of the report under review in light of the requirements in these standards;

Comment: The review should be conducted in the context of market conditions as of the effective date of the opinion in the report being reviewed.

(d) Form an opinion as to the apparent adequacy and relevance of the data and the propriety of any adjustments to the data;
(e) Form an opinion as to the appropriateness of the appraisal methods and techniques used and develop the reasons for any disagreement;
(f) Form an opinion as to whether the analyses, opinions, and conclusions in the report under review are appropriate and reasonable, and develop the reasons for any disagreement.

Comment: Departure from binding requirements (a) through (f) above is not permitted.

An opinion of a different estimate of value from that in the report under review may be expressed, provided the review appraiser:[5]

1. Satisfies the requirements of STANDARD 1;
2. Identifies and sets forth any additional data relied upon and the reasoning and basis for the different estimate of value; and,
3. Clearly identifies and discloses all assumptions and limitations connected with the different estimate of value to avoid confusion in the marketplace.

Standard Rule 3-2

In reporting the results of an appraisal review, an appraiser must:

(a) Disclose the nature, extent, and detail of the review process undertaken;
(b) Disclose the information that must be considered in Standards Rule 3-1 (a) and (b);
(c) Set forth the opinions, reasons, and conclusions required in Standards Rule 3-1 (c) (d), (e) and (f);
(d) Include all known pertinent information;
(e) Include a signed certification similar in content to the following:

I certify that, to the best of my knowledge and belief:

- The facts and data reported by the review appraiser and used in the review process are true and correct.

[5]See Statement on Appraisal Standards Number 1.

- The analyses, opinions, and conclusions in this review report are limited only by the assumptions and limiting conditions stated in this review report, and are my personal, unbiased professional analyses, opinions, and conclusions.
- I have no (or the specified) present or prospective interest in the property that is the subject of this report and I have no (or the specified) personal interest or bias with respect to the parties involved.
- My compensation is not contingent on an action or event resulting from the analyses, opinion, or conclusions in, or the use of, this review report.
- My analyses, opinions, and conclusions were developed and this review report was prepared in conformity with the Uniform Standards of Professional Appraisal Practice.
- I did not (did) personally inspect the subject property of the report under review.
- No one provided significant professional assistance to the person signing this review report. (If there are exceptions, the name of each individual providing significant professional assistance must be stated).

Comment: Departure from binding requirements (a) through (e) above is not permitted.

STANDARD 9 – Business Appraisal

In developing a business or intangible asset appraisal, an appraiser must be aware of, understand, and correctly employ those recognized methods and procedures that are necessary to produce a credible appraisal.

Comment: Standard 9 is directed toward the same substantive aspects set forth in Standard 1, but addresses business and intangible asset appraisal.

Standards Rule 9-1

In developing a business or intangible asset appraisal, an appraiser must:

(a) Be aware of, understand, and correctly employ those recognized methods and procedures that are necessary to produce a credible appraisal;

Comment: Departure from this binding requirement is not permitted. Changes and developments in the economy and in investment theory have a substantial impact on the business appraisal profession. Important changes in the financial arena, securities regulation, tax law and major new court decisions may result in corresponding changes in business appraisal practice.

(b) Not commit a substantial error of omission or commission that significantly affects an appraisal;

Comment: Departure from this binding requirement is not permitted. In performing appraisal services an appraiser must be certain that the gathering of factual information is conducted in a manner that is sufficiently diligent to reasonably ensure that the data that would have material or significant effect on the resulting opinions or conclusions are considered. Further, an appraiser must use sufficient care in analyzing such data to avoid errors that would significantly affect his or her opinions and conclusions.

(c) Not render appraisal services in a careless or negligent manners, such as a series of errors that, considered individually, may not significantly affect the results of an appraisal, but which, when considered in the aggregate, would be misleading.

Comment: Departure from this binding requirement is not permitted. Perfection is impossible to attain and competence does not require perfection. However, an appraiser must not render appraisal services in a careless or negligent manner. This rule requires an appraiser to use diligence and care. The fact that the carelessness or negligence of an appraiser has not caused an error that significantly affects his or her opinions or conclusions and thereby seriously harms a client does not excuse such carelessness or negligence.

Standards Rule 9-2

In developing a business or intangible asset appraisal, an appraiser must observe the following specific appraisal guidelines:

(a) Adequately identify the business enterprise, assets, or equity under consideration, define the purpose and the intended use of the appraisal, consider the elements of the appraisal investigation, consider any special limiting conditions, and identify the effective date of the appraisal;

(b) define the value being considered

  (i) If the appraisal concerns a business enterprise or equity interests, consider any buy-sell agreements, investment letter stock restrictions, restrictive corporate charter or partnership agreement clauses, and any similar features or factors that may have an influence on value.

  (ii) If the appraisal concerns assets, the appraiser must consider whether the assets are:

    (1) Appraised separately; or

    (2) Appraised as parts of a going concern.

Comment: The value of assets held by a business enterprise may change significantly depending on whether the basis of valuation is acquisition or replacement, continued use in place, or liquidation.

(i) If the appraisal concerns equity interests in a business enterprise, consider the extent to which the interests do or do not contain elements of ownership control.

Comment: Special attention should be paid to the attributes of the interest being appraised including the rights and benefits of ownership. The elements of control in a given situation may be affected by law, distribution of ownership interests, contractual relationships, and many other factors. As a consequence, the degree of control or lack of it depends on a broad variety of facts and circumstances which must be evaluated in the specific situation. Equity interests in a business enterprise are not necessarily worth the pro rata share of the business enterprise value as a whole. Conversely, if the value of the whole is not considered, the value of the business enterprise is not necessarily a direct mathematical extension of the value of the fractional interests.

Standards Rule 9-3

In developing a business or intangible asset appraisal relating to an equity interest with the ability to cause liquidation of the enterprise, an appraiser must investigate the possibility that the business enterprise may have a higher value in liquidation than for continued operation as a going concern absent contrary provisions of laws of a competent jurisdiction. If liquidation is the indicated basis of valuation, any real estate or personal property to be liquidated must be valued under the appropriate standard.

Comment: Departure from this binding requirement is not permitted. This rule requires the appraiser to recognize that continued operation of a business is not always the best premise of value, as liquidation may result in a higher value. It should be noted, however, that this should be considered only when the business equity being appraised is in a position to cause liquidation. If liquidation is the appropriate premise of value, then assets such as real estate and tangible personal property must be appraised under Standard 1 and Standard 7, respectively.

Standards Rule 9-4

In developing a business or intangible asset appraisal, an appraiser must observe the following specific appraisal guidelines when applicable:

(a) Consider all appropriate valuation methods and procedures.

(b) Collect and analyze relevant data regarding:
   (i) The nature and history of the business;
   (ii) Financial and economic conditions affecting the business enterprise, its industry, and the general economy;
   (iii) Past results, current operations, and future prospects of the business enterprise;
   (iv) Past sales of capital stock or other ownership interests in the business enterprise being appraised;
   (v) Sales of similar businesses or capital stock of publicly held similar businesses;
   (vi) Prices, terms, and conditions affecting past sales of similar business assets;

Comment: This guideline directs the appraiser to study the prospective and retrospective aspects of the business enterprise to study it in terms of the economic and industry environment within which it operates. Further, sales of securities of the business itself or similar businesses for which sufficient information is available should also be considered.

In certain circumstances, the business appraiser may also collect and analyze data regarding functional and/or economic utility or obsolescence of the business assets.

Economic obsolescence is a major consideration when assets are considered as parts of a going concern. It may also be one of the criteria in deciding that liquidation is the appropriate premise for valuation.

Standards Rule 9-5

In developing a business or intangible asset appraisal, an appraiser must;

(a) select and employ one or more approaches that apply to the specific appraisal assignments.

Comment: This rule requires the appraiser to use all relevant approaches for which sufficient reliable data are available. However, it does not mean that the appraiser must use all approaches in order to comply with the rule if certain approaches are not applicable.

(b) Consider and reconcile the indications of value resulting from the various approaches to arrive at the value conclusion.

Comment: Departure from this binding requirement is not permitted. The appraiser must evaluate the relative reliability of the various indications of value. The appraiser should consider quality and quantity of data leading to each of the indications of value. The value conclusion is the result of the appraiser's judgment and not necessarily the result of a mathematical process.

STANDARD 10 – Business Appraisal, Reporting

In reporting the results of a business or intangible asset appraisal, an appraiser must communicate each analysis, opinion, and conclusion in a manner that is not misleading.

Standard Rule 10-1

Each written or oral business or intangible asset appraisal report must:

(a) Clearly and accurately set forth the appraisal in a manner that will not be misleading.

Comment: Departure from this binding requirement is not permitted.

(b) Contain sufficient information to enable the intended user(s) to understand it. Any specific limiting conditions concerning information should be noted.

Comment: Departure from this binding requirement is not permitted. Any specific limiting conditions should be noted in the engagement letter as well as in the report itself. A failure to observe this rule could cause the intended users of the report to make a serious error even though each analysis, opinion, and conclusion in the report is clearly and accurately stated.

(c) Clearly and accurately disclose any extraordinary assumption that directly affects the appraisal and indicate its impact on value.

Comment: Departure from this binding requirement is not permitted. This rule requires a clear and accurate disclosure of any extraordinary assumptions or conditions that directly affect an analysis, opinion, or conclusion. Examples of such extraordinary assumptions or conditions might include items such as the execution of a pending lease agreement, a typical financing, infusion of additional working capital or making other capital additions, or compliance with regulatory authority rules. The report should indicate whether the extraordinary assumption or condition has a positive, negative, or neutral impact on value.

Standard Rule 10-2

Each written business or intangible asset appraisal report must comply with the following specific reporting guidelines:

(a) Identify and describe the business enterprise, assets, or equity being appraised.
(b) State the purpose and intended use of the appraisal.
(c) Define the value to be estimated.
(d) Set forth the effective date of the appraisal and the date of the report.

Comment: If the appraisal concerns equity, it is not enough to identify the entity in which the equity is being appraised without also identifying the nature of the equity, for example: the number of shares of common or preferred stock. The purpose may be to express an opinion of value but the intended use of the appraisal must also be stated.

The report date is when the report is submitted; the appraisal date or date of value is the effective date of the value conclusion.

(e) Describe the extent of the appraisal process employed;
(f) Set forth all assumptions and limiting conditions that affect the analyses, opinions, and conclusions.
(g) Set forth the information considered, the appraisal procedures followed, and the reasoning that supports the analyses, opinions, and conclusions.
(h) Set forth any additional information that may be appropriate to show compliance with, or clearly identify and explain permitted departures from, the requirements of Standard 9.
(i) Set forth the rationale for the valuation methods and procedures considered and employed.
(j) Include a certification in accordance with S.R. 10-3.

Standards Rule 10-3

Each written business or intangible asset appraisal report must contain a certification that is similar in content to the following:

I certify that, to the best of my knowledge and belief:

- The statements of fact contained in this report are true and correct.
- The reported analyses, opinions, and conclusions are limited only by the reported assumptions and limiting conditions, and are my personal, unbiased professional analyses, opinions, and conclusions.
- I have no (or the specified) present or prospective interest in the property that is the subject of this report, and I have no (or the specified) personal interest or bias with respect to the parties involved.
- My compensation is not contingent on an action or event resulting from the analyses, opinions or conclusions in, or the use of, this report.
- My analyses, opinions, and conclusions were developed, and this report has been prepared, in conformity with the Uniform Standards of Professional Appraisal Practice.

- No one provided significant professional assistance to the person signing this report. (If there are exceptions, the name of each individual providing significant professional assistance must be stated).

Comment: Departure from this binding requirement is not permitted.

Standards Rule 10-4

To the extent that it is both possible and appropriate, each oral business or intangible asset appraisal report (including expert testimony) must address the substantive matters set forth in Standards Rule 10-2 and state conformity with Standard Rule 10-3.

Standard Rule 10-5

An appraiser who signs a business or intangible asset appraisal report prepared by another, even under the label "review appraiser," must accept full responsibility for the contents of this report.

Comment: Departure from this binding requirement is not permitted. This requirement is directed to the employer or supervisor signing the report of an employee or subcontractor. The employer or supervisor signing the report is as responsible as the individual preparing the appraisal for the content and conclusions of the appraisal and the report. Using a conditional label next to the signature of the employer or supervisor, or signing a form report on the line over the words "review appraiser" does not exempt that individual from adherence to these Standards.

This requirement does not address the responsibilities of a review appraiser, the subject of Standard 3.

STATEMENTS ON APPRAISAL STANDARDS

Statements on Appraisal Standards are authorized by the bylaws of The Appraisal Foundation and are specifically for the purpose of clarification, interpretation, explanation, or elaboration of the Uniform Standards of Professional Appraisal Practice (USPAP). Statements have the full weight of a Standards Rule and can only be adopted by the Appraisal Standards Board after exposure and comment.

Index to Statements

SMT-3	Retrospective Value Estimates
SMT-4	Prospective Value Estimates
SMT-5	Confidentiality Rule of Ethics Provision
SMT-6	Reasonable Exposure Time in Market Value Estimates

ADVISORY OPINIONS

Advisory Opinions issued by the Appraisal Standards Board do not establish new standards or interpret existing standards. Advisory opinions are issued to illustrate the applicability of appraisal standards in specific situations and to offer advice from the ASB for the resolution of appraisal issues and problems.

Editor's Note: *The Advisory Opinions noted below are of a general nature. Those not listed deal specifically with the appraisal of real property.*

Index to Advisory Opinions

G-1	Sales History
G-3	Update of an Appraisal
G-6	The Review Appraisal Function
G-10	The Appraiser Client Relationship

All of the above are bound into the booklet containing the Uniform Standards of Professional Appraisal Practice. Ordering information is on page 1 of this document.

American Society of Appraisers
535 Herndon Parkway, Suite 150
Herndon, Virginia 22070
(703) 478-2228

The Appraisal Foundation
1029 Vermont Avenue, N.W., Suite 900
Washington, D.C. 20005-3517
(202) 347-7722

Business Valuation Committee
American Society of Appraisers
2777 South Colorado Boulevard, Suite 200
Denver, Colorado 80202
(303) 758-6148

CERTIFIED BUSINESS APPRAISER

Certified Business Appraiser (CBA) is issued by the Institute of Business Appraisers (IBA). Designees must have a college degree or equivalent, pass a 3 1/2-hour written examination, and successfully complete a peer review of valuation reports issued by the candidate. The IBA requires continuing education and recertification procedures. Approximately 250 individuals hold the CBA designation.

The IBA has developed business valuation standards that are binding on the members of the organization. A copy of those standards has been reproduced here with the permission of the association.

You can receive copies of the standards (publication P-311b) and reach the IBA at Institute of Business Appraisers, PO Box 1447, Boynton Beach, FL 33425, Phone (561) 732-3202

BUSINESS APPRAISAL STANDARDS*

As
Promulgated
by

The Institute Of Business Appraisers, Inc.

May 6, 1998

Copyright (c) 1993, 1998
The Institute of Business Appraisers, Inc.

Publication P-311b

NOTICE

This publication supersedes and replaces the following IBA publications:
P-243 Standards of Business Appraisal Practice
P-244 Standards for Business Appraisal Reports
P-311a Business Appraisal Standards

**Business Appraisal Standards*, The Institute of Business Appraisers, Inc., © 1993, 1998. Reprinted with permission.

2.4 Written Follow-up
2.5 Recordkeeping

STANDARD THREE

3.0 EXPERT TESTIMONY
3.1 Definition
3.2 Mandatory Content
3.3 Conformity
3.4 Recordkeeping

STANDARD FOUR

4.0 LETTER FORM WRITTEN APPRAISAL REPORTS
4.1 Definition
4.2 Conformity
4.3 Mandatory Content
4.4 Distribution of Report
4.5 Valuation Conclusion
4.6 Transmittal Letter
4.7 Recordkeeping

STANDARD FIVE

5.0 FORMAL WRITTEN APPRAISAL REPORTS
5.1 Definition
5.2 Conformity
5.3 Mandatory Content
5.4 Distribution of Report
5.5 Valuation Conclusion
5.6 Transmittal Letter
5.7 Recordkeeping

STANDARD SIX

6.0 PRELIMINARY REPORTS
6.1 Definition
6.2 Conformity
6.3 Usage
6.4 Disclosure
6.5 Departure
6.6 Oral v. Written
6.7 Recordkeeping

FOREWORD

Only a small percentage of individuals representing themselves as business appraisers have been tested and certified by a professional business appraisal institute or society.

Those considering employing a business appraiser are undoubtedly doing so in relation to a matter which can have far-reaching financial or legal ramifications. Beyond the obvious caution that a proper valuation cannot be done without adequate preparation, competency, and documentation, we suggest verification that the individual is certified as a business appraiser and intends to prepare the appraisal in compliance with these standards.

The Institute of Business Appraisers would like to thank those associated with The Appraisal Foundation and the American Society of Appraisers whose efforts toward developing business appraisal standards and ethics have contributed greatly to the product of this Committee.

FOUNDING STANDARDS COMMITTEE

David M. Bishop, CBA, Chairman
Larry R. Cook, CBA, CPA, ABV
James M. Hansen, CBA, CRA
Steven F. Schroeder, CBA, ASA
Raymond C. Miles, CBA, ASA Ex-Officio

PREAMBLE

1. Certain professions, by their nature, and by the way they are perceived by the public, are capable of exerting substantial influence on the public welfare. It is our firm conviction that the practice of business appraisal falls in a similar category.
2. The performance of business appraisal/valuation requires a high degree of skill, imposes upon the appraiser a duty of nonadvocacy to the client and an obligation to the general public as a third party beneficiary of the work. It is our purpose here to articulate standards by which those who aspire to participation and those already established in business appraisal practice may be guided in the ethical and skillful execution of their tasks, and report the results and conclusions of their work in the most effective manner.
3. It is also our purpose to state these standards in such a clear and unequivocal way that the world at large, and especially those who may en-

gage the services of a business appraiser, will know the parameters by which professional competence is to be measured, and by which its professional practitioners wish to be judged.

4. Each standard is qualified as: (i) should, (ii) must, or (iii) shall. Should and must standards are guidelines. While an appraiser may depart from a should standard without a statement of departure, such departure should be made knowingly. In those instances where the appraiser feels a departure from a must standard is warranted, the report shall include a statement of departure. It is the position of the IBA that standards designated shall are those from which departure is not justified.

5. These standards have been developed to provide guidance to appraisers who are members of the Institute of Business Appraisers (IBA) and others performing appraisals of closely held businesses, business ownership interests, or securities. They have also been developed to assist in the evaluation and regulation of members of the IBA through creating uniform practices and procedures. Departures from the standards are not intended to provide a basis for civil liability, and should not be presumed to create evidence that any legal duty has been breached, or to imply the creation of any additional relationships or duties other than those specified herein.

FORMAT

These standards are presented in a naturally progressive format beginning with overall professional conduct and ethics, followed by specific standards applicable to oral reports, expert testimony, letter reports, formal reports, and preliminary reports.

No attempt is made to anticipate every possible scenario or unique circumstance and create standards specific thereto. Conversely, these standards were developed under the premise that the professional business appraiser practicing within the proper standard of care can, on a case-by-case basis, adequately apply these standards in such a manner to result in a competent report while still permitting the flexibility necessary to meet the reasonable requests of the client and the vicissitudes of the assignment.

Within this publication, reference to all individuals has been in the masculine. This is done in the interest of simplicity and is not intended as a gender bias. Terms should be assumed to be in the singular or plural as appropriate to the context in which they are used.

STANDARD ONE

1.0 PROFESSIONAL CONDUCT & ETHICS

1.1 Competence. The achievement of certification as a business appraiser (CBA) is a result of specialized training, study, practice, the successful completion of a proctored examination, and a favorable review of the candidate's actual appraisal reports by The Institute of Business Appraisers' Qualifications Review Committee. To maintain certification, a CBA will adhere to continuing education requirements and periodic recertification as required by IBA.

Prior to accepting an engagement to perform a business appraisal, the appraiser must judge his competence to complete the assignment. Should the appraiser have a meaningful lack of knowledge and experience, the appraiser must immediately disclose that fact to the client. If the client desires the appraiser to continue with the assignment, the appraiser shall take those steps necessary to perform the appraisal in a competent manner, or take those steps necessary to complete the assignment under the supervision of an appraiser who has the requisite skill, or with the permission of the client, refer the engagement to a qualified business appraiser.

It is essential that a business appraiser communicate the research and thought processes which led to his opinions and conclusions in a manner that is clear, meaningful, and not misleading. Said communication, whether oral or written, shall not be rendered in a careless or negligent manner.

The appraiser as an individual must be competent. Software valuation programs and/or excessive reliance on rules of thumb are not surrogates for individual competence.

The professional business appraiser recognizes and understands that compliance with these standards and ethics is an essential part of competence.

1.2 Confidentiality. The very fact an appraiser has been retained to value all or a portion of a business enterprise, or its securities, is in itself confidential. Consequently, it is considered unethical for a business appraiser to disclose either the assignment itself or any of the reasonably identifiable contents of an appraisal report without the client's express permission.

1.3 Disinterestedness. It is unethical for a business appraiser to accept any assignment when the appraiser has a present or contemplated interest in the property being appraised, or a bias for or against any person associated therewith, either directly or indirectly. Such interests include, but are not limited to, present, contemplated or prospective activity with the business enterprise, its officers, directors, or owners, including possible acquirers or investors.

However, if a prospective client, after full disclosure by the appraiser of said interest or bias, still elects to engage the appraiser, the appraiser may accept the assignment. When accepting such an assignment, the business appraiser shall include a Statement of Departure as required by Standard 1.21(b). The Statement of Departure shall include a complete disclosure of the interest or bias.

1.4 Nonadvocacy v. Advocacy. Nonadvocacy is considered to be a mandatory standard of appraisal.

The appraiser's obligation to serve the public interest assures that the integrity of valuations will be preserved. Hence, the appraiser may only be an advocate for his unbiased process and conclusions. The appraiser must be guided by nothing other than his informed judgment, the dictates of the client (as permitted under these standards), applicable administrative rulings, and the law.

In the event the appraiser is engaged to function not as an appraiser but as an advisor or consultant, he may serve as an advocate. In such instances the appraiser shall include a statement of departure which states that any positions taken were taken as an advocate for the client.

1.5 Engagement. Prior to performing an appraisal assignment, a business appraiser should obtain a written agreement signed by the client or his agent. At the very least, the engagement agreement should specify what the appraiser is being engaged to appraise, the function (use) of the appraisal, the purpose (standard of value) including the definition thereof, the effective date of the appraisal, the scope of the appraisal, that the appraisal will be performed on a nonadvocacy basis (see Standard 1.4), the amount of or method for calculating the appraiser's fee, together with the method for payment of same, and an indication of when the client may expect the report.

1.6 Coherence and Production. Appraisal reports must have logical organization. Readers' questions that can reasonably be anticipated should be answered. Data in one part of the report should not contradict other portions without reconciliation.

The appraiser should develop contributing conclusions from the various components of the appraisal process drawing them together in a cross-supporting manner that logically brings the reader to the appraiser's conclusion.

The report should be produced in a manner and style which brings credit to the appraiser and the profession. Typographical errors and the like shall be eliminated. In formal reports, page and exhibit numbers should be used together with a table of contents or index to enhance readability.

1.7 Supportable Opinion. The essence of business appraisal is a supportable opinion.

While it is intuitively logical that on a case-by-case basis certain opinions will be based on the informed, but subjective, judgment of the appraiser to a greater degree than others, the appraiser's goal is to have a supportable opinion. The reader should not be expected to accept critical elements such as adjustments to financial statements, the selected capitalization or discount rates or weightings, without support—even in those instances where the vicissitudes of the assignment dictate that support be primarily based on the informed judgment of the appraiser.

1.8 Replicability. The appraiser's procedures and conclusions in the formal report *must* be presented in sufficient detail to permit the reader to replicate the appraisal process.

1.9 Appropriateness. The standard of value, the type of report and the valuation approaches/methods utilized should be appropriate to the assignment. The material included in the report should be relevant, clear, and cogent.

1.10 Jurisdictional Exception. If any part of these standards is contrary to the law or public policy of any jurisdiction, only that part shall be void and of no force and effect in that jurisdiction.

1.11 Fiduciary Duty to Clients, and Other Duties.

Client The one employing the business appraiser.

Third Parties Others who could be expected to review the report, e.g., attorneys, accountants, lenders, buyers, investors, regulatory agencies, courts, etc.

Public Society at large.

(a) Specialized Character of Business Appraisal. Seldom are others intimately familiar with the process of business appraisal. Therefore, it is anticipated the business appraiser will use his professional abilities properly, as more fully described throughout these standards.

(b) Loyalty, Obedience and Reasonable Skill and Care. Agents have such duties to clients. While no fiduciary or other affirmative duty is owed to others, services provided in accordance with these standards should be clear as to meaning and not be misleading to others.

1.12 Duty to Profession.

(a) Professional Cooperation and Courtesy. It is unethical to damage or attempt to damage the professional reputations or interfere with the performance of other business appraisers practicing within the scope of these standards through false or malicious statement or innuendo.

(b) Conduct. Every member is reminded that his demeanor and general conduct represents his profession and fellow practitioners, and unprofessional conduct damages more than his individual reputation.

(c) Cooperation. Each member shall cooperate fully with the efforts of the Institute and/or its Ethics and Discipline Committee when investigating possible activities which are contrary to these standards.

1.13 Substance v. Form. The form of an appraisal report can be oral or written with variations of each. However, it is only the form of the report that varies. The appraiser's responsibilities to gather data, analyze the data, and draw supportable conclusions as applicable to the type of assignment undertaken does not change. Regardless of whether the final valuation is reported orally, in a summarizing letter report, or a formal report, the appraiser must have first completed an appropriate valuation determination process.

A preliminary report is an exception to the above requirement for a thorough, complete work process. By its nature, a preliminary report results from a more cursory evaluation. (See Standard Six, Preliminary Reports.)

1.14 Professional Fees. The fees charged for the services of an appraiser are a product of the marketplace; however, a business appraiser is ethically denied the selection of a fee that could in itself call to question the objectivity of the appraiser.

(a) Finder's Fees. No appraiser will pay fees, or offer gain in any form, to others to promote the appraiser's work in such a way, or under any circumstances, that will diminish the dignity of, or reflect discredit or disrepute upon, the appraisal profession.

(b) Referral Fees. It is the right of an appraiser and, therefore, not unethical to pay a referral fee to another professional for the referral of appraisal assignments.

(c) Percentage Fees. To accept any engagement for which the compensation is based on a percentage of the valuation conclusion impairs independence and is thus unethical.

1.15 Access to Requisite Data. The business appraiser must decide what documents and/or information are requisite to a competent appraisal.

(a) Reliability of Data. An appraiser may rely upon documents and/or information provided by the client and/or his agents without further corroboration, provided the report clearly states he has done so. This right, however, does not abrogate the appraiser's duty to ask or otherwise inquire regarding information which on its surface clearly appears to be incomplete or otherwise inaccurate.

(b) Pertinent Data. In situations where access to "pertinent" data is denied to the appraiser, the appraiser may, at his option, withdraw from completing the assignment. However, should the appraiser elect to complete the assignment, the report must include a Statement of Departure as required under Standard 1.21(b). Such Statement of Departure must describe the limitation and/or restriction and its potential effect on the appraiser's conclusion.

(c) Essential Data. When the business appraiser is denied access to data considered essential to a proper appraisal, the business appraiser should not proceed with the assignment.

1.16 Valuation Approaches/Methods. The approaches/methods used within a given assignment are a matter that must be determined by the business appraiser's professional judgment. The task is generally decided through consideration of the approaches/methods that are conceptually most appropriate and those for which the most reliable data is available.

1.17 Definitions.

(a) Terms. The appraiser should be careful in the use of ambiguous or esoteric terms. Such terms require definition to prevent the reader from applying a different definition.

(b) Computations. All computations, particularly those used to compute ratios and weightings should be clearly defined.

1.18 Principal Sources and References.

(a) Formal Report. A formal report must include a list of the principal sources of nonconfidential information and references whenever their inclusion will materially contribute to the clarity and understanding of the report.

(b) Oral and Informal Reports. The appraiser's workpapers must include a general description of the principal sources of information and references.

1.19 Site Tours and Interviews.

(a) Tour. Familiarity with an appraisal subject is a compelling necessity to a credible valuation. For this reason, it is desirable that a business appraiser make personal inspections or tours of appraisal subject sites whenever possible. When such activities are not performed, the appraiser's report shall disclose that the appraisal process did not include a site tour.

(b) Interview. An appraiser should not perform an appraisal without interviewing the management and other parties considered appropriate in the circumstances.

1.20 Eligibility of Data. An appraisal shall be based upon what a reasonably informed person would have knowledge of as of a certain date. This shall be known as the appraisal's "date of valuation" or "effective date" and accordingly reflect the appraiser's supportable conclusion as of that date. Information unavailable or unknown on the date of valuation must not influence the appraiser or contribute to the concluding opinion of value.

(a) Imminent Change. The appraiser is sometimes faced with the knowledge of a material imminent change in the business; a change not known of on the "date of valuation," but known as of the appraisal's "report" date. In such an event, the imminent change (positive or negative) should not affect the valuation conclusion, unless a reasonably informed person could have anticipated the imminent change. However, it is not uncommon for an appraiser to disclose such a change within the narrative portion of the report.

(b) Data on Guideline Companies. When an appraiser selects guideline companies, the data on the companies judged sufficiently similar should be information knowable, although perhaps not yet compiled, on or before appraisal's date of valuation. Additionally, the data on the guideline companies should be for the same accounting period; however, if it is as of a different period, said different period must be on or before the appraisal's date of valuation.

This restriction should apply whether the guideline companies are specific companies or aggregate industry statistics or ratios.

1.21 Departure. A business appraiser may be engaged to perform an appraisal assignment that calls for something different from the work that would routinely result from the appraiser's compliance with all must standards; provided, that prior to entering into an agreement to perform such an assignment:

(a) The appraiser is of the opinion that the assignment is not so limited in scope that the resulting report would tend to mislead or confuse the client or other anticipated readers; and

(b) The appraiser has advised the client that the assignment calls for something different than that which would normally result from compliance with applicable standards and, therefore, the report shall include a statement of departure.

1.22 Hypothetical Reports. An analysis or appraisal may be prepared under a hypothetical assumption, or series thereof, even though they may appear improbable. However, such a report must clearly state (i) the hypothetical assumption and (ii) the purpose of the analysis or appraisal, and any opinion of value must clearly be identified as resulting from a hypothetical assumption.

1.23 Dissenting Opinion.

(a) Dissenting Opinion With Other Appraisers. Collaborating appraisers, and review appraisers must sign the report. When a signing appraiser disagrees in whole or in part with any or all of the findings of other appraisers, said dissenting opinion must be included in the report, signed by the dissenting appraiser.

(b) Dissenting Opinion With Case Law and/or Administrative Regulation. As any other member of society, appraisers are required to comply with statutory law and statutory definitions as they may exist from time to time and from jurisdiction to jurisdiction. However, case law and/or administrative regulations do not have the same force as statutory law. Therefore, the business appraiser may, when he believes it is warranted, express within the appraisal report a dissenting opinion to case law and/or an administrative regulation.

1.24 Membership Designations. It is considered unethical conduct for any individual to explicitly or implicitly indicate he is a Certified Business Appraiser (CBA) when he has not been awarded the designation.

(a) Certified Business Appraisal Reports. An appraisal report may be considered a "Certified Report" when it is signed by a Certified Business Appraiser who is taking technical responsibility for its content.

(b) Certification of Firms. The designation Certified Business Appraiser (CBA) is awarded to individuals, not business enterprises; therefore, it is unethical for an appraiser to explicitly or implicitly indicate that the firm is certified.

(c) Misuse of Certification. Each Certified Business Appraiser is honorbound to refrain from any use of his professional designation in connection with any form of activity that may reflect discredit upon his designation, or the organization that conferred it, or deceive his client, or the public. As with actual appraisal conclusions, this has been left as a matter of individual judgment and conscience; those who abuse this privilege could be subject to disciplinary action by IBA's Ethics and Discipline Committee.

1.25 Certification. Each written report must contain a certification signed by the appraiser. Additional appraisers signing the report must accept responsibility for the full contents of the report. [In the event of a dissenting opinion, see Standard 1.23(a).] The certificate must be similar in content to the following:

(a) That to the best of the appraiser's knowledge, the statements of fact contained in the report are true and correct.

(b) That the reported analyses, opinions, and conclusions are limited only by the reported assumptions and limiting conditions, and are the appraiser's personal, unbiased professional analyses, opinions, and conclusions.

(c) That the appraisal was performed on a basis of nonadvocacy, including a statement that the appraiser has no present or contemplated interest in the property appraised and has no personal bias with respect to the parties involved, or a complete disclosure of any such interest or bias.

(d) That the appraiser's compensation is not contingent on an action or event resulting from the analyses, opinions, or conclusions in, or the use of, the report.

(e) That the appraiser's analyses, opinions, and conclusions were developed and that the report has been prepared in conformity with the Business Appraisal Standards of The Institute of Business Appraisers.

(f) That no one provided significant professional assistance to the person signing the report. However, if there are exceptions to this, then the name of each individual providing significant professional assistance must be disclosed.

1.26 Qualifications of the Appraiser. The reader cannot fully judge the quality of the appraisal report without being given the opportunity to judge the appraiser's qualifications. Therefore, each appraisal report <u>must</u> include the appraiser's qualifications in a manner the appraiser believes accurately presents his appraisal experience, certification, professional activities, and other qualifications.

1.27 Force and Effect. These standards shall be in full force and effect on the date of their issuance. (Earlier compliance is encouraged.) Any and all prior standards regarding business appraisal practices, reports, conduct, or ethics are superseded. Future amendments, to be effective, <u>shall</u> be initiated and passed in accordance with Standard 1.29.

1.28 Enforcement. The enforcement of these standards, including amendments or modifications as may occur in accordance with Standard 1.29, <u>shall</u> be the responsibility and duty of all members as to their own performance, and otherwise by the standing Ethics and Discipline Committee of The Institute of Business Appraisers and/or such other individuals or committees as are designated from time to time by the governing body of The Institute of Business Appraisers.

1.29 Amendments to Standards. The Standards Committee of The Institute of Business Appraisers is a standing committee. Certified members desiring to propose amendments, additions, or deletions to these standards should submit a clear expression of the proposed change to The Institute of Business Appraisers, Attention: Chairperson, Standards Committee. The chairperson reserves the right to return any submitted change for further clarification as to the precise change proposed. The chairperson shall distribute copies of the proposed change to the members of the Standards Committee for their opinions on the proposed change. Should two-thirds or more of the Committee support the change, it shall be endorsed by the Committee and an exposure draft will be provided to all CBAs. The exposure draft shall provide for a thirty-day period for the vote of all CBAs. In the event that those certified members who vote "No" exceeds 50% of all CBAs (those voting plus those not voting), the Committee's vote will be overruled and the proposed change will die for lack of support. Otherwise, the change will be adopted as of the first day of the month following the date copies of the amendments are provided to all members.

1.30 Signing Reports. Each written report *must* be signed by the appraiser and any other appraisers, including those signing as a "Review Appraiser" or "Collaborating Appraiser," *shall* accept responsibility for the full content of the report. [In the event of a dissenting opinion, see Standard 1.23(a).]

(a) Exception. Should the policy of a given firm be that all reports are to be signed by a person authorized to sign reports on behalf of the firm, an exception to Standards 1.30 and 1.25 is permitted. However, in this event:

(i) The designated signer shall take technical responsibility for the full content of the report; and

(ii) The report may not be considered a "Certified Appraisal Report" unless a Certified Business Appraiser taking technical responsibility signs the report.

(iii) The fact that a given appraisal report is signed under 1.30(a) is not intended in any way to justify or excuse deviation from any standard that would otherwise apply.

STANDARD TWO

2.0 ORAL APPRAISAL REPORTS

2.1 Usage. In general written reports are preferred; however, oral appraisal reports are permitted when ordered by the client.

2.2 Mandatory Content. When presenting an oral report, the business appraiser shall in a manner that is clear and not misleading communicate the following:

(a) Introduction. Identify the client, and set forth the property being appraised, the purpose and function of the appraisal, the definition of the standard of value, and the effective date of the appraisal.

(b) Assumptions and Limiting Conditions. Disclose any extraordinary assumptions or limiting conditions that in the appraiser's judgment affected the value.

(c) Disinterestedness. That the appraisal was performed on a basis of nonadvocacy, including a statement that the appraiser has no present or contemplated interest in the property appraised and has no personal bias with respect to the parties involved, or a complete disclosure of any such interest or bias. [See Standard 1.3]

(d) Valuation Conclusion. Represents a concluding opinion of value expressed as:

(i) A statement of a specific opinion of value; or

(ii) A range of values; or

(iii) A preliminary estimate which must include a statement that an opinion of value resulting from a formal report might be different and that difference might be material. (See also Standard Six, Preliminary Reports)

2.3 Conformity. Oral appraisal reports should comply with all applicable sections of Standard One, Professional Conduct and Ethics.

2.4 Written Follow-up. By its nature, the oral report is less detailed than the written report. Therefore, whenever feasible, it is suggested that oral reports be followed by a written presentation of the salient features of the oral report. In general, the written follow-up should include:

(a) Assumptions and Limiting Conditions. All applicable assumptions and limiting conditions.

(b) Support. In general, a brief presentation of the information considered, the appraisal approaches used, and the research and thought processes that support the appraiser's analyses, opinions, and conclusions.

(c) Appraiser's Certification as specified in Section 1.25.

2.5 Recordkeeping. An appraiser should retain written records of appraisal reports for a period of at least five (5) years after preparation or at least two (2) years after final disposition of any judicial proceeding in which the appraiser gave testimony, whichever period expires last.

STANDARD THREE

3.0 EXPERT TESTIMONY

3.1 Definition. Expert testimony is an oral report given in the form of testimony in a deposition and/or on the witness stand before a court of proper jurisdiction or other trier of fact.

3.2 Mandatory Content. The appraiser shall answer all questions put to him in a manner that is clear and not misleading. When giving testimony, the appraiser shall not advocate any position that is incompatible with the appraiser's obligation of nonadvocacy; i.e., it is unethical for the appraiser to suppress any facts, data, or opinions which are adverse to the case his client is trying to establish, or to overemphasize any facts, data, or opinions which are favorable to his client's case, or in any other particulars become an advocate. The expert witness must at least comply in a manner that is clear and not misleading with the following:

(a) Introduction. Identify the client, and set forth the property being appraised, the purpose and function of the appraisal, the definition of the standard of value, and the effective date of the appraisal.

(b) Assumptions and Limiting Conditions. Disclose any extraordinary assumptions or limiting conditions that in the appraiser's judgment affected the value.

(c) Disinterestedness. That the appraisal was performed on a basis of nonadvocacy, including a statement that the appraiser has no present or contemplated interest in the property appraised and has no personal bias with respect to the parties involved, or a complete disclosure of any such interest or bias. (See Standard 1.3)

(d) Valuation Conclusion. Any concluding opinion of value may be expressed as:

(i) A statement of a specific opinion of value; or

(ii) A range of values; or

(iii) A preliminary estimate which must include a statement that an opinion of value resulting from a formal report may be different and that difference may be material. (See also Standard Six, Preliminary Reports.)

3.3 Conformity. Expert testimony reports should comply with all applicable sections of Standard One, Professional Conduct and Ethics.

3.4 Recordkeeping. An appraiser should retain written records of appraisal reports for a period of at least five (5) years after preparation or at least two (2) years after final disposition of any judicial proceeding in which the appraiser gave testimony, whichever period expires last.

STANDARD FOUR

4.0 LETTER FORM WRITTEN APPRAISAL REPORTS

4.1 Definition. An appraiser's written report can be in the form of a letter report or a formal report. The letter report, which is shorter than the formal report, presents conclusions together with brief generalized comments. This type of report is often referred to as a short-form report, letter opinion, or an informal report.

By its nature, the letter form report is an instrument of brevity. It should contain at least a summary of the material factors that led to its conclusions, but it is usually intended by the parties to reduce the normal appraisal burden of writing a comprehensive report, and thereby allow the client to realize some economic benefit. However, the appraiser is still required to perform materially the same investigation and analysis as would be required for a comprehensive formal report and maintain in his file the workpapers necessary to support the conclusions stated in the letter report.

4.2 Conformity. The letter form written report must comply with all applicable provisions of Business Appraisal Standards, Standard One, Professional Conduct and Ethics.

4.3 Mandatory Content. All letter form written appraisal reports shall minimally set forth in a manner that is clear and not misleading:

(a) Identify the client, and set forth a description of the business enterprise, security, or other tangible and/or intangible property being appraised.

(b) Form of the organization and if incorporated, the state of incorporation, together with a description, adequate to the assignment, of all classes of securities outstanding and a list of shareholders whose interest should, in the appraiser's judgment be specified. If a partnership, the type and the state of filing, together with a list of those partners, whether general or limited, whose interest should, in the appraiser's judgment, be specified.

(c) The purpose (standard of value) of the appraisal.

(d) The function (use) of the appraisal.

(e) The definition of the standard of value that is the purpose of the appraisal.

(f) The effective ("as of") date of the appraisal.

(g) The date the appraisal report was prepared.

(h) The report's assumptions and limiting conditions.

(i) Any special factors that affected the opinion of value. Such factors include, but are not limited to, buy-sell agreements, restrictive stock agreements, corporate articles, bylaws and resolutions, partnership agreements, litigation, regulatory compliance, or environmental hazards.

(j) Applicable discounts and premiums such as minority interest, control, marketability or lack thereof.

(k) A certification consistent with the intent of section 1.25.

4.4 Distribution of Report. The letter report should include a clear statement of the expected distribution of the report.

4.5 Valuation Conclusion. The letter report must include a clear statement of the appraiser's concluding opinion of value expressed as appropriate to the assignment:

(a) A statement of a specific opinion of value; or

(b) A range of values; or

(c) A preliminary estimate which must include a statement that an opinion of value resulting from a formal report might be different and that difference might be material. (See also Standard Six, Preliminary Reports.)

4.6 Transmittal Letter. If a transmittal letter is used, it should include a summary of the engagement. It may be structured in the form of a letter, an executive summary, or a similar rendering. However, regardless of the structure used, if a transmittal is used, it shall refer to the report in a manner sufficient to discourage any attempt to remove and use the transmittal without the report.

4.7 Recordkeeping. An appraiser should retain written records of appraisal reports for a period of at least five (5) years after preparation or at least two (2) years after final disposition of any judicial proceeding in which the appraiser gave testimony, whichever period expires last.

STANDARD FIVE

5.0 FORMAL WRITTEN APPRAISAL REPORTS

5.1 Definition. The formal appraisal report is a comprehensive business appraisal report prepared to contain at a minimum, the requirements described within this standard. It is sometimes called the long form, narrative, or comprehensive report.

5.2 Conformity. The formal written report must comply with all applicable provisions of Business Appraisal Standards, Standard One, Professional Conduct and Ethics.

5.3 Mandatory Content. All formal appraisal reports shall minimally set forth the following items in a manner that is clear and not misleading, including detail sufficient to permit the reader to reasonably replicate the appraiser's procedures:

(a) Identify the client, and set forth a description of the business enterprise, security, or other tangible and/or intangible property being appraised.

(b) Form of the organization and if incorporated, the state of incorporation, together with a description, adequate to the assignment, of all classes of securities outstanding and a list of shareholders whose interest should, in the appraiser's judgment be specified. If a partnership, the type and the state of filing, together with a list of those partners, whether general or limited, whose interest should, in the appraiser's judgment, be specified.

(c) The purpose (standard of value) of the appraisal.

(d) The function (use) of the appraisal.

(e) The definition of the standard of value that is the purpose of the appraisal.

(f) The effective ("as of") date of the appraisal.

(g) The date the appraisal report was prepared.

(h) The report's assumptions and limiting conditions.

(i) The principal sources and references used by the appraiser.

(j) The consideration of relevant data regarding:

(i) The nature and history of the business.

(ii) The present economic conditions and the outlook affecting the business, its industry, and the general economy.

(iii) Past results, current operations, and future prospects of the business.

(iv) Past sales of interests in the business enterprise being appraised.

(v) Sales of similar businesses or interests therein, whether closely held or publicly held.

(vi) The valuation approaches/methods considered and rejected, the approaches/methods utilized, and the research, sources, computations, and reasoning that supports the appraiser's analyses, opinions, and conclusions.

(vii) Any special factors that affected the opinion of value. Such factors include, but are not limited to, buy-sell agreements, restrictive stock agreements, corporate articles, bylaws and resolutions, partnership agreements, litigation, regulatory compliance, or environmental hazards.

(viii) Applicable discounts and premiums such as minority interest, control, marketability or lack thereof.

(ix) When valuing a majority interest in a business on a "going concern" basis, consider whether the business' highest value may be achieved on a liquidation basis.

(k) A Certification consistent with the intent of section 1.25.

5.4 Distribution of Report. The formal report should include a clear statement of the expected distribution of the report.

5.5 Valuation Conclusion. The formal report must include a clear statement of the appraiser's concluding opinion of value expressed as appropriate to the assignment:

(a) A statement of a specific opinion of value; or

(b) A range of values.

5.6 Transmittal Letter. If a transmittal letter is used, it should include a summary of the engagement. It may be structured in the form of a letter, an executive summary, or a similar rendering. However, regardless of the structure, if used, the transmittal shall refer to the report in a manner sufficient to discourage any attempt to remove and use the transmittal without the report.

5.7 Recordkeeping. An appraiser should retain written records of appraisal reports for a period of at least five (5) years after preparation or at least two (2) years after final disposition of any judicial proceeding in which the appraiser gave testimony, whichever period expires last.

STANDARD SIX

6.0 PRELIMINARY REPORTS

6.1 Definition. A brief oral or written report reflecting the appraiser's limited opinion.

A preliminary report must clearly identify any valuation as a "limited" opinion of value as the appraiser has not performed the detailed investigation and analysis essential to a cogent appraisal. [See Standard 6.5]

6.2 Conformity. The preliminary report must comply with all applicable provisions of Business Appraisal Standards, Standard One, Professional Conduct and Ethics.

6.3 Usage. The preliminary report has use when a client desires the appraiser's limited opinion.

6.4 Disclosure. The presentation of a preliminary opinion without disclosing its limitations is unethical.

6.5 Departure. If an appraiser makes a preliminary report without including a clear statement that it is preliminary, there is the possibility a user of the report could accord the report and its limited opinion of value a greater degree of accuracy and reliability than is inherent in the preliminary report process. Therefore, all preliminary reports shall include a Statement of Departure in accordance with Standard 1.21(b). The Statement of Departure shall include a statement that the report is preliminary and the conclusion subject to change following a proper appraisal and that said change could be material.

6.6 Oral v. Written. All preliminary reports whether oral or written are subject to Standard Six.

6.7 Recordkeeping. An appraiser should retain written records of appraisal reports for a period of at least five (5) years after preparation or at least two (2) years after final disposition of any judicial proceeding in which the appraiser gave testimony, whichever period expires last.

CERTIFIED VALUATION ANALYST

The Certified Valuation Analyst (CVA) credential is issued by the National Association of Certified Valuation Analysts. Designees must hold a valid CPA certificate in a state jurisdiction, be a member of a state CPA Society of the AICPA, and complete a 40-hour training program prescribed by the association. Subsequently, the designee must complete a take home examination that is expected to take 30 to 50 hours to complete. There are no experience requirements as part of the initial certification process. Presently, there are more than 3,000 designated members, with a total membership of approximately 3,800 members.

There is an elected membership-based Executive Advisory Board with responsibility over the other boards, that includes veto power over the other board decisions. The Executive Advisory Board is accountable to the National Association of Certified Valuation Analysts' (NACVA) Board of Directors, whose composition is determined by the shareholders of NACVA. The board of directors has ultimate veto power over the executive advisory board, as well as the subsidiary boards. These boards are:

- Certification Board—responsible for credentials and certification policy and procedures. This committee is also responsible for recertification.
- Education Board—oversees the content of NACVA's curriculum and training, excluding conferences and symposiums.
- Membership Board—responsible for maintaining membership integrity, which includes enforcement of standards and member benefits.
- Government Valuation Analyst Board—responsible for supporting and overseeing NACVA's GVA designation.

The NACVA can be reached at

National Association of Certified Valuation Analysts
Brickyard Towers, Suite 330
1245 E. Brickyard Road
Salt Lake City, UT 84106
(801) 486-0600

NACVA has developed standards that are imposed on the membership. The standards are reproduced with permission of the association.

National Association of Certified Valuation Analysts

Professional Standards

As of May 31, 1998

CONTENTS

PREAMBLE

1.1 **General.** All members of the National Association of Certified Valuation Analysts (NACVA), an association of Certified Public Accountants and other business valuation professionals who perform valuation services, will comply with the standards and definitions of the AICPA's Code of Professional Conduct and Statement on Standards for Consulting Services (SSCS). Under the SSCS, litigation support and valuation services are considered "transaction" consulting services when the practitioner's function is to provide services related to a specific client transaction, generally in conjunction with a third party. NACVA members will comply with the business valuation standards as promulgated by the AICPA and NACVA. NACVA will adopt changes and interpretations of the standards when necessary to avoid conflicts and ambiguities between the Standards of Practice issued by the AICPA and NACVA.

1.2 **Conclusions of Value.** Conclusions of value can be expressed as an Opinion of Value, as a single number, or an Estimate of Value, as a single number or a range of values. Where, in the professional judgment of the Valuation Analyst, an Opinion of Value can not be expressed, the valuation analyst may report an Estimate of Value.

1.3 **Other Valuation Services.** Any other services provided by a valuation analyst are not subject to NACVA standards. Such services may, however, be subject to other standards, such as the SSCS.

1.4 **Litigation Engagements.** Generally, opinions of expert witnesses in litigation engagements are subject to discovery and/or cross-examination. In such engagements, when a valuation analyst is expressing an Opinion or Estimate of Value, all NACVA standards apply, except for the Reporting Standards.

1.5 **Purpose of Standards.** These standards have been developed to provide guidelines to the members of NACVA.

GENERAL STANDARDS

2.1 The following Rules from the **AICPA *Code of Professional Conduct*** shall apply (see Appendix No. 1):

2.1.1 *Rule 102—Integrity and Objectivity,* as modified by SSCS No. 1

2.1.2 *Rule 201—General Standards*

2.1.3 *Rule 202—Compliance with Standards*

2.1.4 *Rule 301—Confidential Client Information*

2.1.5 *Rule 302—Contingent Fees*

2.1.6 *Rule 501—Acts Discreditable*

2.2 The following Standards from the **AICPA *Statement on Standards for Consulting Services*** (SSCS) shall apply (see Appendix No. 2):

2.2.1 *Statement on Standards for Consulting Services No. 1 – Consulting Services: Definitions and Standards* (SSCS No. 1).

2.3 **Independence.** A valuation analyst shall not express an Opinion of Value or Estimate of Value unless the valuation analyst and the valuation analyst's firm state either of the following:

a. *"I (We) have no financial interest or contemplated financial interest in the property that is the subject of this report.*"; or

b. *"I (We) have a* (specified) *financial interest or contemplated financial interest in the property that is the subject of this report."*

A valuation analyst or the valuation analyst's firm may only state a conclusion of value associated with independence statement 2.3 b. above with the written consent of the client and full disclosure of the financial interest, present or contemplated, in the valuation analyst's report.

DEVELOPMENT STANDARDS

3.1 **Identification.** In developing a conclusion of value, a valuation analyst must define the assignment and determine the scope of work necessary by identifying the following:

a. Subject to be valued;
b. Interest to be valued;
c. Valuation date;
d. Purpose of the valuation;
e. Standard of value;
f. Premise of value;
g. Assumptions, limiting conditions and scope limitations; and
h. Ownership size, nature, restrictions, and agreements.

3.2. **Fundamental Analysis.** In developing a conclusion of value, the valuation analyst must consider and, when applicable, perform research and analysis of the following factors:

a. The nature of the business and the history of the enterprise;
b. The economic outlook in general and the condition and outlook of the specific industry in particular;

c. The book value of the interest to be valued and the financial condition of the business;
d. The earning capacity of the enterprise;
e. The dividend paying capacity of the enterprise;
f. Whether or not the enterprise has goodwill or other intangible value;
g. Sales of interests and the size of the block of interest to be valued; and
h. The market price of interests of enterprises engaged in the same or a similar line of business having interests actively traded in a free and open market.

3.3 **Scope Limitations.** In developing a conclusion of value, the valuation analyst must identify and evaluate limitations on the scope of work, which affect the research, analysis, and/or level of reliance the valuation analyst places on the valuation results.

3.4 **Valuation Approaches and Methods.** Valuation methods are commonly categorized into the asset-based approach, the market approach, the income approach, or a combination of the foregoing. Professional judgment must be used to select the methods to consider and the methodology that best indicates the value of the business interest.

3.5 **Financial Statement Adjustments.** The historical financial statements should be analyzed and, if appropriate, adjusted to reflect the hypothetically transferable asset value, income, cash flows, and/or benefit stream, as applicable, to be consistent with the valuation methodologies selected by the valuation analyst.

3.6 **Earnings Determination.** The valuation analyst should select the appropriate benefit stream, such as pre-tax or after-tax income and/or cash flows, and select appropriate projection models to be consistent with the valuation methodologies selected by the valuation analyst.

3.7 **Capitalization/Discount Rate.** The valuation analyst must consider appropriate capitalization/discount rates, if applicable. Capitalization/discount rates are used to convert a benefit stream to an indicated present value. Incorporated in these rates are components, which reflect the risk associated with the subject to be valued, such as an investment in a privately held entity, and the likelihood of realizing the benefit stream.

3.8 **Premiums and Discounts.** The valuation analyst must consider appropriate premiums and discounts, if applicable. These are factors that can impact value, such as the value of a specific business versus the value of a partial interest in a specific business. If applied, the base upon which the premiums and/or discounts are applied should be clearly defined.

3.9 **Documentation.** Documentation must be retained for all information relied upon in the valuation process. Inclusion of such information in the report satisfies this standard.

REPORTING STANDARDS

4.1 **Overview.** One of the final stages in the valuation process is the communication of the results of the valuation to the client or other user of the report. The form of any particular report will depend on the nature of the engagement, its purpose, its findings, and the needs of the decision-makers who receive and rely upon it. NACVA has adopted the following standards for reporting on valuations. The purpose of these standards is to establish minimum reporting criteria. The objective of these standards is to ensure consistency and quality of valuation reports issued by members of NACVA.

4.2 **Opinion of Value Reporting Standards.**

4.2.1 A written report expressing an Opinion of Value should be well written, communicate the results, and identify the information relied upon in the valuation process. The wording used in the report should effectively communicate important thoughts, methods, and reasoning, as well as identify the supporting documentation in a simple and concise manner, so that the user of the report can replicate the process followed by the valuation analyst.

4.2.2 Any reporting of an Opinion of Value must be in writing and set forth the following information concerning the valuation engagement and its results:

- Identification of the subject being valued;
- Description of the interest being valued;
- Valuation date;
- Report date;
- Purpose of the valuation;
- Identification of the standard of value;
- Identification of the premise of value;
- Identification of the assumptions, limiting conditions, and scope limitations;
- Conclusion as to Opinion of Value;
- Limitations on use of the report;
- Responsible valuation analyst signature;
- A statement of independence;

- Enterprise background and description;
- Ownership size, nature, restrictions, and agreements;
- A description of the fundamental analysis;
- Valuation approaches and methodologies;
- Historical financial statement summaries, when applicable;
- Adjustments to historical financial statements, when applicable;
- Adjusted financial statement summaries, when applicable; and
- Projected/forecasted financial statements including the underlying assumptions, when applicable.

4.2.3 *Assumptions, Limiting Conditions, and Scope Limitations.* All valuation cases vary as to specific assumptions, limiting conditions, and scope. The valuation analyst must identify material matters considered.

4.2.4 *Responsible Valuation Analyst Signature.* The valuation analyst who has primary responsibility for the conclusion of value must sign the report. If an individual does not sign the report, the individual or individuals who have primary responsibility for the Conclusion of Value must be identified in the report.

4.2.5 *Statement that the Report is in Accordance with NACVA Standards.* A statement similar to the following should be included in the valuation analyst's report:

"This valuation and report were completed in accordance with the National Association of Certified Valuation Analysts standards for conducting and reporting on business valuations."

4.3 **Estimate of Value Reporting Standards.** Valuation analysts may be requested to report a valuation conclusion where, in the professional judgment of the valuation analyst, an Opinion of Value cannot be expressed. In such instances, the valuation analyst may conclude that value can be expressed as a range of values or a single number, and label the value conclusion "Estimate of Value." Such a report must be in writing and include all the information required in a report on Opinion of Value plus the following statement:

"An Estimate of Value is not an Opinion of Value and such difference may be material."

4.4 **Litigation Engagements Reporting Standards.** Generally, reporting as an expert witness in the litigation engagement is subject to discovery and/or cross-examination. When in a litigation engagement and when the valuation analyst's expression of a conclusion of value is subject to discovery and/or cross-examination, NACVA's Reporting Standards do not apply.

OTHER GUIDELINES AND REQUIREMENTS

5.1 Besides NACVA's Professional Standards, valuation analysts may also find it necessary to consider guidelines and/or other requirements established by other organizations, such as

- Department of Labor (DOL)
- Internal Revenue Service (IRS)
- Federal and state laws
- The Appraisal Foundation (USPAP)

5.2 **Department of Labor.** The DOL has developed guidelines and other requirements that apply to business valuations for ESOPs. Accordingly, a report for the valuation of an ESOP should discuss applicable DOL guidelines and requirements.

5.3 **Internal Revenue Service.** The IRS has guidelines and other requirements regarding business valuations. Accordingly, a report for a tax-related valuation should discuss applicable IRS guidelines and other requirements.

5.4 **Federal and State Laws.** The valuation analyst must be aware of applicable federal and state law and judicial requirements.

5.5 **Uniform Standards of Professional Appraisal Practice.** The Appraisal Foundation has issued standards (USPAP) for appraisals. These standards are required to be followed for certain federally related transactions.

EFFECTIVE DATE

6.1 These Professional Standards are effective for engagements accepted on or after May 31, 1998.

NACVA Standards Committee*

Questions and Answers About NACVA's Standards

In response to frequently asked questions, to better explain how the new Standards apply to everyday practice and to begin a process of providing formal interpretations of the Standards, the Standards Committee is providing the following list of questions and answers. These answers are the Standards Committee's intent for interpretation of the Standards. The Membership Board, Executive Advisory Board and/or the Membership have not approved the Committee's answers. Significant disagreements, if any, that arise from the Standards Committee's published answers to Members' questions will be submitted to a formal interpretation or Standards amendment process.

98-1. ***What are the types of services recognized by NACVA's Standards?***

The new Standards recognize two broad types of services. These are "Conclusions of Value" and "Other Valuation Services." NACVA's Professional Standards apply specifically to "Conclusions of Value." The AICPA's general and consulting standards adequately cover all situations that are defined as "Other Valuation Services." Proper ethical conduct and due professional care standards apply to everything a CPA and a CVA does. We will be held accountable to the highest standards of conduct prescribed by each of the organizations to which we belong.

98-2. ***What are the levels for Conclusions of Value?***

Conclusions of Value include two recognized levels: "Opinion of Value" or "Estimate of Value." The Standards Committee did not invent these terms. They were defined and recognized by other appraisal organizations before NACVA was founded. An Opinion of Value is intended to be the most unambiguous expression of value and, therefore, can only be expressed as a single value. An Estimate of Value may be stated when, in the sole professional judgment of the Valuation Analyst, an Opinion of Value can not be stated. An Estimate of Value may be stated as a range of values.

*1998 National Association of Certified Valuation Analysts. (801) 486–0600. Reprinted with permission.

98-3. ***Are verbal reports of an Opinion of Value or Estimate of Value allowed under the new Standards?***

Verbal reports stating a Conclusion of Value (an "Opinion of Value" or an "Estimate of Value") are allowed only in a litigation engagement. However, other verbal expressions of value, which are not "Opinions of Value" or "Estimates of Value," are permitted under Other Valuation Services. NACVA's Professional Standards do not govern written or verbal expressions of value, which are not Conclusions of Value as defined in the Standards. Other Valuation Services are governed by the AICPA's general and consulting standards.

98-4. ***What are some examples of Other Valuation Services?***

Preliminary estimates of value, indications of value, calculations of value or consultations regarding the value of a business are examples of expressions of value permitted as Other Valuation Services. These expressions may be stated either verbally or in writing. The valuation analyst should use caution, however, to be certain that the client and other users do not consider these expressions or services as rendering an "Opinion of Value" or an "Estimate of Value." It is strongly recommended that written expressions in such situations include an appropriate disclaimer.

98-5. ***When does a member know that the litigation waiver applies? Aren't all engagements potentially litigation engagements?***

All engagements are not considered potential litigation engagements. The litigation waiver is only to apply when the Valuation Analyst is specifically engaged as an expert witness or a consultant in conjunction with a lawsuit, which either has been or is to be filed within the context of the engagement. For the litigation waiver to apply the Conclusion of Value must be subject to discovery and/or cross-examination. The General Standards and Development Standards apply to all engagements when expressing a Conclusion of Value. When not expressing a Conclusion of Value, the AICPA general and consulting standards apply.

98-6. ***Why can't an Opinion of Value be expressed as a range?***

An Opinion of Value is intended to be the most unambiguous expression of a Conclusion of Value. As such, a range of values is simply not appropriate. The Standards Committee believes that a range is better suited for an Estimate of Value, where the valuation analyst has some reservation as to the specific singular value of the business interest.

98-7. ***May a Valuation Analyst issue a "qualified" report?***

No. A Valuation Analyst must define the standard of value, premise of value, assumptions, limiting conditions, and scope limitations for each engagement. Disclosure of these items in the report is all the qualification that is allowed, or needed.

98-8. ***Does a financial interest include payments for other services performed by the Valuation Analyst or his firm, such as audit or tax preparation fees?***

The answer to this question is restated in 98-13.

98-9. ***What is NACVA's position on using the weighted average of different valuation methods?***

NACVA has taken no official position on the use of weighted averages. It should be noted, however, that the Internal Revenue Service, the Tax Court, and many noted authors discourage such a practice.

98-10. ***Can a firm sign a report as the Valuation Analyst?***

Yes. The individual or individuals who have primary responsibility for the Conclusion of Value must be identified, however. This issue was the item of most concern to NACVA's membership. The new standards allow for either an individual or firm signature of the report. The term "Valuation Analyst", as used in the Standards, refers to both the firm and/or the individuals involved.

98-11. ***What happened to NACVA's Glossary of Terms?***

For the time being, NACVA has dropped development of its Glossary in favor of a group effort to develop a single Glossary for the benefit of NACVA, the AICPA, the ASA, and the IBA. The group is called the C.L.A.R.E.N.C.E. Group. It expects to have a joint Glossary in the near future.

98-12. ***Why did NACVA eliminate the "short-form" report?***

The appropriate length of discussion for any item in a written report was never established by NACVA under any prior version of our standards. The reference to short-form or long-form in the prior standards was therefore meaningless. The new standards avoid misunderstandings and misconceptions by eliminating use of the terms "short-form" and "long-form." The result is complete freedom for members to vary the length of discussion of each item included in the report and the format of the report as necessary to clearly reflect the specific circumstances. The member should use his or her professional judgment. NACVA's emphasis is on the quality of the report and on proper disclosure, not on length.

98-13. ***Are NACVA's Standards for Independence different than the AICPA Standards for Audits, Compilations, and Reviews?***

Yes. NACVA's Standard for Independence follows USPAP and other independence standards, which are established and generally accepted in appraisal practice. The term "financial interest" in NACVA's standards includes a direct equity ownership interest in the subject or client, a loan or note payable from the subject or client and/or an account receivable in excess of one year from the subject or client. If a member or the member's firm has a financial interest in the subject, he or she may still express a conclusion of value, but the financial interest must be fully disclosed in the report. The fact that a member or the member's firm performs other services for the subject or client, including audit or tax preparation services, does not impair independence under NACVA's Standards.

98-14. ***What is the difference between a consulting valuation engagement and an engagement that includes a Conclusion of Value?***

NACVA's Development and Reporting Standards apply only when a member is expressing a Conclusion of Value. A Conclusion of Value is stated as either: 1) an *"Opinion of Value,"* or 2) an *"Estimate of Value."* In such cases, a member is required to fully comply with all NACVA Standards. The AICPA General and Consulting Standards apply when a member is providing any other type of valuation service, such as calculating a value or assisting in determining an asking or offering price for a particular business. Results or conclusions in consulting engagements may be stated either orally or in writing. In consulting engagements, do not use the terms: *"Opinion of Value"* or *"Estimate of Value."* A member may use terms such as "indicated value," "indicated asking price," "indicated offering price," "preliminary estimate of value," "calculated value," etc. NACVA's Development and Reporting Standards do not apply to consulting engagements. If the results of a consulting engagement are stated in writing, NACVA strongly recommends that the writing contain an appropriate disclaimer, such as the following:

> *This engagement does not provide a Conclusion of Value as defined by the Professional Standards of the National Association of Certified Valuation Analysts. More analysis and/or disclosure would be required*

to express such a conclusion. Therefore, this engagement should not be referred to, used, or relied upon outside of the specific consulting purpose for which it was stated.

98-15. ***Do NACVA's Standards apply to reports for valuing economic losses or damages?***

No. NACVA, the AICPA, and USPAP do not have specific standards applicable to writing such reports. However, the AICPA Code of Professional Conduct and Statements on Standards for Consulting Services (SSCS) apply to everything an AICPA member or a NACVA member does. If the report is used in Federal Court, Rule 26(a)(2)(B) may be applicable.

98-16. ***Do other AICPA reporting requirements, i.e., SSARS, apply when a CPA includes historical or prospective financial statements in the valuation report?***

There is an exemption in the Statements on Standards for Accounting and Review Services (SSARS) for financial statements submitted in conjunction with litigation (AICPA Professional Standards, AR Section 9100.77). NACVA has a similar exemption for reporting before a trier of fact. Outside of litigation engagements, however, there is currently no authoritative answer to be found. Some experts say SSARS is applicable, some experts say it is not. The Accounting and Review Services Committee of the AICPA is expected to release an exposure draft providing guidance sometime soon. Until then, the treatment of such financial statements in a valuation report is subject to the professional judgment of the member. Disclosure of who prepared the statements is required to be included in the valuation report, however.

Chapter 16

Marketing the Divorce Practice

Divorce litigation is still one of the great growth industries in the United States. Expectations are that this trend will continue into the next century. As you may be aware, most accounting publications have indicated that litigation support services and business valuation have been two of the fastest growing consulting services for CPA firms over the last five years. Is there a correlation? We think there is. In our many lectures and teaching sessions around the country, we find that most individuals who are involved with business valuation training work mainly in the area of marital litigation.

The marital litigation market is very much of a local based marketplace. Although many marital disputes have need for forensic accountants and/or business valuation experts, most of these engagements are relatively small and are best served by practitioners in the same area as the litigation. Certainly there are very large divorce cases where significant expertise is required of the valuation expert, but these are the exceptions, not the norm. In short, the local practitioners generally handle the local cases.

Keeping that in mind, it should be obvious that the major focus of any marketing program should start in your local service area. We have regular contact with family lawyers from all over the United States. Many of these practitioners handle the day-to-day marital litigation in their home location. When we have the opportunity to discuss with these lawyers the types of services that CPAs and credentialed business valuation individuals can provide to them, many times we are told that no one in their community seems to be interested in this work. Interestingly enough, when we talk to CPAs, they tell us that the local attorneys use out-of-town experts. Strangely enough, many times both the attorney and the CPA come from the same market area. Is the attorney using out-of-town experts because he or she does not want to use the local expert, or is it because the attorney does not know that the local CPA is interested and qualified to do this type of work?

To begin our journey into marketing these services, first let us examine the types of services that we can provide, and then be certain that we have a clear understanding of what attorneys are looking for when they retain a marital litigation/business valuation expert.

TYPE OF SERVICES

Confining ourselves only to marital litigation matters, the CPA is uniquely qualified to provide a number of services to the parties to a divorce and the attorneys involved. Remember, not every service can and should be provided by every CPA who is interested in marital litigation matters. Some CPAs do not get involved in any accounting or tax aspects of marital litigation. As we review the myriad of services required in marital litigation, keep one important premise in mind. You may not be everything to everyone, on every case. Know your strengths as well as your limitations.

Some of the services required in most marital litigation matters and which are many times performed by CPAs include:

- Determination of net spendable income available to the parties. It is very interesting how little people really know about the differences between what they believe they earn and what they have to spend. When we get into the area of discretionary spending, this distinction becomes even more blurred. How many times have you heard somebody say that they made *x* dollars on their W-2, without a recognition that the actual dollars received were significantly less than *x* dollars. Many people have no idea how to read a tax return, and the adjusted gross income numbers are meaningless. A net spendable income analysis can allow the parties and their respective attorneys to know what dollars are available to be divided between the parties.
- Hand in hand with the net spendable income analysis is the standard of living analysis. How many times have you seen a situation where there are much lower reported earnings than the apparent lifestyle would seem to consume? What about the self-employed individual who shows little or no profits on the Schedule C, yet lives a fairly nice lifestyle. Or the owner of the small corporation who is able to finance many of his or her personal costs through expenses that are paid from the corporation. A standard of living analysis is necessary in many marital litigation matters.
- Asset tracing services may be required where there is either premarital/postmarital property, or where there is a community property issue, with claims of separate property.
- Tax advice and counsel. It may seem that the complexity of taxation as it relates to divorce has become simpler, but we are not sure that we agree with that premise. With the issues of basis in property, as well as other issues relating to taxable

versus nontaxable transactions, most middle-sized divorces today require some level of tax advice.

- Business valuation. Many divorce cases that may need the foregoing services do not need business valuation services. But where the parties do in fact have an interest in a closely held business, most states require a valuation of that property for purposes of the property settlement.

Keeping that listing of services in mind and prior to beginning your marketing efforts, determine what services you feel that you are qualified to provide in your marketplace. Once that has been determined, then you can focus your marketing.

WHAT ATTORNEYS LOOK FOR

In our many discussions with lawyers across the country we have asked what they look for when they are involved with the selection of an expert witness. Over the years the following four responses continue to surface:

- **Qualifications.** First and foremost, most attorneys say that they are interested in the qualifications of the potential expert. What does that expert possess in terms of training and experience that will provide the attorney and the underlying client with benefit? As mentioned previously, the attorneys do not expect every expert to be expert in every area of the potential matters, but they do need to know what you can and cannot do. What is your prior experience? What types of services have you provided in the past? If this is the first time that you are going to provide a specific service, what specialized training have you completed that would qualify you to perform the service needed on this particular engagement?
- **Designations.** Do you have any specialty designations? How did you get them? What do they mean? What distinguishes one designation from another? How many other people have this designation? This has become a much more heated topic. There have been several tax court decisions over the last few years where the court stated that just being a CPA did not indicate that there was competency to provide business valuation services. This trend seems to be escalating.
- **Presentation Skills.** Presentation skills are very important to an expert witness. You can have all of the business valuation expertise in existence, but if you are unable to convey that knowledge and expertise, both in writing as well as orally, you are not very valuable to the attorney. In the long view, it is your presentation skills that will get you the second, third, and fourth engagement in your local community.
- **Credibility.** If your presentation is not credible, it will not be believed. If it is not believed, it will have little or no positive impact on the outcome of the marital litigation. We must look at the concept of objectivity and integrity spelled out in the

American Institute of Certified Public Accountants (AICPA) standards. Some of the attributes that help the expert maintain credibility are:

- **Objective and Unbiased.** Under the Rule 702 definition of an expert, you are testifying to assist the trier of fact with issues in which you have special skills. You do not represent either party to the matter but are expected to be unbiased in the presentation of your opinions.
- **Beyond Reproach.** You cannot be thought of as the expert who provides the "made as instructed" opinion. People must respect you for both your technical competence and your fairness.
- **Trustworthy.** You will be dealing in highly emotional situations. You will also have access to a great deal of personal, confidential information. Both the attorneys and the clients have to trust in your judgment and common sense.
- **A Voice of Reason.** You are not being asked to be an expert so that you can have the highest valuation conclusion, nor are you expected to bring in the lowest valuation conclusion. You are expected to be reasonable. Remember the old saying "Bulls make money, bears make money, but pigs get taken to slaughter."
- **Wise.** As an expert, in order to maintain your credibility, you will be called upon to demonstrate your wisdom.

Now that we know what the attorneys are looking for in an expert witness, let us examine how we can build a marketing plan to help us sell these services.

IDENTIFY THE MARKET AND THE COMPETITION

What is your potential market? Depending on where you practice, the market could be geographically very small, with a large population, or it could be very broad geographically, with a small population. Practicing in Manhattan, New York, requires different marketing strategies than practicing in Manhattan, Kansas. It is different because of the density of the population as well as the density of competition. The first step in any successful marketing program is to determine the market segment that you want to reach. If you want to provide marital litigation services, it seems clear that your target market is attorneys who handle divorce cases. Obviously, the more cases that any specific lawyer handles increases the chances that that attorney would need to retain expert services. Most local bar associations publish membership directories that often list areas of concentration or specialization. Get a copy of your local directory and pinpoint the individuals and firms that you want to target. Once you have that information, you can plan how to get your name in front of those people.

At the same time that you are identifying your targets, you should be identifying your local competition. In fact, your local competition might be a good referral source for you. Discuss how your competitor handles cases where there is a conflict. Where does the case get referred? Perhaps you can work out a long-term working relationship to help on those conflict situations.

LET THE USERS KNOW YOU WANT THE WORK

Many attorneys do not know that qualified local people can provide these services. Your first marketing goal must be to get out the message that you are qualified and you do want to provide these types of services. This is not the time to be overly shy. You need to prepare a curriculum vitae (CV) that demonstrates why the attorney should hire you. Think about the qualities that attorneys look for when selecting an expert witness, and try to tailor your promotional materials to emphasize those qualities.

MAKING CONTACT

The most successful contact is a personal contact. Nothing can replace the opportunity for you to meet and discuss your qualifications on a one-to-one basis. How do you get the opportunity to meet with the attorney? First, if you already know the attorney (perhaps you have mutual clients), it should be no problem for you to invite the attorney to a breakfast or lunch meeting. If you currently provide marital litigation services to an attorney, ask if he will refer you to his colleagues. If you do not know the attorney, perhaps a good approach would be to send a personal letter, and then follow up with a telephone call to ask for the opportunity to meet. Keep the letter very short and to the point. Remember, you want the recipient to read the letter rather than toss it in the trash.

During the initial meeting be certain that you have a copy of your CV with you, and be prepared to discuss your qualifications and experience. Explain what you have done to make yourself a qualified expert. If possible, be prepared to provide references, either other attorneys that you have worked with or perhaps clients that you have provided similar services to, but in a nonlitigation environment.

Speaking Engagements

There is no better way to demonstrate your presentation skills than having the opportunity to make presentations that discuss areas of your expertise. How do you get the opportunity to make these types of presentations? Think about all of the various organizations that have regular meetings and that have speakers at those meetings. This can range from local bar association meetings, state bar meetings, continuing legal education programs, to Rotary or other service clubs. Believe me, if you know anyone who is the program chairman of a group, that individual is always looking for someone to provide an entertaining and informative discussion. Do not use the speaking opportunity to be a self-promoting commercial, but use the program to provide useful information. What you really are demonstrating are your presentation skills.

Contact the state bar or whatever other organization provides continuing legal education for the bar. Volunteer to lead programs, or better yet, to develop a program in an area of need. Every opportunity that you have to appear in front of your target audience is an additional opportunity to demonstrate your skills in front of your potential clients.

Volunteer or Pro Bono Work

In many jurisdictions there is a need for these types of services in small divorces where the parties might not have the financial ability to retain experts. Many bar associations have committees that provide pro bono legal services for these types of matters. Consider letting the local bar and/or the local court know that you are willing to provide volunteer services in these cases. Usually the issues are relatively simple, and the time commitment is not excessive. However, this type of activity will give you the opportunity to meet members of the bar who are working in the same areas that you want to be involved in. Plus, you are providing a significant benefit to your community.

Newsletters or Brochures

An initial caveat before we continue: Newsletters, brochures and other marketing tools are just that, they are tools. They rarely create opportunity, but they do reinforce contacts. If you are going to use a newsletter, make certain that it is a quality piece that will be read by the attorney. There are two ways to have a newsletter: You can purchase one, or you can create your own, in-house. Each of these approaches has its own downside.

A commercially prepared newsletter may be very generic and not meet the needs of your individual practice. In addition, many commercially prepared newsletters are territory limited, and you may not be able to purchase a specific newsletter because one of your competitors already has purchased the market.

If you choose to create your own newsletter, there are actually two problems you must overcome. The first is the time commitment to create, write, and edit a quality newsletter. There must be a significant commitment to this activity. Second, you must determine how often you want the newsletter to be distributed, and then set firm deadlines on the production of each newsletter. If you are going to successfully use a newsletter, your audience must come to expect the receipt of that newsletter and look forward to it.

Brochures and other advertising pieces tend to be "leave behind" pieces, and are useful to remind the attorney about what services you can provide. We do not believe that these pieces create new relationships. That takes place with personal contact.

SUMMARY

If you want your practice to grow, you will need to market that practice. Marketing is not a generic, one-size-fits-all approach. You need to tailor your efforts to the local market conditions as well as the types of services that you want to provide. Nothing replaces personal contact in acquiring new clients and expanding your practice.

Appendix A

Library and Reference Materials

The following library and other reference materials are useful to the business valuation professionals. Certainly every personal library does not require every volume listed. The more sophisticated the valuation practice that you have, the more sophisticated your library needs to be. Refer to Chapter 5, Data Collection and Analysis where some of these materials are discussed in further detail. Some of the newsletters are very timely in a business valuation practice. We strongly recommend Shannon Pratt's *Business Valuation Update* to provide you with monthly updates concerning the business valuation community. In addition, *Fair Share* provides a focus on marital litigation issues. The *Business Valuation Review* is a very worthwhile quarterly publication that presents both good practice tips and very scholarly articles on emerging business valuation techniques. We have attempted to provide a telephone number where you can obtain the materials. You must understand that new materials are being published on a regular basis.

BOOKS

Asset Valuation, James R. Eck, William Gary Baker, David J. Ensign, Shepard's/McGraw-Hill (800) 262-4729.

Business Valuation Body of Knowledge, Shannon P. Pratt, John Wiley & Sons, Inc., (800) 825-8763.

Conduction of a Valuation of a Closely-Held Business, AICPA Consulting Services Practice Aid 93-3.

Cost of Capital, Shannon P. Pratt, John Wiley & Sons, Inc. (800) 825-8763.

Equitable Distribution Law and Practice, Gerald D. McLellan, John Wiley & Sons, Inc. (800) 825-8763.

Financial Valuation: Businesses and Business Interests, James H. Zukin, Maxwell MacMillan.

Guide to Business Valuations, Jay E. Fishman, Shannon P. Pratt, J. Clifford Griffith, D. Keith Wilson, Practitioners Publishing Company, (800) 323-8724.

Guide to Divorce Engagements, Shannon P. Pratt, et al., Practitioners Publishing Company, (800) 323-8724.

Handbook of Business Valuation, Thomas L. West, Jeffrey D. Jones, John Wiley & Sons, Inc., (800) 825-8763.

How to Price a Profitable Company, 2nd Edition, Paul Baron, American Management Association, (800) 262-9699.

Intellectual Property—Licensing and Joint Venture Profit Strategies, Gordon V. Smith, Russell L. Parr, John Wiley & Sons, Inc., (800) 825-8763.

Intellectual Property Infringement Damages, a Litigation Support Handbook, Russell L. Parr, John Wiley & Sons, Inc., (800) 825-8763.

IRS Guide for Income, Estate and Gift Taxes, Commerce Clearing House.

Quantifying Marketability Discounts, Z. Christopher Mercer, Peabody Publishing, LP, (901) 685-2120.

Technology Licensing—Corporate Strategies for Maximizing Value, Russell L. Parr, Patrick H. Sullivan, John Wiley & Sons, Inc., (800) 825-8763.

Understanding Business Valuation—A Practical Guide to Valuing Small to Medium Sized Businesses, Gary R. Trugman, AICPA (888) 777-7077

Valuation—Measuring and Managing the Value of Companies, Tom Copeland, Tim Koller, Jack Murrin, John Wiley & Sons, Inc., (800) 825-8763.

Valuation of the Closely Held Business, 2nd Edition, James Alerding, Research Institute of America

Valuation and Distribution of Marital Property, Matthew Bender & Company, Inc., (800) 223-1940.

Valuation of Divorce Assets, Barth H. Goldberg, West Publishing Company, (800) 328-4880.

The Valuation Expert in Divorce Litigation—a Handbook for Attorneys and Accountants, Robert B. Moriarty, David J. Zaumeyer, American Bar Association, (800) 285-221.

The Valuation of Hospitals and Medical Centers—Analyzing and Measuring Hospital Assets and Market Value, James J. Unland, Probus Publishing Company, (800) 998-4644.

Valuation of Intellectual Property and Intangible Assets, 2nd Edition, Gordon V. Smith, Russell L. Parr, John Wiley & Sons, Inc., (800) 825-8763.

The Valuation of Privately-Held Businesses, Irving L. Blackman, Probus Publishing Company, (800) 998-4644.

Valuation Strategies in Divorce, Robert D. Feder, John Wiley & Sons, Inc., (800) 825-8763.

Value of Pensions in Divorce, Marvin Snyder, John Wiley & Sons, Inc., (800) 825-8763.

Valuing Accounting Practices, Robert F. Reilly, Robert P. Schweihs, John Wiley & Sons, Inc., (800) 825-8763.

Valuing a Business, The Analysis and Appraisal of Closely Held Companies, 3rd Edition, Shannon P. Pratt, Richard F. Riley, Robert P. Schweihs, Irwin Professional Publishing, (800) 634-3966.

Valuing Financial Institutions, Z. Christopher Mercer, Business One Irwin, (800) 634-3966.

Valuing Professional Practices and Licenses: A Guide for the Matrimonial Practitioner, Ronald L. Brown, Prentice Hall, (800) 922-0579.

Valuing Small Businesses and Professional Practices, 3rd Edition, Shannon P. Pratt, Richard F. Riley, Robert P. Schweihs, McGraw-Hill, (800) 262-4729.

PERIODICALS AND DATABASES

Almanac of Business and Industrial Financial Ratios, Leo Troy, Prentice Hall, (800) 922-0579.

Bizcomps, Jack Sanders, Asset Business Appraisal, (619) 457-0366

Business Valuation Review, the American Society of Appraisers, (303) 758-6148.

Business Valuations by Industry, Walter Jurek, Quality Services Company, (800) 266-3888.

Construction Industry Annual Financial Survey, the Construction Financial Management Association, (609) 683-5000.

Cost of Capital Quarterly, Ibbotson Associates, (312) 616-1620.

CPA Expert, AICPA (888) 777-7077

CPA Litigation Service Counselor, Harcourt Brace, (800) 831-7799.

Done Deals, World M&A Network, (202) 628-7767.

Executive Compensation Reports, Harcourt Brace, (800) 831-7799.

Fair Share, Aspen Law Publishing, (800) 638-8437.

Federal Reserve Bulletin, the Board of Governors of the Federal Reserve System, (202) 452-3244 or 3245.

Federal Tax Valuation Digest, Idelle A. Howitt, Warren, Gorham & Lamont of the RIA Group, (800) 950-1210.

Financial Studies of the Small Business, Financial Research Associates, (800) 422-3782.

Goodwill Registry, The Healthcare Group, Inc., (610) 828-3658.

Handbook of Small Business Valuation Formulas and Rules of Thumb, Glenn Desmond, Valuation Press, (800) 544-2678.

Merger and Acquisition Sourcebook, Quality Services Company, (800) 266-3888.

Mergerstat Review, Mergerstat, Houlihan, Lokey Howard & Zukin, (800) 455-8871.

Mergerstat Transaction Roster, Mergerstat, Houlihan, Lokey Howard & Zukin, (800) 455-8871.

Officer Compensation Report, Panel Publishers, a division of Aspen Publishers, Inc., (212) 597-0200.

Partnership Spectrum, Partnership Profiles, Inc., (800) 634-4614.

Physician Marketplace Statistic, the American Medical Association, (800) 621-8335.

Physicians Compensation and Production Survey, the Medical Group Management Association, (303) 799-1111.

Pratt's Stats, Business Valuation Resources, (888) BUS-VALU.

Principia, Morningstar, Inc., (312) 424-4288.

RMA Annual Statement Studies, Robert Morris Associates, (800) 677-7621.

Shannon Pratt's Business Valuation Update, Business Valuation Resources, (888) 287-8258.

Socioeconomic Characteristics of Medical Practices, the American Medical Association, (800) 621-8335.

Standard Industrial Classification Manual, Executive Office of the President Office of Management and Budget, (202) 512-1800.

Stocks, Bonds, Bills and Inflation, Ibbotson Associates, (312) 616-1620.

The Survey of Dental Practices—Income from the Private Practice of Dentistry, American Dental Association, (312) 440-2568.

The Survey of Law Firm Economics, Altman Weil Pensa Publications, Inc., (610) 359-9900.

U.S. Global Trade Outlook 1995–2000, U.S. Department of Commerce, (202) 512-1800.

WEFA Industrial Monitor, John Wiley & Sons, Inc., (800) 825-8763.

Appendix B

Forms

SAMPLE ENGAGEMENT LETTER

Date

Name
Company
Address
Address

Re: **Valuation Engagement re XYZ, Inc., as of _____**

Dear Mr.:

This letter will confirm our engagement by you to provide professional services related to the above-captioned matter. Our engagement is for the purposes of determining the fair market value of a __% interest, as well as a __% interest in XYZ, Inc. as of ____________. The purpose of our valuation is for a marital dissolution. Our report will not address any potential environmental matters unless they are brought to our attention. In that event, you agree that appropriate environmental experts will be retained, and copies of those reports will be provided to us for inclusion in our valuation report.

We will use our professional judgment in determining what records and documents will be reviewed and relied on for the purpose of forming our opinions. Any financial information provided to us will be accepted at its face value. We will not provide any attestation to those financial statements. Appropriate firm resources will be used on this engagement, as we deem necessary. Mr. ____, a partner in the ______ office, will be the client service partner. Ms. _________, a partner in the firm, will be responsible for the valuation engagement.

It is expressly understood that any reports or other documents produced to us or by us will not be provided to any third parties, with the exception of the parties to this matter, and their respective Counsel, without our written consent.

Our fees for this engagement will be billed at our standard hourly rates. Ms. _____'s billing rate is $___.00 per hour, with lower billing rates for other engagement personnel. We will also bill for all out-of-pocket expenses incurred as part of this engagement.

It is impossible to accurately estimate fees in matters such as this. However, we have estimated that the cost of the valuation will range between $______ and $______. Fees will be billed on a monthly basis, and are due and payable upon presentation. Due to the prohibitions of our profession regarding contingent fee arrangements, we will discontinue an engagement where substantial fees are outstanding. Fees unpaid 30 days past the billing date are subject to an interest charge of 1.5% per month. In the event that any collection action is required to collect unpaid balances due us, reasonable attorney fees and costs shall be recoverable by us.

Our valuation services are provided on a retainer basis. We request a retainer fee of $_____, which will be applied to the final billing. Any unused portion of the retainer will be returned to you upon our collection of all outstanding fees and costs related to this matter.

If the above accurately reflects the terms and conditions of our engagement, please sign the enclosed duplicate of this letter and return it to Ms. ______. We look forward to working with you on this matter.

Very truly yours,

CPA Firm

CPA Firm
Address
Address

Gentlemen:

The above accurately reflects our engagement agreement and I accept the above terms and conditions.

____
Name

Date ____________

Date Mailed or Delivered ______________________________ *Office Use Only*
*Date Returned*______ *Client #*_____

SAMPLE VALUATION INFORMATION QUESTIONNAIRE

Contents

The Questionnaire has been completed by____
(Print name and title)

The foregoing individual or individuals represent that the information provided in the questionnaire, as well as the information provided in the form of financial reports, legal documents, and any other form of information, is complete, accurate, and the most current information available in relation to the valuation date.

Signature ____ Date ________________

Instructions

1. All listed questions are as of the valuation date unless instructed otherwise. If more than one entity is being valued, this questionnaire will need to be completed for each entity.
2. All listed questions must be answered or this form will be considered incomplete and not valid. Some questions may not pertain to your business. Please read the question, and if it is not relative to your business indicate with N/A.
3. If sufficient space has not been provided on the form, please respond on a separate attached sheet with the number and letter (if applicable) of the question being answered.
4. There is a section of this questionnaire that requests certain information. Not all requests will pertain to your business. Please indicate by checking the boxes provided if the information requested has been provided, not provided, or is not applicable. Also, if more than one entity is being valued we will need each request answered for each entity.

Information about the Business

Description

1. Name of business ____
   a. Address of business ____
      ____
   b. Telephone number ____
   c. Fax number ____
   d. Primary contact at the business ______________________________
   e. Date for which valuation is requested __________________________
   f. Date of filing (Marital Dissolution cases only) ____________________
   g. What is the purpose of this valuation? i.e. Estate tax, gifting, divorce, purchase, etc. ____
   h. Number of years the business has been in operation _____

2. On a separate sheet, please provide a complete and detailed history and description of the business including nature of the business, operations, products, etc.
3. a. Have any valuations of this business been prepared in the five years prior to the date of this valuation, and up through the date of completion of this questionnaire? **Yes_____ No_____**
   b. **If 3a is yes, please provide copies.**
4. Please list your CPA firm, corporate counsel, and primary banking relationships:
   ____
   ____
   ____

Structure and Ownership Information

5. a. Is the entity a (please check one):
   _____ Regular corporation _____"S" corporation
   _____ Partnership _____ Proprietorship
   _____ Other (describe) _____ Limited liability company
   b. Please list the owners, their ownership at the valuation date, and their relationship to each other: (**Please use Schedule A attached.**)
   c. Has the ownership changed since the date of valuation, or anytime in the five years preceding the date of valuation? **Yes_____ No_____**
   d. **If 5c is yes, please complete Schedule B attached.**
   e. Are there any members of the board of directors who are not owners? **Yes _____ No _____**
   f. If 5e is yes, please complete the following:

Name	*Title*	*Relationship to Business*	*Years of Service on the Board*
________	________	________	________
________	________	________	________

   g. Is the present board different from the board at the valuation date? If yes, please complete the following schedule. _________

Name	*Prior Title*	*New Title*	*Relationship to the Business*	*Date of Change*
________	________	________	________	________
________	________	________	________	________
________	________	________	________	________

   h. Are the officers and key management people in good health? **Yes _____ No _____**
   If no, please explain. ______________________________________
   ____
   ____

6. Equity structure and transactions
   a. If the company is a corporation, does it have more than one class of stock? **Yes _____ No _____ N/A _____ If yes, please provide details of the structure of each class of stock.**
   b. If the Company is a partnership, does it have a partnership agreement? **Yes _____ No _____**
   c. Does the entity have a buy/sell or stock redemption agreement? **Yes _____ No _____**
   d. If other than a corporation, are there any options or similar agreements to sell, trade, or offer equity interests? **Yes _____ No _____ If yes, please provide details.**
   e. Are there any restrictions on the sale or transfer of securities or equity interests in the business of any equity holders? **Yes _____ No _____ If yes, please provide details.**
   f. Is there a legend on stock certificates of the business? **Yes _____ No_____**
   g. Has the company entered into any negotiations and/or offers of equity in another business? **Yes _____ No _____ If yes, please provide details.**

Information about Sales/Customers

7. a. How does the Company sell, advertise, or market its products or services?
   ____
   ____
   ____
   b. Does the business sell through salespersons or manufacturer's representatives, distributors, or other means? ______________________
   ____
   ____
   ____
8. Please detail standard sales terms, discounts offered, return and allowance policies. ____
   ____
   ____
9. Are any sales on consignment? **Yes _____ No _____**
10. Does the business warehouse its inventory? **Yes _____ No _____**
11. a. Are maintenance agreements included in the sales terms? **Yes _____ No _____** If so, please provide copies.
    b. Are express or implied warranties offered in the sales terms? **Yes _____ No _____**
12. a. Please describe your typical customer. ______________________
    ____
    ____

b. Why do you feel these customers buy from you? ____________________

____

____

c. Please describe your current customer relationships—good, bad, or fair? Explain.

____

____

____

____

____

d. Please list the names of the company's five (5) largest customers and their location, sales volume, and the number of years the customer has been with your company on the following schedule:

Name	*City/State/Location*	*Sales Volume*	*Number of Years as a Customer*
1.			
2.			
3.			
4.			
5.			

e. Has the business gained or lost any business from a principal customer in the past five years? **Yes** _____ **No** _____

f. If 12e is yes, please complete the following schedule:

Gained or Lost	*Customer Name*	*Year Gained or Lost*	*Annual Sales Volume*	*Why was business lost*
1.				
2.				
3.				
4.				
5.				
6.				
7.				
8.				

g. How will these gains or losses affect future operations? _____

13. a. Has the business ever experienced product liability problems?
Yes _____ **No** _____ **N/A** _____

b. If 13a is yes, please explain.________________________________

____

____

14. Does the business lease any of its products to customers?
Yes _____ **No** _____**N/A** _____

15. Does the business have any foreign business? **Yes** _____ **No** _____ **N/A** _____

a. If yes, what is the percentage? ______________________________

16. Are any new products planned or anticipated? **Yes** _____ **No** _____ **N/A** _____
17. Are any existing products or lines of business planned to be discontinued? **Yes** _____ **No** _____
    If question 16 or 17 is yes, please provide detail. ____________________
    ____
    ____

Information about Personnel

18. How many people are employed by your business?
    full time _____
    part time _____
    seasonal _____
19. Briefly describe past and current employee relations (that is, contentious, harmonious, strike, etc.). Also, discuss employee turnover and indicate whether any of the employees are unionized. ____________________
    ____
    ____
    ____
    ____
20. Are there any deferred compensation arrangements between the business and owners, employees, or independent contractors? **Yes** _____ **No** _____ **If yes, please describe in detail.** ____________________
21. Do any employees have employment contracts? **Yes**_____ **No** _____ **If yes, please provide copies of the contracts.**
22. Please list the ten highest paid nonofficer employees, their annual compensation, and their position in the Company

Name	*Position*	*Annual Compensation*
____________	________	$ ________
____________	________	$ ________
____________	________	$ ________
____________	________	$ ________
____________	________	$ ________
____________	________	$ ________
____________	________	$ ________
____________	________	$ ________
____________	________	$ ________

23. Please list any qualified or nonqualified retirement plans (keogh, corporate pension, or profit sharing, etc.).
    ____
    ____
    a. If there is a retirement plan, is it a defined benefit plan? ____________________
    ____

b. If so, is it overfunded or underfunded?
By what amount? _____ Please provide actuarial report.

24. **Compensation**
    a. For each of the five years dating back from the date of valuation, please list the information requested on attached **Schedule C** regarding each officer, shareholder, and/or equity owner:
    b. Is compensation paid to any related party who is not an officer or shareholder (i.e., spouse, parent, or child)? **Yes** _____ **No**_____
    If 24b is yes, please provide the same details as requested on **Schedule C** attached.
    c. How are bonuses determined?____
    ____
    ____
    d. Please list the types of fringe benefits received by any equity owner, officer, or related party and the annual cost and/or value of such benefits.__________
    ____
    ____

Information about Related Parties

25. a. Does the business lease property or equipment, business or personal, from/to related parties? **Yes** _____ **No** _____**If yes, please provide details.**
    b. Is it leased at market rates? **Yes** _____ **No** _____**If not, please explain.**
    ____
    ____
26. Has any individual or entity guaranteed any debts or liabilities of the business?
    Yes _____ **No** _____ **If yes, please provide details.**
27. Has the business guaranteed debts and liabilities of another individual or entity?
    Yes _____ **No**_____ **If yes, please provide details.**
28. Please detail any other related party transactions, contracts, etc., and whether they are at market rates. If not at market, please indicate what market is. _____
    ____
29. Please provide details of any loans that the business has to/from its shareholders, directors, officers, employees, or related parties.

Loan from *business date*	*To whom*	*Amount*	*Interest Rate*	*Maturity Date*
________	________	________	________	________
________	________	________	________	________
________	________	________	________	________
________	________	________	________	________
________	________	________	________	________

Please provide copies of loan documents.

Information about the Industry and Economy

30. Please provide a detailed description of the industry or industries in which the business operates. ____________________

____

31. What are the SIC (Standard Industry Classification) codes applicable to this business? ____________________

____

32. What industry organizations does the business belong to? (Please fill out the following schedule.)

Name	*City/ State Location (if known)*	*Telephone (if known)*	*Contact (if known)*	*Are you an active member?*
______	______	______	______	______
______	______	______	______	______
______	______	______	______	______
______	______	______	______	______
______	______	______	______	______

33. What industry publications do you receive?

Name	*Publisher (if known)*	*Location of Publisher City/State (if known)*
______	______	______
______	______	______
______	______	______

34. What substitute products are available for the company product line? ________

____

____

35. Please describe any important business relationships that significantly influence sales—customers, suppliers, agents, attorneys, accountants, engineers, consultants, etc.? ____________________

____

____

   a. In relation to the foregoing question, have any such relationships been discontinued during the last five years? ____________________

   ____

   ____

36. What is the economic climate in your **market** area? ____________________

____

37. What is the economic climate in your **industry**? ____________________

____

____

38. Please compare the strengths and weaknesses of the **industry** and business in which the company operates versus five years ago.
Strengths today ____________________

____

Strengths five years ago ______________________________

____

____

Weaknesses today ______________________________

____

____

Weaknesses five years ago ______________________________

____

____

Information about Competitors

39. a.

Primary Competitors	*Location*	*Market Share*
________	________	________
________	________	________
________	________	________
________	________	________
________	________	________
________	________	________
________	________	________
________	________	________
________	________	________
________	________	________

b. Do any of these competitors manufacture products or provide services that make your company's products or services obsolete or less competitive? Please explain why. ______________________________

____

____

40. Please list up to five publicly held businesses that you consider comparable to your own.
    1. ______________________________
    2. ______________________________
    3. ______________________________
    4. ______________________________
    5. ______________________________

Information about Financial Statements

41. Please describe the credit rating of the business's principal customers.
    Strong _____ **Fair** _____ **Weak** _____
    a. Please detail the historical bad debt sales return/allowance experience of the business for the past five years.

Year Ended	*Bad Debt Expense*	*Sales Returns/Allowances*
_________	_________________	____________________
_________	_________________	____________________
_________	_________________	____________________

42. Were there any material unusual or nonrecurring items of income or expense during the past five-year period? (e.g. settlement in a lawsuit) **Yes** _____ **No** _____
43. a. List locations where the business has facilities (offices, plants, etc.).

Location	*Owned or Leased*	*Most recent fiscal year sales at location (Approximate if exact unknown)*

b. Are there any subsidiaries, operating investments, or affiliated companies? **Yes**_____ **No** _____ **If yes, please provide a financial statement and federal tax return as of the valuation date and the fiscal year prior to the valuation date.** Also complete for each the "Information about the Business" section of this questionnaire.

44. Does the business have any assets or liabilities not recorded on the books? **Yes** _____ **No** _____

If the foregoing is answered yes, please complete the following table.

Description	*Fair Market Value*	*Is There an Appraisal? Yes/No*
____________________	_____________	_______________
____________________	_____________	_______________
____________________	_____________	_______________
____________________	_____________	_______________
____________________	_____________	_______________

45. List any nonoperating assets such as aircraft, boats, art, real estate investments, and any other assets not primarily used in the operation of the entity on the following schedule.

Description	*Cost*	*Book Value*	*Estimated Fair Market Value*	*Debt Outstanding*	*Annual Net Income Loss*
_________	_____	_____	_____	_____	_____
_________	_____	_____	_____	_____	_____
_________	_____	_____	_____	_____	_____
_________	_____	_____	_____	_____	_____
_________	_____	_____	_____	_____	_____

46. List any excess operating assets not needed to operate the entity (i.e. (1) an owned but closed service station of a company operating service stations (2) a drill press no longer being used by a manufacturer).

Description	*Cost*	*Book Value*	*Estimated Fair Market Value*	*Debt Outstanding*
____________	_____	_____	_____	_____
____________	_____	_____	_____	_____
____________	_____	_____	_____	_____
____________	_____	_____	_____	_____
____________	_____	_____	_____	_____

47. a. What are the future annual capital spending needs of your business for five years into the future?
    Year 1 ______________________________
    Year 2 ______________________________
    Year 3 ______________________________
    Year 4 ______________________________
    Year 5 ______________________________
    b. Does the business have any current substantial capital needs?
    Yes _____ **No** _____ **If yes, please provide details.**
48. What is the overall condition of the company's equipment? ______________
    ____
    ____
    a. Is there any inefficient or obsolete equipment? **Yes** _____ **No** _____ If yes, please explain ______________________________
    ____
    ____
    b. What is the likelihood of major repairs of the company's equipment? _____
    ____
    ____
    c. Have there been any machinery and equipment appraisals prepared in the last five years? **Yes** _____ **No**_____ **If yes, please provide copies.**
49. If not detailed in the financial statements, have any dividends or other distributions to equity owners been paid during the five-year period?
    Yes _____ **No**_____ **N/A**_____
    a. If the foregoing answer is yes, in what years, in what amounts, and to whom were the dividends or distributions paid?

Dividend or Distribution Amount	*In What Year Were Dividends or Distributions Declared/Paid*	*To Whom Paid*
____________	________	____________
____________	________	____________
____________	________	____________
____________	________	____________

50. Do you have any deferred charges? **Yes** _____ **No** _____ If yes, please fill out the following table.

Nature of Deferral	*Amount*	*Real Value*
________________	_____	_____
________________	_____	_____
________________	_____	_____
________________	_____	_____
________________	_____	_____

51. Please detail insurance coverages (liability, property, etc.). Why? __________
____
____
____

52. What are your future plans for expansion, if any? ____________________
____

53. Have there been any current strategic plans, long-range plans, or business plans developed? **Yes**_____ **No** _____ **(Please provide copies.)**
54. Have there been any current projections or forecasts prepared? **Yes** _____ **No** _____ **(Please provide copies.)**

Information about Contingencies

55. Has the business been audited by the IRS, OSHA, EPA, EEOC, or any federal or state agency in the past five years? **Yes** _____ **No** _____**If yes, please detail the results and provide copies of any reports.**
56. Has the business had any environmental or hazardous waste studies, audits, investigations, etc., in the past five years? **Yes** _____ **No** _____ **If yes, please provide copies of any reports or studies.**
57. Does the business have difficulty complying with environmental regulations? **Yes** _____ **No** _____
58. Is there any material litigation pending against the business? **Yes** _____ **No** _____
59. Is there any legislation pending or recently enacted that could have a material effect on the operation of the business? **Yes** _____ **No** _____
    If the answer is yes to any of the foregoing questions, please explain. _______
    ____
    ____

THE FOLLOWING QUESTIONS RELATE TO CASH BASIS BUSINESSES ONLY. **Professional practice, services business, or businesses on a cash basis, please provide the following information.**

60. a. Accounts receivable as of the date of the valuation. $__________________
    b. Accounts receivable as of the most current date. $__________________
        i. What percentage is uncollectible?
        As of the date of valuation _____%
        As of the most current date _____%
        ii. Must any additional work be performed before any of these receivables can be collected? **Yes** _____ **No** _____. If yes, please explain (including estimates of cost to complete). ______________________________

        ____

        ____
    c. Liabilities
        i. Accounts Payable $_____
        ii. Other current liabilities (detail) ______________________________

        ____
        iii. Current portion of long-term debt ______________________________
        iv. Long-term liabilities (detail) ______________________________
    d. Work in process
        i. Amount ______________________________
        ii. What percentage is billable? ______________________________
    e. Escrow amounts? ______________________________
    f. Do you have cases on a contingent fee basis? **Yes** _____ **No** _____

Business Valuation Questionnaire
Schedule A
List of Owners

Owner	Position/ Title	Date of Birth	% Owned	# of Shares Owned	Years of service or Involvement	Relationship (i.e., son, sister, unrelated, etc.)	On Board of Directors Yes or No
		__/__/__	______%				
		__/__/__	______%				
		__/__/__	______%				
		__/__/__	______%				
		__/__/__	______%				
		__/__/__	______%				
		__/__/__	______%				
		__/__/__	______%				
		__/__/__	______%				

Teasury shares ____________

Total shares outstanding ____________

Business Valuation Questionnaire
Schedule B
Changes in Ownership

Date of Ownership Change	Current Owner	Previous Owner	# of Shares Transferred	Relationship of Current Owner to Previous Owner	Nature of Transaction (i.e., gift, sell, estate, etc.)

Business Valuation Questionnaire
Schedule C
Executive Compensation

Name	Date of Birth	Title	Salary	Bonus	Other Compensation	Total Compensation
YEAR 1 (most recent year)						
YEAR 2						
YEAR 3						
YEAR 4						
YEAR 5						

SIMPLIFIED DATA COLLECTION CHECKLIST

BUSINESS VALUATION
DATA COLLECTION CHECKLIST

Entity Name____
Completed by ______________________________ Date __________

In connection with the valuation of the entity named hereon, please provide the information listed below. Only those items marked need to be provided.

Financial Statements

__ Annual financial statements for the last __ years
__ Interim financial statements from the last annual statement to the most recent date
__ Federal income tax returns for the last __ years
__ Forecasts, projections, or budgets prepared for any future periods
__ Other
__ Listing of subsidiaries or other businesses in which this entity has an ownership interest, together with the foregoing financial information

Other Financial Information

__ Listing of cash accounts and other investments
__ Aged accounts receivable at last annual statement date, as well as last interim date
__ Inventory listing and valuation, including details of any adjustments related to LIFO Inventory Valuation Methods
__ Fixed asset listing, and/or depreciation schedules
__ List of items comprising significant other asset balances
__ Aged accounts payable listing at last annual statement date and at last interim date
__ Analysis of significant accrued liabilities
__ Detailed listing of all notes payable and interest-bearing debt to include
    Date of indebtedness
    Repayment terms and interest rate
    Holder of indebtedness
__ Schedule of sales by product for each period that a financial statement is provided
(Only required if F/S does not present detailed information)
__ Schedule of significant expense captions on income statements
(Only required if F/S does not present detailed information)
__ Schedule of shareholder, director, and officers compensation for last __ years
__ Copies of sales, capital, or operating budgets

__ Copies of business plan
__ Schedule of key man insurance
__ Copies of prior appraisals of fixed assets, and/or entity, prepared within last __ years

Other Operating Data

__ Product brochures, price lists, catalogs, and other product information
__ List of stockholders or owners of entity
__ Organization chart
__ List of 10 largest customers and suppliers, and the percentage of sales/purchases for each of the last __ years
__ Details of previous transfers of ownership interest in the entity during the last 10 years

Legal Documents

__ Copies of significant leases and loans
__ Copies of shareholder or other ownership agreements, to include buy/sell agreements, stock options, or other similar agreements
__ Minutes of the board of directors meetings for the prior __ years
__ Copies of key employee employment contracts
__ Copies of significant purchase or sales contracts
__ Copies of franchise or dealership agreements
__ Details of any pending litigation that has the potential of impacting the operations of the company
__ Details of any employee benefit plans, to include profit sharing, pension, 401k, and employee stock option plans
__ Collective bargaining agreements
__ Reports of examinations conducted by IRS, EEOC, EPA, OSHA, or other government agencies
__ Details regarding intangible assets owned by entity to include patents, copyrights, trademarks, or others
__ History of entity from inception to current date
__ Resumes of key management personnel

Appendix C

Revenue Rulings

REVENUE RULING 59–60

SECTION 1. PURPOSE.

The purpose of this Revenue Ruling is to outline and review in general the approach, methods and factors to be considered in valuing shares of the capital stock of closely held corporations for estate tax and gift tax purposes. The methods discussed herein will apply likewise to the valuation of corporate stocks on which market quotations are either unavailable or are of such scarcity that they do not reflect the fair market value.

SECTION 2. BACKGROUND AND DEFINITIONS.

.01 All valuations must be made in accordance with the applicable provisions of the Internal Revenue Code of 1954 and the Federal Estate Tax and Gift Tax Regulations. Sections 2031(a), 2032, and 2512(a) of the 1954 Code (sections 811 and 1005 of the 1939 Code) require that the property to be included in the gross estate, or made the subject of a gift, shall be taxed on the basis of the value of the property at the time of death of the decedent, the alternate date if so elected, or the date of gift.

.02 Section 20.2031-1(b) of the Estate Tax Regulations (section 81.10 of the Estate Tax Regulations 105) and section 25.2512-1 of the Gift Tax Regulations (section 86.19 of Gift Tax Regulations 108) define fair market value, in effect, as the price at which the property would change hands between a willing buyer and a willing seller when the former is not under any compulsion to buy and the latter is not under any compulsion to sell, both parties having reasonable knowledge of relevant facts. Court decisions frequently state in addition that the hypothetical buyer and seller are assumed to be able, as well as willing, to trade and to be well informed about the property and concerning the market for such property.

.03 Closely held corporations are those corporations the shares of which are owned by a relatively limited number of stockholders. Often the entire stock issue is held by one family. The result of this situation is that little, if any, trading in the shares takes place. There is, therefore, no established market for the stock and such sales as occur at irregular intervals seldom reflect all of the elements of a representative transaction as defined by the term "fair market value."

SECTION 3. APPROACH TO VALUATION.

.01 A determination of fair market value, being a question of fact, will depend upon the circumstances in each case. No formula can be devised that will be generally applicable to the multitude of different valuation issues arising in estate and gift tax cases. Often, an appraiser will find wide differences of opinion as to the fair market value of a particular stock. In resolving such differences, he should maintain a reasonable attitude in recognition of the fact that valuation is not an exact science. A sound valuation will be based upon all the relevant facts, but the elements of common sense, informed judgment and reasonableness must enter into the process of weighing those facts and determining their aggregate significance.

.02 The fair market value of specific shares of stock will vary as general economic conditions change from "normal" to "boom" or "depression," that is, according to the degree of optimism or pessimism with which the investing public regards the future at the required date of appraisal. Uncertainty as to the stability of continuity of the future income from a property decreases its value by increasing the risk of loss of earnings and value in the future. The value of shares of stock of a company with very uncertain future prospects is highly speculative. The appraiser must exercise his judgment as to the degree of risk attaching to the business of the corporation which issued the stock, but that judgment must be related to all of the other factors affecting value.

.03 Valuation of securities is, in essence, a prophesy as to the future and must be based on facts available at the required date of appraisal. As a generalization, the prices of stock which are traded in volume in a free and active market by informed persons best reflect the consensus of the investing public as to what the future holds for the corporations and industries represented. When a stock is closely held, is traded infrequently, or is traded in an erratic market, some other measures of value must be used. In many instances, the next best measure may be found in the prices at which the stocks of companies engaged in the same or a similar line of business are selling in a free and open market.

SECTION 4. FACTORS TO CONSIDER.

.01 It is advisable to emphasize that in the valuation of the stock of closely held corporations or the stock of corporations where market quotations are either lacking or too scarce to be recognized, all available financial data, as well as all relevant factors affecting the fair market value, should be considered. The following factors, although not all-inclusive are fundamental and require careful analysis in each case:

(a) The nature of the business and the history of the enterprise from its inception.

(b) The economic outlook in general and the condition and outlook of the specific industry in particular.

(c) The book value of the stock and the financial condition of the business.

(d) The earning capacity of the company.

(e) The dividend-paying capacity.

(f) Whether or not the enterprise has goodwill or other intangible value.

(g) Sales of the stock and the size of the block of stock to be valued.

(h) The market prices of stock of corporations engaged in the same or a similar line of business having their stocks actively traded in a free and open market, either on an exchange or over-the-counter.

.02 The following is a brief discussion of each of the foregoing factors:

(a) The history of a corporate enterprise will show its past stability or instability, its growth or lack of growth, the diversity or lack or diversity of its operations, and other facts needed to form an opinion of the degree of risk involved in the business. For an enterprise which changed its form of organization but carried on the same or closely similar operations of its predecessor, the history of the former enterprise should be considered. The detail to be considered should increase with approach to the required date of appraisal, since recent events are of greatest help in predicting the future; but a study of gross and net income and of dividends covering a long prior period, is highly desirable. The history to be studied should include, but need not be limited to, the nature of the business, its products or services, its operating and investment assets, capital structure, plant facilities, sales records and management, all of which should be considered as of the date of the appraisal, with due regard for recent significant changes. Events of the past that are unlikely to recur in the future should be discounted, since value has a close relation to future expectancy.

(b) A sound appraisal of closely held stock must consider current and prospective economic conditions as of the date of appraisal, both in the national economy and in the industry or industries with which the corporation is allied. It is important to know that the company is more or less successful than its competitors in the same industry, or that it is maintaining a stable position with respect to competitors. Equal or even greater significance may attach to the ability of the industry with which the company is allied to compete with other industries. Prospective competition which has not been a factor in prior years should be given careful attention. For example, high profits due to the novelty of its product and the lack of competition often lead to increasing competition. The public's appraisal of the future prospects of competitive industries or of competitors within an industry may be indicated by price trends in the markets for commodities and for securities. The loss of the manager of a so-called "one-man" business may have a depressing effect upon the value of the stock of such business, particularly if there is a lack of trained personnel capable of succeeding to the management of the enterprise. In valuing the stock of this type of business, therefore, the effect of the loss of the manager on the future expectancy of the business, and the absence of management-succession potentialities are pertinent factors to be taken into consideration. On the other hand, there may be factors which offset, in whole or in part, the loss of the manager's services. For instance, the nature of the business and of its assets may be such that they will not be impaired by the loss of the manager. Furthermore, the loss may be adequately covered by life insurance, or competent management might be employed on the basis of the consideration paid for the former manager's services. These, or other offsetting factors, if found to exist, should be carefully weighed against the loss of the manager's services in valuing the stock of the enterprise.

(c) Balance sheets should be obtained, preferably in the form of comparative annual statements for two or more years immediately preceding the date of appraisal, together with a balance sheet at the end of the month preceding that date, if corporate accounting will permit. Any balance sheet descriptions that are not self-explanatory, and balance sheet items comprehending diverse assets or liabilities, should be clarified in essential detail by supporting supplemental schedules. These statements usually will disclose to the appraiser (1) liquid position (ratio of current assets to current liabilities); (2) gross and net book value of principal classes of fixed assets; (3) working capital; (4) long-term indebtedness; (5) capital structure; and (6) net worth. Consideration also should be given to any assets not essential to the operation of the business, such as investments in securities, real estate, etc. In general, such nonoperating assets will command a lower rate of return than do the operating assets, although in exceptional cases the reverse may be true. In computing the book value per share of stock, assets of the investment type should be revalued on the basis of their market price and the book value adjusted accordingly. Comparison of the company's balance sheets over several years may reveal, among other facts, such developments as the acquisition of additional production facilities or subsidiary companies, improvement in financial position, and details as to recapitalizations and other changes in the capital structure of the corporation. If the corporation has more than one class of stock outstanding, the charter or certificate of incorporation should be examined to ascertain the explicit rights and privileges of the various stock issues including: (1) voting powers, (2) preference as to dividends, and (3) preference as to assets in the event of liquidation.

(d) Detailed profit-and loss statements should be obtained and considered for a representative period immediately prior to the required date of appraisal, preferably five or more years. Such statements should show (1) a gross income by principal items; (2) principal deductions from gross income including major prior items of operating expenses, interest, and other expense on each item of long-term debt, depreciation, and depletion if such deductions are made, officers' salaries, in total if they appear to be reasonable or in detail if they seem to be excessive, contributions (whether or not deductible for tax purposes) that the nature of its business and its community position require the corporation to make, and taxes by principal items, including income and excess profits taxes; (3) net income available for dividends; (4) rates and amounts of dividends paid on each class of stock; (5) remaining amount carried to surplus; and (6) adjustments to, and reconciliation with, surplus as stated on the balance sheet. With profit and loss statements of this character available, the appraiser should be able to separate recurrent from nonrecurrent items of income and expense, to distinguish between operating income and investment income, and to ascertain whether or not any line of business in which the company is engaged is operated consistently at a loss and might be abandoned with benefit to the company. The percentage of earnings retained for business expansion should be noted when dividend-paying capacity is considered. Potential future income is a major factor in many valuations of closely held stocks, and all information concerning past income which will be helpful in predicting the future should be secured. Prior earnings records usually are the most reliable guide as to the future expectancy, but resort to arbitrary five-or-ten-year averages without regard to current trends or future prospects will not produce a realistic valuation. If, for instance, a record of progressively increasing or decreasing income is found, then greater weight may be accorded the most recent years' profits in estimating earning power. It will be helpful, in judging risk and the extent to which a business is a marginal operator, to consider deductions from income and net income in terms of percentage of sales. Major categories of cost and expense to be so analyzed include the consumption of raw materials and supplies in the case of manufacturers, processors, and fabricators; the cost of purchased merchandise in the case of merchants; utility services; insurance; taxes; depletion or depreciation; and interest.

(e) Primary consideration should be given to the dividend-paying capacity of the company rather than to dividends actually paid in the past. Recognition must be given to the necessity of retaining a reasonable portion of profits in a company to meet competition. Dividend-paying capacity is a factor that must be considered in an appraisal, but dividends actually paid in the past may not have any relation to dividend-paying capacity. Specifically, the dividends paid by a closely held family company may be measured by the income needs of the stockholders or by their desire to avoid taxes on dividend receipts, instead of by the ability of the company to pay dividends. Where an actual or effective controlling interest in a corporation is to be valued, the dividend factor is not a material element, since the payment of such dividends is discretionary with the controlling stockholders. The individual or group in control can substitute salaries and bonuses for dividends, thus reducing net income and understating the dividend-paying capacity of the company. It follows, therefore, that dividends are less reliable criteria of fair market value than other applicable factors.

(f) In the final analysis, goodwill is based upon earning capacity. The presence of goodwill and its value, therefore, rests upon the excess of net earnings over and above a fair return on the net tangible assets. While the element of goodwill may be based primarily on earnings, such factors as the prestige and renown of the business, the ownership of a trade or brand name, and a record of successful operation over a prolonged period in a particular locality, also may furnish support for the inclusion of intangible value. In some instances it may not be possible to make a separate appraisal of the tangible and intangible assets of the business. The enterprise has a value as an entity. Whatever intangible value there is, which is supportable by the facts, may be measured by the amount by which the appraised value of the tangible assets exceeds the net book value of such assets.

(g) Sales of stock of a closely held corporation should be carefully investigated to determine whether they represent transactions at arm's length. Forced or distress sales do not ordinarily reflect fair market value nor do isolated sales in small amounts necessarily control as the measure of value. This is especially true in the valuation of a controlling interest in a corporation. Since, in the case of closely held stocks, no prevailing market prices are available, there is no basis for making an adjustment for blockage. It follows, therefore, that such stocks should be valued upon a consideration of all the evidence affecting the fair market value. The size of the block of stock itself is a relevant factor to be considered. Although it is true that a minority interest in an unlisted corporation's stock is more difficult to sell than a similar block of listed stock, it is equally true that control of a corporation, either actual or in effect, representing as it does an added element of value, may justify a higher value for a specific block of stock.

(h) Section 2031(b) of the Code states, in effect, that in valuing unlisted securities the value of stock or securities of corporations engaged in the same or a similar line of business which are listed on an exchange should be taken into consideration along with all other factors. An important consideration is that the corporations to be used for comparisons have capital stocks which are actively traded by the public. In accordance with section 2031(b) of the Code, stocks listed on an exchange are to be considered first. However, if sufficient comparable companies whose stocks are listed on an exchange cannot be found, other comparable companies which have stocks actively traded in on the over-the-counter market also may be used. The essential factor is that whether the stocks are sold on an exchange or over-the-counter there is evidence of an active, free public market for the stock as of the valuation date. In selecting corporations for comparative purposes, care should be taken to use only comparable companies. Although the only restrictive requirement as to comparable corporations specified in the statute is that their lines of business be the same or similar, yet it is obvious that consideration must be given to other relevant factors in order that the most valid comparison possible will be obtained. For illustration, a corporation having one or more issues of preferred stock, bonds, or debentures in addition to its common stock should not be considered to be directly comparable to one having only common stock outstanding. In like manner, a company with a declining business and decreasing markets is not comparable to one with a record of current progress and market expansion.

SECTION 5. WEIGHT TO BE ACCORDED VARIOUS FACTORS.

The valuation of closely held corporate stock entails the consideration of all relevant factors as stated in section 4. Depending upon the circumstances in each case, certain factors may carry more weight than others because of the nature of the company's business. To illustrate:

(a) Earnings may be the most important criterion of value in some cases whereas asset value will receive primary consideration in others. In general, the appraiser will accord primary consideration to earnings when valuing stocks of companies which sell products or services to the public; conversely, in the investment or holding type of company, the appraiser may accord the greatest weight to the assets underlying the security to be valued.

(b) The value of the stock of a closely held investment or real estate holding company, whether or not family owned, is closely related to the value of the assets underlying the stock. For companies of this type the appraiser should determine the fair market values of the assets of the company. Operating expenses of such a company and the cost of liquidating it, if any, merit consideration when appraising the relative values of the stock and the underlying assets. The market values of the underlying assets give due weight to potential earnings and dividends of the particular items of property underlying the stock, capitalized at rates deemed proper by the investing public at the date of appraisal. A current appraisal by the investing public should be superior to the retrospective opinion of an individual. For these reasons, adjusted net worth should be accorded greater weight in valuing the stock of a closely held investment or real estate holding company, whether or not family owned, than any of the other customary yardsticks of appraisal, such as earnings and dividend paying capacity.

SECTION 6. CAPITALIZATION RATES.

In the application of certain fundamental valuation factors, such as earnings and dividends, it is necessary to capitalize the average of current results at some appropriate rate. A determination of the proper capitalization rate presents one of the most difficult problems in valuation. That there is no ready or simple solution will become apparent by a cursory check of the rates of return and dividend yields in terms of the selling prices of corporate shares listed on the major exchanges of the country. Wide variations will be found even for companies in the same industry. Moreover, the ratio will fluctuate from year to year depending upon economic conditions. Thus, no standard tables of capitalization rates applicable to closely held corporations can be formulated. Among the more important factors to be taken into consideration in deciding upon a capitalization rate in a particular case are: (1) the nature of the business; (2) the risk involved; and (3) the stability or irregularity of earnings.

SECTION 7. AVERAGE OF FACTORS.

Because valuations cannot be made on the basis of a prescribed formula, there is no means whereby the various applicable factors in a particular case can be assigned mathematical weights in deriving the fair market value. For this reason, no useful purpose is served by taking an average of several factors (for example, book value, capitalized earnings, and capitalized dividends) and basing the valuation on the result. Such a process excludes active consideration of other pertinent factors, and the end result cannot be supported by a realistic application of the significant facts in the case except by mere chance.

SECTION 8. RESTRICTIVE AGREEMENTS.

Frequently, in the valuation of closely held stock for estate and gift tax purposes, it will be found that the stock is subject to an agreement restricting its sale or transfer. Where shares of stock were acquired by a decedent subject to an option reserved by the issuing corporation to repurchase at a certain price, the option price is usually accepted as the fair market value for estate tax purposes. See Rev. Rul. 54-76, C.B. 1954-1, 194. However, in such case the option price is not determinative of fair market value for gift tax purposes. Where the option, or buy and sell agreement, is the result of voluntary action by the stockholders and is binding during the life as well as at the death of the stockholders, such agreement may or may not, depending upon the circumstances of each case, fix the value for estate tax purposes. However, such agreement is a factor to be considered, with other relevant factors, in determining fair market value. Where the stockholder is free to dispose of his shares during life and the option is to become effective only upon his death, the fair market value is not limited to the option price. It is always necessary to consider the relationship of the parties, the relative number of shares held by the decedent, and other material facts, to determine whether the agreement represents a bona fide business arrangement or is a device to pass the decedent's shares to the natural objects of his bounty for less than an adequate and full consideration in money or money's worth. In this connection see Rev. Rul. 157 C.B. 1953-2, 255, and Rev. Rul. 189, C.B. 1953-2, 294.

SECTION 9. EFFECT ON OTHER DOCUMENTS.

Revenue Ruling 54-77, C.B. 1954-1, 187, is hereby superseded.

SOURCE: Rev. Rul. 59-60, 1959-1, C.B. 237.

REVENUE RULING 68-609

The "formula" approach may be used in determining the fair market value of intangible assets of a business only if there is no better basis available for making the determination; A.R.M. 34, A.R.M. 68, O.D. 937, and Revenue Ruling 65-192 superseded.

SECTION 1001.—DETERMINATION OF AMOUNT OF AND RECOGNITION OF GAIN OR LOSS

26 CFR 1.1001-1: Computation of gain or loss.
(Also Section 167; 1-167(a)-3.) Rev. Rul. 68-609[1]

The purpose of this Revenue Ruling is to update and restate, under the current statute and regulations, the currently outstanding portions of A.R.M. 34, C.B. 2, 31 (1920), A.R.M. 68, C.B. 3, 43 (1920), and O.D. 937, C.B. 4, 43 (1921).

The question presented is whether the "formula" approach, the capitalization of earnings in excess of a fair rate of return on net tangible assets, may be used to determine the fair market value of the intangible assets of a business.

The "formula" approach may be stated as follows:

A percentage return on the average annual value of the tangible assets used in a business is determined, using a period of years (preferably not less than five) imme-

[1]Prepared pursuant to Rev. Proc. 67-6, C.B. 1967-1, 576.

diately prior to the valuation date. The amount of the percentage return on tangible assets, thus determined, is deducted from the average earnings of the business for such period and the remainder, if any, is considered to be the amount of the average annual earnings from the intangible assets of the business for the period. This amount (considered as the average annual earnings from intangibles), capitalized at a percentage of, say, 15 to 20 percent, is the value of the intangible assets of the business determined under the "formula" approach.

The percentage of return on the average annual value of the tangible assets used should be the percentage prevailing in the industry involved at the date of valuation, or (when the industry percentage is not available) a percentage of 8 to 10 percent may be used.

The 8 percent rate of return and the 15 percent rate of capitalization are applied to tangibles and intangibles, respectively, of businesses with a small risk factor and stable and regular earnings; the 10 percent rate of return and 20 percent rate of capitalization are applied to businesses in which the hazards of business are relatively high.

The above rates are used as examples and are not appropriate in all cases. In applying the "formula" approach, the average earnings period and the capitalization rates are dependent upon the facts pertinent thereto in each case.

The past earnings to which the formula is applied should fairly reflect the probable future earnings. Ordinarily, the period should not be less than five years, and abnormal years, whether above or below the average, should be eliminated. If the business is a sole proprietorship or partnership, there should be deducted from the earnings of the business a reasonable amount for services performed by the owner or partners engaged in the business. See *Lloyd B. Sanderson Estate v. Commissioner,* 42. F. 2d 160 (1930). Further, only the tangible assets entering into net worth, including accounts and bills receivable in excess of accounts and bills payable, are used for determining earnings on the tangible assets. Factors that influence the capitalization rate include (1) the nature of the business, (2) the risk involved, and (3) the stability or irregularity of earnings.

The "formula" approach should not be used if there is better evidence available from which the value of intangibles can be determined. If the assets of a going business are sold upon the basis of a rate of capitalization that can be substantiated as being realistic, though it is not within the range of figures indicated here as the ones ordinarily to be adopted, the same rate of capitalization should be used in determining the value of intangibles.

Accordingly, the "formula" approach may be used for determining the fair market value of intangible assets of a business only if there is no better basis therefor available.

See also Revenue Ruling 59-60, C.B. 1959-1, 237, as modified by Revenue Ruling 65-193, C.B. 1965-2, 370, which sets forth the proper approach to use in the valuation of closely held corporate stocks for estate and gift tax purposes. The general approach, methods, and factors, outlined in Revenue Ruling 59-60, as modified, are equally applicable to valuations of corporate stocks for income and other tax purposes as well as for estate and gift tax purposes. They apply also to problems involving the determination of the fair market value of business interests of any type, including partnerships and proprietorships, and of intangible assets for all tax purposes.

A.R.M. 34, A.R.M. 68, and O.D. 937 are superseded, since the positions set forth therein are restated to the extent applicable under current law in this Revenue Ruling. Revenue Ruling 65-192, C.B. 1965-2, 259, which contained restatements of A.R.M. 34 and A.R.M. 68, is also superseded.

SOURCE: Rev Rul. 68-609, 1968-2, C.B. 327.

REVENUE RULING 77-287

SECTION 1. PURPOSE.

The purpose of this Revenue Ruling is to amplify Rev. Rul. 59-60, 1959-1 C.B. 237, as modified by Rev. Rul. 65-193, 1965-2 C.B. 370, and to provide information and guidance to taxpayers, Internal Revenue Service personnel, and others concerned with the valuation, for Federal tax purposes, of securities that cannot be immediately resold because they are restricted from resale pursuant to Federal securities laws. This guidance is applicable only in cases where it is not inconsistent with valuation requirements of the Internal Revenue Code of 1954 or the regulations thereunder. Further, this ruling does not establish the time at which property shall be valued.

SECTION 2. NATURE OF THE PROBLEM.

It frequently becomes necessary to establish the fair market value of stock that has not been registered for public trading when the issuing company has stock of the same class that is actively traded in one or more securities markets. The problem is to determine the difference in fair market value between the registered shares that are actively traded and the unregistered shares. This problem is often encountered in estate and gift tax cases. However, it is sometimes encountered when unregistered shares are issued in exchange for assets or the stock of an acquired company.

SECTION 3. BACKGROUND AND DEFINITIONS.

.01 The Service outlined and reviewed in general the approach, methods, and factors to be considered in valuing shares of closely held corporate stock for estate and gift tax purposes in Rev. Rul. 59-60, as modified by Rev. Rul. 65-193. The provisions of Rev. Rul. 59-60, as modified, were extended to the valuation of corporate securities for income and other tax purposes by Rev. Rul. 68-609, 1968-2 C.B. 327.

.02 There are several terms currently in use in the securities industry that denote restrictions imposed on the resale and transfer of certain securities. The term frequently used to describe these securities is "restricted securities," but they are sometimes referred to as "unregistered securities," "investment letter stock," "control stock," or "private placement stock." Frequently these terms are used interchangeably. They all indicate that these particular securities cannot lawfully be distributed to the general public until a registration statement relating to the corporation underlying the securities has been filed, and has also become effective under the rules promulgated and enforced by the United States Securities & Exchange Commission (SEC) pursuant to the Federal securities laws. The following represents a more refined definition of each of the following terms along with two other terms—"exempted securities" and "exempted transactions."

(a) The term "restricted securities" is defined in Rule 144 adopted by the SEC as "securities acquired directly or indirectly from the issuer thereof, or from an affiliate of such issuer, in a transaction or chain of transactions not involving any public offering."

(b) The term "unregistered securities" refers to those securities with respect to which a registration statement, providing full disclosure by the issuing corporation, has not been filed with the SEC pursuant to the Securities Act of 1933. The registration statement is a condition precedent to a public distribution of securities in interstate commerce and is aimed at providing the prospective investor with a factual basis for sound judgment in making investment decisions.

(c) The terms "investment letter stock" and "letter stock" denote shares of stock that have been issued by a corporation without the benefit of filing a registration statement with the SEC. Such stock is subject to resale and transfer restrictions set forth in a letter agreement requested by the issuer and signed by the buyer of the stock when the stock is delivered. Such stock may be found in the hands of either individual investors or institutional investors.

(d) The term "control stock" indicates that the shares of stock have been held or are being held by an officer, director, or other person close to the management of the corporation. These persons are subject to certain requirements pursuant to SEC rules upon resale of shares they own in such corporations.

(e) The term "private placement stock" indicates that the stock has been placed with an institution or other investor who will presumably hold it for a long period and ultimately arrange to have the stock registered if it is to be offered to the general public. Such stock may or may not be subject to a letter agreement. Private placements of stock are exempted from the registration and prospectus provisions of the Securities Act of 1933.

(f) The term "exempted securities" refers to those classes of securities that are expressly excluded from the registration provisions of the Securities Act of 1933 and the distribution provisions of the Securities Exchange Act of 1934.

(g) The term "exempted transactions" refers to certain sales or distributions of securities that do not involve a public offering and are excluded from the registration and prospectus provisions of the Securities Act of 1933 and distribution provisions of the Securities Exchange Act of 1934. The exempted status makes it unnecessary for issuers of securities to go through the registration process.

SECTION 4. SECURITIES INDUSTRY PRACTICE IN VALUING RESTRICTED SECURITIES.

.01 *Investment Company Valuation Practices.* The Investment Company Act of 1940 requires open-end investment companies to publish the valuation of their portfolio securities daily. Some of these companies have portfolios containing restricted securities, but also have unrestricted securities of the same class traded on a securities exchange. In recent years the number of restricted securities in such portfolios have increased. The following methods have been used by investment companies in the valuation of such restricted securities:

(a) Current market price of the unrestricted stock less a constant percentage discount based on purchase discount;

(b) Current market price of unrestricted stock less a constant percentage discount different from purchase discount;

(c) Current market price of the unrestricted stock less a discount amortized over a fixed period;

(d) Current market price of the unrestricted stock; and

(e) Cost of the restricted stock until it is registered.

The SEC ruled in its Investment Company Act Release No. 5847, dated October 21, 1969, that there can be no automatic formula by which an investment company can value the restricted securities in its portfolios. Rather, the SEC has determined that it is the responsibility of the board of directors of the particular investment company to determine the "fair value" of each issue of restricted securities in good faith.

.02 *Institutional Investors Study.* Pursuant to Congressional direction, the SEC undertook an analysis of the purchases, sales, and holding of securities by financial institutions, in order to determine the effect of institutional activity upon the securities market. The study report was published in eight volumes in March 1971. The fifth volume provides an analysis of restricted securities and deals with such items as the characteristics of the restricted securities' purchasers and issuers, the size of transactions (dollars and shares), the marketability discounts on different trading markets, and the resale provisions. This research project provides some guidance for measuring the discount in that it contains information, based on the actual experience of the marketplace, showing that, during the period surveyed (January 1, 1966, through June 30, 1969), the amount of discount allowed for restricted securities from the trading price of the unrestricted securities was generally related to the following four factors:

(a) *Earnings.* Earnings and sales consistently have a significant influence on the size of restricted securities discounts according to the study. Earnings played the major part in establishing the ultimate discounts at which these stocks were sold from the current market price. Apparently earnings patterns, rather than sales patterns, determine the degree of risk of an investment.

(b) *Sales.* The dollar amount of sales issuers' securities also has a major influence on the amount of discount at which restricted securities sell from the current market price. The results of the study generally indicate that the companies with the lowest dollar amount of sales during the test period accounted for most of the transactions involving the highest discount rates, while they accounted for only a small portion of all transactions involving the lowest discount rates.

(c) *Trading Market.* The market in which publicly held securities are traded also reflects variances in the amount of discount that is applied to restricted securities purchases. According to the study, discount rates were greatest on restricted stocks with unrestricted counterparts traded over-the-counter, followed by those with unrestricted counterparts listed on the American Stock Exchange, while the discount rates for those stocks with unrestricted counterparts listed on the New York Stock Exchange were the smallest.

(d) *Resale Agreement Provisions.* Resale agreement provisions often affect the size of the discount. The discount from the market price provides the main incentive for a potential buyer to acquire restricted securities. In judging the opportunity cost of freezing funds, the purchaser is analyzing two separate factors. The first factor is the risk that the underlying value of the stock will change in a way that, absent the restrictive provisions, would have prompted a decision to sell. The second factor is the risk that the contemplated means of legally disposing of the stock may not materialize. From the seller's point of view, a discount is justified where the seller is relieved of the expenses of registration and public distribution, as well as of the risk that the market will adversely change before the offering is completed. The ultimate agreement between buyer and seller is a reflection of these and other considerations. Relative bargaining strengths of the parties to the agreement are major considerations that influence the resale terms and consequently the size of discounts in restricted securities transactions. Certain provisions are often found in agreements between buyers and sellers that affect the size of discounts at which restricted stocks are sold. Several such provisions follow, all of which, other than number (3), would tend to reduce the size of the discount:

(1) A provision giving the buyer an option to "piggyback," that is, to register restricted stock with the next registration statement, if any, filed by the issuer with the SEC;

(2) A provision giving the buyer an option to require registration at the seller's expense;

(3) A provision giving the buyer an option to require registration, but only at the buyer's own expense;

(4) A provision giving the buyer a right to receive continuous disclosure of information about the issuer from the seller;

(5) A provision giving the buyer a right to select one or more directors of the issuer;

(6) A provision giving the buyer an option to purchase additional shares of the issuer's stock; and

(7) A provision giving the buyer the right to have a greater voice in operations of the issuer, if the issuer does not meet previously agreed upon operating standards.

Institutional buyers can and often do obtain many of these rights and options from the sellers of restricted securities, and naturally, the more rights the buyer can acquire, the lower the buyer's risk is going to be, thereby reducing the buyer's discount as well. Small buyers may not be able to negotiate the large discounts or the rights and options that volume buyers are able to negotiate.

.03 *Summary.* A variety of methods have been used by the securities industry to value restricted securities. The SEC rejects all automatic or mechanical solutions to the valuation of restricted securities, and prefers, in the case of the valuation of investment company portfolio stocks, to rely upon good faith valuations by the board of directors of each company. The study made by the SEC found that restricted securities generally are issued at a discount from the market value of freely tradable securities.

SECTION 5. FACTS AND CIRCUMSTANCES MATERIAL TO VALUATION OF RESTRICTED SECURITIES.

.01 Frequently, a company has a class of stock that cannot be traded publicly. The reason such stock cannot be traded may arise from the securities statutes, as in the case of an "investment letter" restriction; it may arise from a corporate charter restriction; or perhaps from a trust agreement restriction. In such cases, certain documents and facts should be obtained for analysis.

.02 The following documents and facts, when used in conjunction with those discussed in Section 4 of Rev. Rul. 59-60, will be useful in the valuation of restricted securities:

(a) A copy of any declaration of trust, trust agreement, and any other agreements relating to the shares of restricted stock;

(b) A copy of any document showing any offers to buy or sell or indications of interest in buying or selling the restricted shares;

(c) The latest prospectus of the company;

(d) Annual reports of the company for 3 to 5 years preceding the valuation date;

(e) The trading prices and trading volume of the related class of traded securities 1 month preceding the valuation date, if they are traded on a stock exchange (if traded over-the-counter, prices may be obtained from the National Quotations Bureau, the National Association of Securities Dealers Automated Quotations (NASDAQ), or sometimes from broker-dealers making markets in the shares);

(f) The relationship of the parties to the agreements concerning the restricted stock, such as whether they are members of the immediate family or perhaps whether they are officers or directors of the company; and

(g) Whether the interest being valued represents a majority or minority ownership.

SECTION 6. WEIGHING FACTS AND CIRCUMSTANCES MATERIAL TO RESTRICTED STOCK VALUATION.

All relevant facts and circumstances that bear upon the worth of restricted stock, including those set forth above in the preceding Sections 4 and 5, and those set forth in Section 4 of Rev. Rul. 59-60, must be taken into account in arriving at the fair market value of such securities. Depending on the circumstances of each case, certain factors may carry more weight than others. To illustrate:

.01 Earnings, net assets, and net sales must be given primary consideration in arriving at an appropriate discount for restricted securities from the freely traded shares. These are the elements of value that are always used by investors in making investment decisions. In some cases, one element may be more important than in other cases. In the case of manufacturing, producing, or distributing companies, primary weight must be accorded earnings and net sales; but in the case of investment or holding companies, primary weight must be given to the net assets of the company underlying the stock. In the former type of companies, value is more closely linked to past, present, and future earnings while in the latter type of companies, value is more closely linked to the existing net assets of the company. See the discussion in Section 5 of Rev. Rul. 59-60.

.02 Resale provisions found in the restriction agreements must be scrutinized and weighted to determine the amount of discount to apply to the preliminary fair market value of the company. The two elements of time and expense bear upon this discount; the longer the buyer of the shares must wait to liquidate the shares, the greater the discount. Moreover, if the provisions make it necessary for the buyer to bear the expense of registration, the greater the discount. However, if the provisions of the restricted stock agreement make it possible for the buyer to "piggyback" shares at the next offering, the discount would be smaller.

.03 The relative negotiation strengths of the buyer and seller of restricted stock may have a profound effect on the amount of discount. For example, a tight money situation may cause the buyer to have the greater balance of negotiation strength in a transaction. However, in some cases the relative strengths may tend to cancel each other out.

.04 The market experience of freely tradable securities of the same class as the restricted securities is also significant in determining the amount of discount. Whether the shares are privately held or publicly traded affects the worth of the shares to the holder. Securities traded on a public market generally are worth more to investors than those that are not traded on a public market. Moreover, the type of public market in which the unrestricted securities are traded is to be given consideration.

SECTION 7. EFFECT ON OTHER DOCUMENTS.

Rev. Rul. 59-60, as modified by Rev. Rul. 65-193, is amplified.

SOURCE: Rev. Rul. 77-287, 1977-2, C.B. 319.

REVENUE RULING 83-120

SECTION 1. PURPOSE.

The purpose of this Revenue Ruling is to amplify Rev. Rul. 59-60, 1959-1 C.B. 237, by specifying additional factors to be considered in valuing common and preferred stock of a closely held corporation for gift tax and other purposes in a recapitalization of closely held businesses. This type of valuation problem frequently arises with respect to estate planning transactions wherein an individual receives preferred stock with a stated par value equal to all or a large portion of the fair market value of the individual's former stock interest in a corporation. The individual also receives common stock which is then transferred, usually as a gift, to a relative.

SECTION 2. BACKGROUND

.01 One of the frequent objectives of the type of transaction mentioned above is the transfer of the potential appreciation of an individual's stock interest in a corporation to relatives at a nominal or small gift tax cost. Achievement of this objective requires preferred stock having a fair market value equal to a large part of the fair market value of the individual's former stock interest and common stock having a nominal or small fair market value. The approach and factors described in this Revenue Ruling are directed toward ascertaining the true fair market value of the common and preferred stock and will usually result in the determination of a substantial fair market value for the common stock and a fair market value for the preferred stock which is substantially less than its par value.

.02 The type of transaction referred to above can arise in many different contexts. Some examples are:

(a) *A* owns 100% of the common stock (the only outstanding stock) of *Z* Corporation which has a fair market value of 10,500x. In a recapitalization described in section 368(a)(1)(E), *A* receives preferred stock with a par value of 10,000x and new common stock, which *A* then transfers to *A*'s son *B*.

(b) *A* owns some of the common stock of *Z* Corporation (or the stock of several corporations) the fair market value of which stock is 10,500x. *A* transfers this stock to a new corporation *X* in exchange for preferred stock of *X* corporation with a par value of 10,000x and common stock of corporation, which *A* then transfers to *A*'s son *B*.

(c) *A* owns 80 shares and his son *B* owns 20 shares of the common stock (the only stock outstanding) of *Z* Corporation. In a recapitalization described in section 368(a)(1)(E), *A* exchanges his 80 shares of common stock for 80 shares of new preferred stock of *Z* Corporation with a par value of 10,000x. *A*'s common stock had a fair market value of 10,000x.

SECTION 3. GENERAL APPROACH TO VALUATION

Under section 25.2512-2(f)(2) of the Gift Tax Regulations, the fair market value of stock in a closely held corporation depends upon numerous factors, including the corporation's net worth, its prospective earning power, and its capacity to pay dividends. In addition, other relevant factors must be taken into account. See Rev. Rul. 59-60. The weight to be accorded any evidentiary factor depends on the circumstances of each case. See section 25.2512-2(f) of the Gift Tax Regulations.

SECTION 4. APPROACH TO VALUATION—PREFERRED STOCK.

.01 In general the most important factors to be considered in determining the value of preferred stock are its yield, dividend coverage, and protection of its liquidation preference.

.02 Whether the yield of the preferred stock supports a valuation of the stock at par value depends in part on the adequacy of the dividend rate. The adequacy of the dividend rate should be determined by comparing its dividend rate with the dividend rate of high-grade publicly traded preferred stock. A lower yield than that of high-grade preferred stock indicates a preferred stock value of less than par. If the rate of interest charged by independent creditors to the corporation on loans is higher than the rate such independent creditors charge their most credit worthy borrowers, then the yield on the preferred stock should be correspondingly higher than the yield on high quality preferred stock. A yield which is not correspondingly higher reduces the value of the preferred stock. In addition, whether the preferred stock has a fixed dividend rate and is nonparticipating influences the value of the preferred stock. A publicly traded preferred stock for a company having a similar business and similar assets with similar liquidation preferences, voting rights, and other similar terms would be the ideal comparable for determining yield required in arm's-length transactions for closely held stock. Such ideal comparables will frequently not exist. In such circumstances, the most comparable publicly traded issues should be selected for comparison and appropriate adjustments made for differing factors.

.03 The actual dividend rate on a preferred stock can be assumed to be its stated rate if the issuing corporation will be able to pay its stated dividends in a timely manner and will, in fact, pay such dividends. The risk that the corporation may be unable to timely pay the stated dividends on the preferred stock can be measured by the coverage of such stated dividends by the corporation's earnings. Coverage of the dividend is measured by the ratio of the sum of pretax and preinterest earnings to the sum of the total interest to be paid and the pretax earnings needed to pay the after-tax dividends. *Standard & Poor's Ratings Guide,* 58 (1979). Inadequate coverage exists where a decline in corporate profits would be likely to jeopardize the corporation's ability to pay dividends on the preferred stock. The ratio for the preferred stock in question should be compared with the ratios for high quality preferred stock to determine whether the preferred stock has adequate coverage. Prior earnings history is important in this determination. Inadequate coverage indicates that the value of preferred stock is lower than its par value. Moreover, the absence of a provision that preferred dividends are cumulative raises substantial questions concerning whether the stated dividend rate will, in fact, be paid. Accordingly, preferred stock with noncumulative dividend features will normally have a value substantially lower than a cumulative preferred stock with the same yield, liquidation preference, and dividend coverage.

.04 Whether the issuing corporation will be able to pay the full liquidation preference at liquidation must be taken into account in determining fair market value.

This risk can be measured by the protection afforded by the corporation's net assets. Such protection can be measured by the ratio of the excess of the current market value of the corporation's assets over its liabilities to the aggregate liquidation preference. The protection ratio should be compared with the ratios for high quality preferred stock to determine adequacy of coverage. Inadequate asset protection exists where any unforeseen business reverses would be likely to jeopardize the corporation's ability to pay the full liquidation preference to the holders of the preferred stock.

.05 Another factor to be considered in valuing the preferred stock is whether it has voting rights and, if so, whether the preferred stock has voting control. See, however, Section 5.02 below.

.06 Peculiar covenants or provisions of the preferred stock of a type not ordinarily found in publicly traded preferred stock should be carefully evaluated to determine the effects of such covenants on the value of the preferred stock. In general, if covenants would inhibit the marketability of the stock or the power of the holder to enforce dividend or liquidation rights, such provisions will reduce the value of the preferred stock by comparison to the value of preferred stock not containing such covenants or provisions.

.07 Whether the preferred stock contains a redemption privilege is another factor to be considered in determining the value of the preferred stock. The value of a redemption privilege triggered by death of the preferred shareholder will not exceed the present value of the redemption premium payable at the preferred shareholder's death (i.e., the present value of the excess of the redemption price over the fair market value of the preferred stock upon its issuance). The value of the redemption privilege should be reduced to reflect any risk that the corporation may not possess sufficient assets to redeem its preferred stock at the stated redemption price. See Section .03 above.

SECTION 5. APPROACH TO VALUATION—COMMON STOCK

.01 If the preferred stock has a fixed rate of dividend and is nonparticipating, the common stock has the exclusive right to the benefits of future appreciation of the value of the corporation. This right is valuable and usually warrants a determination that the common stock has substantial value. The actual value of this right depends upon the corporation's past growth experience, the economic condition of the industry in which the corporation operates, and general economic conditions. The factor to be used in capitalizing the corporation's prospective earnings must be determined after an analysis of numerous factors concerning the corporation and the economy as a whole. See Rev. Rul. 59-60, at page 243. In addition, after-tax earnings of the corporation at the time the preferred stock is issued in excess of the stated dividends on the preferred stock will increase the value of the common stock. Furthermore, a corporate policy of reinvesting earnings will also increase the value of the common stock.

.02 A factor to be considered in determining the value of the common stock is whether the preferred stock also has voting rights. Voting rights of the preferred stock, especially if the preferred stock has voting control, could under certain circumstances increase the value of the preferred stock and reduce the value of common stock. This factor may be reduced in significance where the rights of common stockholders as a class are protected under state law from actions by another class of shareholders, see *Singer v. Magnavox Co.,* 380 A.2d 969 (Del. 1977), particularly where the common shareholders, as a class, are given the power to disapprove a proposal to allow preferred stock to be converted into common stock. See ABA-ALI Model Bus. Corp. Act, Section 60 (1969).

SECTION 6. EFFECT ON OTHER REVENUE RULINGS

Rev. Rul. 59-60, as modified by Rev. Rul. 65-193, 1965-2 C.B. 370 and as amplified by Rev. Rul. 77-287, 1977-2 C.B. 319, and Rev. Rul. 80-213, 1980-2 C.B. 101, is further amplified.

SOURCE: Rev. Rul. 83-120, 1983-2 C.B. 170

REVENUE RULING 93-12

Issue

If a donor transfers shares in a corporation to each of the donor's children, is the factor of corporate control in the family to be considered in valuing each transferred interest, for purposes of section 2512 of the Internal Revenue Code?

Facts

P owned all of the single outstanding class of stock of *X* corporation. *P* transferred all of *P*'s shares by making simultaneous gifts of 20 percent of the shares to each of *P*'s five children, *A, B, C, D,* and *E.*

Law and Analysis

Section 2512(a) of the Code provides that the value of the property at the date of the gift shall be considered the amount of the gift.

Section 25.2512-1 of the Gift Tax Regulations provides that, if a gift is made in property, its value at the date of the gift shall be considered the amount of the gift. The value of the property is the price at which the property would change hands between a willing buyer and a willing seller, neither being under any compulsion to buy or to sell, and both having reasonable knowledge of relevant facts.

Section 25.2512-2(a) of the regulations provides that the value of stocks and bonds is the fair market value per share or bond on the date of the gift. Section 25.2512-2(f) provides that the degree of control of the business represented by the block of stock to be valued is among the factors to be considered in valuing stock where there are no sales prices or bona fide bid or asked prices.

Rev. Rul. 81-253, 1981-1 C.B. 187, holds that, ordinarily, no minority shareholder discount is allowed with respect to transfers of shares of stock between family members if, based upon a composite of the family members' interest at the time of the transfer, control (either majority voting control or de facto control through family relationships) of the corporation exists in the family unit. The ruling also states that the Service will not follow the decision of the Fifth Circuit in *Estate of Bright v. United States,* 658 F.2d 999 (5th Cir. 1981).

In *Bright,* the decedent's undivided community property interest in shares of stock, together with the corresponding undivided community property interest of the decedent's surviving spouse, constituted a control block of 55 percent of the shares of a corporation. The court held that, because the community-held shares were subject to a right of partition, the decedent's own interest was equivalent to 27.5 percent of the outstanding shares and, therefore, should be valued as a minority interest, even though the shares were to be held by the decedent's surviving spouse as trustee of a testamentary trust. See also, *Propstra v. United States,* 680 F.2d 1248 (9th Cir. 1982). In addition, *Estate of Andrews v. Commissioner,* 79 T.C. 938 (1982), and *Estate of Lee v. Commissioner,* 69 T.C. 860 (1978), *nonacq.,* 1980-2C.B. 2, held that the corporation shares owned by other family members cannot be attributed to an individual family member for determining whether the individual family member's share should be valued as the controlling interest of the corporation.

After further consideration of the position taken in Rev. Rul. 81-253, and in light of the cases noted above, the Service has concluded that, in the case of a corporation with a single class of stock, notwithstanding the family relationship of the donor, the donee, and other shareholders, the shares of other family members will not be aggregated with the transferred shares to determine whether the transferred shares should be valued as part of a controlling interest.

In the present case, the minority interests transferred to *A, B, C, D,* and *E* should be valued for gift tax purposes without regard to the family relationship of the parties.

Holding

If a donor transfers shares in a corporation to each of the donor's children, the factor of corporate control in the family is not considered in valuing each transferred interest for purposes of section 2512 of the Code. For estate and gift tax valuation purposes, the Service will follow *Bright, Propstra, Andrews,* and *Lee* in not assuming that all voting power held by family members may be aggregated for purposes of determining whether the transferred shares should be valued as part of a controlling interest. Consequently, a minority discount will not be disallowed solely because a transferred interest, when aggregated with interest held by family members, would be a part of a controlling interest. This would be the case whether the donor held 100 percent or some lesser percentage of the stock immediately before the gift.

Effect on Other Documents

Rev. Rul. 81-253 is revoked. Acquiescence in issue one of *Lee,* 1980-2 C.B. 2.

SOURCE: Rev. Rul. 93-12, 1993-1, C.B. 202.

Index

Index

Index